The Bedside 'Guardian' 26

The Englishman's Castle

THE BEDSIDE
'GUARDIAN'
26

A selection from
The 'Guardian' 1976-77

Edited by
W. L. Webb

With an Introduction by
J. K. Galbraith

Cartoons by
Gibbard and Bryan McAllister

COLLINS
St James's Place, London
1977

William Collins Sons & Co Ltd
London · Glasgow · Sydney · Auckland
Toronto · Johannesburg

First published 1977
© Guardian Newspapers Ltd, 1976
ISBN 0 00 211394 5
Set in Monotype Imprint
Made and Printed in Great Britain by
William Collins Sons & Co Ltd Glasgow

Introduction

In the last ten or twenty years I have not been an unqualified
admirer of British journalism. I don't, of course, dwell on the
superbly vulgar achievements of the lesser Sunday press. They
have their counterpart in most countries – in our case it is the
magazines on abnormal and subnormal psychology and sexual
function and dysfunction. Rather I have in mind the immoderate,
often apocalyptic tone which, especially in the last decade, has
crept into much political writing. My neighbour, friend and fellow
Anglophile Anthony Lewis, long the head of the London Bureau
of the *New York Times*, has recently commented on this quality
with much sorrow:

> The British remain pre-eminently a moderate-minded people.
> Opinion polls on this political issue or that show a majority for
> middle-of-the-road views. Individuals are as reasonable as ever,
> and as kind.
>
> But somehow, in the national dialogue, the voices of reason
> are submerged. The strident and the bloody-minded dominate.

With this I agree.

Literary and artistic comment is much better; British book,
theatre and arts reviewing must surely be the most literate,
responsible and demanding of any in the world, the most certain,
in my experience, to skewer carelessness or error. But here too
one detects a tendency for assertion and exaggeration to replace
careful argument, and not always by journalists alone. My
examples tend always to be depressingly personal. I remember
being taken severely to task some months ago – it was by J. H.
Plumb, who combines journalism with quite reputable scholarship
in his own areas of historical knowledge – for attributing prime
importance, along with the great movement in economic thought,
to mechanical inventions as a cause of the Industrial Revolution.
Not for a century, Plumb averred, had anyone argued such nonsense. This, of course, *was* nonsense. Technology is still held to be
vastly significant in initiating this great period of change. Lofty,
ill-informed assertiveness is bad journalism, and it has an adverse

5

effect even when directed at someone else.

There is a glib and easy explanation for these trends. Money could be part of it. Budgets, one is told, are tight. Thought is cheaper than travel, research and reporting. Certainly no exchange is so disastrous. Not everyone is up to thinking. The tendency for the incapable is to compensate with clamorous overstatement or, if all else fails, imaginative prediction of imminent and violent catastrophe. American columnists, the aspiring Lippmanns, are a useful study in this regard. Waugh's William Boot, the greatest journalist of his age, was unknown until he was moved, so much against his will, from his reflective pieces on badgers to the actual scene of revolutionary intrigue in Ishmaelia. Years ago when I was an editor, which is to say a writer, for *Fortune*, I was considered to have a special affinity for what were called 'think pieces'. This category, to my great distress, was thought deeply inferior. Much better to get and pass on hard information. I realize now that the instinct of my colleagues was sound.

Also, these are difficult days in Britain. The confidence of only a generation back has given way to the seemingly unresolvable problems of the present – I say 'seemingly' for I do not think things are all that bad – and revered economists come from afar to regale their reactionary audiences with the news that Britain will be the next Chile, Callaghan the next Allende and that Margaret Thatcher may just not be the next Pinochet. This produces, as one might expect, a defensive and assertive response. We know exactly how bad we are; but everybody else is nasty too.

The trouble with such generalizations is, of course, the exceptions. There is a great deal of good newspaper writing in Britain, in the good Sunday papers in particular. And there is the *Guardian*. Past writers of these prefaces have regularly described themselves as *Guardian* readers and told of their pleasure in having numerous of their favourite pieces preserved. My pleasure is different; I get the paper only when I am in England. My delight is in articles that otherwise I would have missed. Nancy Banks-Smith is far better on American elections as television comedy and a spectator sport than anything I've ever read in the local press. I've long admired Keith Joseph, though from a safe distance, as one of those men whose courage is almost totally unmarred by judgement. Peter Jenkins here affirms what I had wished to believe: in office he might try to carry out Milton Friedman's ideas, something that no one ever imagined that Nixon, Ford or their Friedmanite acolytes would dream of doing in their eight years of power. (Though they did, of course, go far enough to get themselves defeated.) Jonathan Steele is wonderfully right in saying that numerous American liberals, in their fear of being thought soft on Communism, can be dangerously more belligerent than conservatives who merely fear Communism. I was brought up in Canada as a republican – note the small 'r'. There was much pleasure for me here in the consistently amused and sometimes hilarious view of the higher folk-rites of royalty. I greatly liked Caroline Tisdall's piece on whales which did not play to any of my political or anthropological likes or dislikes.

But I think my response is to a more general quality which *Guardian* writers seem still to share. There is very little here of the bloodymindedness that Tony Lewis quite rightly regrets. Most of these writers, I would judge, still feel that even if things are bad they can be improved, and that solid effort is still worthwhile, and moderation and compassion are not athwart all civilized change. All agree that those who deal in calamity should be answered not in kind but with sympathy that is appropriate to their handicap. And that while one should be unforgiving of error, one should also be exceedingly careful in assertion or rebuke. That requires that you be right. And most of all, these essays show that men and women can be intelligent while also being amused and amusing.

The editors of these volumes seem determined to call them bedside reading. I thought them all well worth reading while sitting up in broad daylight. For getting off to sleep there is an infinity of other work I would recommend first.

Broadway's opening knights

Sir John Gielgud said, 'How do you do?' Sir Ralph Richardson's first words were to tell me about the celebrated New York hotel where they only changed the sheets once every five years. He had stayed there often.

We met for lunch at the Algonquin, a place still possessed by the spirit of Dorothy Parker and of the 1920s, but, Dorothy Parker or not, immediately on the entry of the two knights the place was possessed by them. By Richardson in this manner – by receiving the engulfing attentions of passers-by and what appeared to be the assembled management with resonant cries of: 'How nice. How kind of you.' By Gielgud in this manner – by walking determinedly towards the dining room and separating himself, which was a feat, from the instant recognition and adulation which afflicts actors in New York. They were in town to play in the National Theatre's production of Pinter's *No Man's Land*, which had been first to Toronto and Washington, and then come to Broadway. The American management takes the risk, if risk there is, and the National takes a cut of the gross. Gielgud and Richardson are old and good friends, who first acted together in 1931. What follows is a selected account of the talk over an amiable lunch.

GIELGUD: 'Speakeasies. I was here in 1928. We used to go to little gratings. I went with someone who had a password. I was terrified I was going to be poisoned by bath-tub gin. It was rather fun really. I had no money.'
RICHARDSON (who made his first visit later, in the thirties): 'I hated New York. I was in fear. I loathed it.'
GIELGUD: 'How funny. I was thrilled.'

I had rather expected Sir Ralph to be thrilled too, since in youth he had a famous reputation for climbing high ledges. What about the ledges of New York?
RICHARDSON: '*Bit* high, outside my gambit or range. I used to love climbing upon high things.'

9

GIELGUD: 'Harold Lloyd complex.'

RICHARDSON: 'There was a high mast at Portsmouth when I was in the navy. I was always shinning up it.'

Lamb, spinach and claret were ordered. Vast American salads were offered and declined, but still came. The conversation turned to a man who had modelled six pages of magazine photographs and had not even been given the clothes he wore, only the bowler hat and the umbrella. This was felt to be unjust.

GIELGUD: 'The only way to get good clothes now is to do television. They give you a new suit for television and you keep it and that keeps you going.'

RICHARDSON: 'My salary at Lowestoft was £2 10s, and the tradition was that a Shakespearean actor had to be in possession of two pairs of tights, one brown, one black, and a juvenile wig and an old man's wig.'

We talked about *No Man's Land* and the Kennedy Center at Washington where it was performed. Richardson liked the Center. Gielgud detested it. But hadn't he laid a cornerstone 10 years ago?

GIELGUD: 'I did. With President Johnson. In the rain.'

Did Americans lose some nuances of *No Man's Land*?

GIELGUD: 'It's a great pity. It makes it difficult for us. You have to take it on the chin. Google. Jack Straw's Castle. They don't know cricket (or Hampstead), you see. They don't know the word *pouf*. They don't know the word *bent*.'

I said I was terrified by the play.

GIELGUD (amusedly?): 'Good.'

RICHARDSON: 'If you haven't a sense of being terrified you're not a complete chap.' (Then, addressing a waiter urgently summoned), 'I love bread so much; I want it to be taken out of my temptation. I have made a vow. I am going to give up my beautiful rolls.' The waiter gazed in perplexity at the basket of bread, reflected, and then took it away from the table and from temptation.

GIELGUD (watching the bread go): 'Bread is soggy in this country.'

RICHARDSON: 'My toast this morning was not.'

GIELGUD: 'Like damp sheets.'

Food was served with American vigour, which disrupted the fluency of conversation. Sir Ralph enquired where I lived in London.

COLEMAN: 'There is a scrap iron dealer in the mews at the back.'

RICHARDSON (beaming): 'How charming. Do you do anything else? Macmillan's a nice chap to talk to. When he really wants to smile at you . . .'

GIELGUD: 'Like A. E. Matthews. A great sort of bloodhound.'

RICHARDSON: 'Aaah.' (Then, to me) 'May I take your elbow out of your salad? Don't you think Harold Wilson makes quite nice company?'

GIELGUD: 'I always dread him.'

RICHARDSON: 'I find him a taking fellow.'

GIELGUD: 'I find Bernard Levin fascinating.'

RICHARDSON: 'Levin? He's not a Prime Minister.'

GIELGUD: 'He knows so many things.'

RICHARDSON (at large): 'I'm glad you like Wilson personally. I'm glad he's not our headmaster any more. But I think he would be wonderful where he came from – the Board of Trade.'

There had also been a previous slight allusion to President Ford.

RICHARDSON: 'These chaps are not bad, are they? Don't they have an Opposition bench here? Couldn't he (Ford) sit on it the same as Heath?'

I thought he would be just an ex-President and have a pension.

RICHARDSON: 'He'd have to start at the bottom again. He could arrive down at the back door and try to creep in.'

I asked about inherited genius. Sir John said he was lucky to have not only the Terrys as ancestors, on his English side, because apart from Ellen Terry they had no humour. 'That sort of property basket background gave me such gifts as I possess – wearing costume, speaking well.' But that had been much enhanced by the Slavic temperament of his father's Lithuanian family.

Sir Ralph's parents were art students who met in Paris.

RICHARDSON: 'My family were sort of manufacturers – leather, Fry's cocoa, Richardson's the shipbuilders. My grandfather had an awful lot of sons. He had a factory. My father asked could he be excused and go to Paris. My grandfather was a very humane chap, and he had lots of sons going into the works, so he said well, with great sorrow, if you're going to take up this awful job, well, do it.'

GIELGUD (with the acuity of *No Man's Land* suddenly in his voice): 'Were your parents separated, or was your father dead?'

RICHARDSON: 'No, my father sort of never died. They separated when he was art master at Cheltenham, the Ladies' College.'

GIELGUD: 'And you went with her?'

RICHARDSON: 'My other brothers went with him.'

GIELGUD: 'Are your brothers dead, your brothers?'

RICHARDSON: 'They are.'

GIELGUD: 'Were you fond of your brothers?'

RICHARDSON: 'Not very. I was fond of one, when I was young.'

At this point two strangers came up to the table.

FIRST STRANGER: 'We just wanted to say on behalf of two generations how glad we are to see you back again in New York.'

RICHARDSON (formally replying): 'I think that's a *marvellous* speech. Thank you very much indeed. Very kind.'

The strangers passed.

RICHARDSON: 'They deliver the current speech. Very sweet. They know you . . . In London you might be working down a coal mine. Your barber, who's cut your hair for years, you may be in a very big success in London, he'll say, "Well, how are you getting on, sir? I suppose you must be retired now."'

GIELGUD: 'Americans are very courteous.'

RICHARDSON: 'In the old days, Tallulah Bankhead fans would come in and take over. Stand in groups at the stage door and sit down in your dressing room, and tell you how to marry. Everything. Even I was told a bit of that in the matinee idol days. I'm sure Larry (Olivier) was.'

GIELGUD: 'I thought I would end up playing ambassadors in Hollywood. Aubrey Smith stuff. And the writers, Dodie Smith, Hemingway, Isherwood, all sat in little cubicles, loathing each other and loathing the work.'

I asked about the theatre as ritual.

RICHARDSON: I love ritual. Well, I do. The work we do in the theatre is a ritual, a kind of mass. What I mean by ritual – it is repeated over and over again. It isn't a separate adventure like a film.'

GIELGUD: 'One knew this (the theatre) was a dignified occupation; whereas in film you have to lie about all day, and suddenly come to life for five minutes.'

RICHARDSON: 'I've never given a good performance, that has satisfied me, in any play. No actor ever has. No, and if one gets near to it one is terrified, because one thinks, "Tomorrow night I'll be bloody awful." You dread tomorrow.'

GIELGUD: 'An audience can suddenly delight you. You know, the moment the curtain goes up. The first two or three minutes.

RICHARDSON: 'Two or three minutes, Johnny, is putting it very long. I know within half a minute. Da-da da-da da-da. Does it go musically or is it jumping? And you can never recover from it.'

Sir John considered. Sir Ralph drank coffee from his saucer.

What about delightful audiences?

RICHARDSON: 'I'm rather inclined to think of them as a cage of bloody tigers that will bite you, and will put you out of the stage door if they can. It's no good cracking the whip, or saying, "Go back," with a revolver; but you must never let them command. They'll see you out of the stage door.'

GIELGUD: 'But then if you have a certain charisma, which presumably you have as a leading actor, the chances are they'll be on your side, and you have a certain unfair advantage.'

RICHARDSON: 'If you believe that, which I think you do, you're a very lucky man.'

They went to their separately waiting Cadillacs, provided by the American management. 'See you tonight, Johnny.' 'See you tonight, Ralph.'

Sir Ralph surveyed his immense limousine, letting his gaze move from front to back. 'Usually about that size,' he said. 'Or longer.'

15 November, 1976   **Terry Coleman**

Breakfast time bust-up in Chapter Road

Get off the tube at Dollis Hill, one stop before the much-derided wastes of Neasden, and it's all happening right there, with the police lining the entrance to the station as though gathered outside the church for a colleague's wedding. On the left, across the road, is the corner store – Khusema Newsagent and Confectionary – and in front stand a band of middle-class stalwarts bearing a red banner with the legend 'Haldane Society of Socialist Lawyers'.

Opposite between two red brick semis, are the blue wire gates of the Grunwick film processing plant, just wide enough for a bus to get through. There is no sign written up, but there is no doubt that this is the focus of attention, the reason why a few hundred people – police, journalists, cameramen, MPs, and assorted 'militants' – should find themselves at this early hour in Chapter Road, NW2.

In front of the gates are four diminutive Asian ladies, one with a placard saying mildly: 'Mr Ward exploits everyone, leave him.' Behind her is a distinguished black man with large lenses and a printed poster saying: 'Apex official picket, Apex demands recognition.' Beside him is an even more distinguished gent with a megaphone looking uncommonly like Wilfred Hyde White. Can this be the Ealing comedies team of long ago filming *Passport To Neasden*?

The bowler hat (initialled inside with J. F. F. P.-M.) and the grey tie, the stiff white collar, and the pin-stripe, not to mention the articulate and kindly upper-class voice, all go to indicate that this, in fact, is John Platt-Mills, QC, inveighing, as he has done all his life, against the evils of businesses 'built on slavery and sweated labour'. He is soon replaced at the megaphone by a working-class bloke who surveys the meagre crowd, where the police outnumber the pickets at least two to one, and tells them: 'If I was leader of a union – and you know why I'm not (pause for laughter) – I'd say that 5000 or 10,000 pickets ought to be here.'

The serried row of police, on either side of the narrow leafy road along the pavement, look glum. Above the factory, the Union

Jacks and loyalist tea-towels hang limply in the morning damp.

Earlier a bus with non-union labour had come down the road and swung into the factory, but now everyone is calm and good humoured. Half a dozen MPs are standing with the pickets. A journalist approaches Stan Thorne, MP, and asks him why he jumped back as the bus came by. 'The bus,' says Stan judiciously, 'seemed to be travelling too fast for me to have a word with the driver.'

At this moment the gates begin to open and the bus starts backing out. The driver, no working-class lad he, misjudges the space and backs the bus straight towards the opposite pavement where the Haldane Society lawyers are in grave danger of being crushed against Mr Khusema's shopfront. Only the opportune intervention of the redoubtable Ms Pat Arrowsmith who attempted to throw herself under the rear wheels of the bus, thus drawing the attention of the police and subsequently of the driver to the dangers of the situation, prevents a disaster. (The bus stops in time.)

Emerging from the factory with the bus comes Mr John Gorst, MP. I ask him if he would care to comment. 'It's rather difficult to see what's happening,' he said plaintively. 'Surely,' I said, 'you can see that this bus is backing into the crowd.' 'It is rather a problem, isn't it?' he sighed, turning back into the factory.

The activities of the bus have thrown everyone into a feverish state. The police no longer fully control the street. An anguished officer calls out: 'Hold your positions,' as though faced with an imminent retreat by his men. One policeman starts shoving the distinguished black man on the picket line, and when order is finally restored, a picket leader announces that Audrey Wise, MP, has been arrested, and an ironic cheer goes up.

A television team starts interviewing Ian Mikardo who is always ready with a quote, when suddenly a riot breaks out afresh down the street, and the cameraman rushes off, leaving poor Mikardo in mid-sentence, and the interviewer trying to pacify him. Finally the MPs have to leave, to go to a meeting of the Parliamentary Labour Party. They promise they will raise the matter with Merlyn Rees. But once they have gone, the police clear the street again – journalists and cameramen and lawyers and 'militants' are all treated alike. 'Get out of it,' says the officer.

We move away – just in time. For the bus is coming down the street again, with another load of strike-breaking labour. Only the four frail Asian ladies stand in its path, and they are shepherded aside by the police. The gates open, swallow up the bus, and close again. A train rattles by on the Watford line.

22 June, 1977   **Richard Gott**

The Mecca of the West

'You won't find any foreigners here,' one Arab was heard saying to another in the heart of Arab London. And indeed, at the height of the summer season there are parts of the city such as Earls Court or Bayswater which might almost be Kasr al-Nil Street in Cairo, or Phoenicia Street in Beirut.

Arabs from many different countries stroll up and down in animated groups, at the leisurely pace of people who have nothing very much to do. Some, from Saudi Arabia and the Persian Gulf, wear flowing robes and headgear, their women veiled or exotically masked. The newsstands are dominated by *al-Ahram*, *al-Anwar*, *al-Ray*, *al-Amm* and a score of other journals from the Middle East. The shops sell *hommos*, and other Arab foods. Former hamburger stalls now offer *shawarma*, mutton grilled on revolving spits, instead.

It is Ramadan, and a grocer has pasted up appropriate verses from the Koran. An enterprising estate agent has renamed his premises *al-Khalij*, the Gulf. A hoarding bears an advertisement, in Arabic, for 'the longest lasting fruit gum in the world.' 'Foreigners' – that is, Englishmen – really are few and far between.

London has experienced such sudden 'invasions' before. Since the Second World War, Americans, Germans, Japanese have, each in their turn, drawn a special, and often ungracious, attention to themselves. The causes have been various – the numbers in which the visitors come, their novelty, their behaviour, or just the memories they arouse of unpleasant things past. But 1976 will undoubtedly go down as the Year of the Arabs. These new invaders

16

seem to fall into a special category of their own.

They appear not just as super-rich tourists, whose money is admittedly as welcome as their manner of spending it is often distasteful, but as humiliating reminders of Britain's fallen place in the world, as yet another threat to its flagging economy, if not its heritage and whole way of life.

You can hardly open your newspaper these days without reading of some new Arab 'takeover'. Hotels, hospitals, and historic mansions all seem to be falling like nine-pins into the hands of the new-rich potentates from the fabulous shores of the Persian Gulf.

A princeling from the obscure sheikhdom of Ras al-Khaimah, whose few thousand inhabitants used to live off fishing and the issue of eccentric postage stamps, is now the principal shareholder in the Dorchester Hotel; Mahdi Tajir, the billionaire tycoon from Dubai, and United Arab Emirates Ambassador to London, has acquired Meryworth Castle and a string of other choice properties, The middling rich are busy snapping up all available properties in the £100,000 to £300,000 range in Mayfair. They often pay cash down. Lower down the scale, the great mass of ordinary London Arabs are buying up whole tracts of Kensington for £20,000 to £50,000 a flat. Arabs have probably now acquired some 10,000 properties in Britain, most of them in the London area, at a cost of £100 million for this year alone.

The Arab tourists fill up the smart hotels which, if not already bought by other Arabs, are busy 'Arabising' themselves to cope with the invasion. They have Arabic-speaking staff and menus, in both Arabic and English, that cater for the special tastes of their guests. Each Arab country has its own favourite hotel. You tend to find Saudis in the Grosvenor; Kuwaitis at the Churchill and the Portman; Lebanese at the Hilton and Londonderry; Gulf Arabs at the Gloucester; and Iraquis at the Penta.

From the hotels, the Arabs descend in droves on Oxford Street and the great London stores – also reputed to be targets of Arab takeover bids – and make those extraordinary purchases which leave not just the impoverished British, but the Arabs' nearest competitors, American tourists, wide-eyed with amazement. There is hardly anyone, it seems, who has not this year seen an Arab buy a hundred suits at once, or his veiled womenfolk bear off armfuls of gorgeous evening dresses without thought for price, nor apparently for size either, and certainly with no opportunity to wear them except in the seclusion of their own quarters.

Other daytime expeditions will take the Arabs to Harley Street or the more expensive hospitals. If they are not undergoing treatment themselves they are visiting relatives and friends who are. Should the new Wellington Hospital be their destination, they will be greeted by an Arab girl at the reception and notices in Arabic – with English, French, and German thrown in for form's sake – will guide them round its hushed and carpeted interior; the patients, who are almost entirely Arab, can order their guests any food they should desire and invite them to watch Arabic films on closed-circuit television. As another outing they might go to the Curzon Cinema to see the Arabic-only version of *The Message*, banned in most Arabic countries, which relates the life of the Prophet Mohammed. On Fridays they might go to a service conducted outside the mosque being built in Regent's Park; but it will not be many of them who do. In the evening, the Arab visitors, now almost exclusively male and wearing Western dress, are likely to head for a nightclub or a casino. If it is Crockford's to which they may have been drawn by sumptuous advertisements in Arabic magazines, they can retire to an 'Arab room' with Egyptian hostesses in attendance. If it is to the Omar Khayyam nightclub, they will find an ambience, decor, floorshow, staff, and clientele so completely Oriental – Arabic, Persian and Turkish – that it must come as a surprise, upon re-emergence in the small hours, to rediscover that this is Regent Street, London.

Such, by and large, is Arab London as most Londoners probably see it. It is certainly an obvious and important part of it. But, Arabs complain, it is all the British ever care to see. In the West, they point out, the word 'Arab' has become virtually synonymous with oil-rich, and, for the British, the Arab-made-flesh does not seem to extend beyond those *keffiyah*- and *abbaya*-clad hordes who, this year, have descended on the British capital in greater numbers than ever before. They come essentially from the Gulf, and it is mainly they who commit those solecisms which, in addition to great wealth, Londoners are apt to attribute to all Arabs. It is they who supposedly graze goats in back gardens;

wreak havoc with the interiors of elegant apartments; deafen neighbours with noisy children and transistors; squat in Mayfair entrances; hang exotic washing over fashionable balconies; shop-lift, with hundreds of pounds on their persons, at Harrods and Marks and Spencer's; think that they can get off with local girls by brandishing £20 notes.

Many complex ingredients have gone into the making of Arab London, and it would not be much more accurate to call the Gulf Arabs – even if they all really did behave like that – representative of Arab London than it is to describe as 'oil sheikhs' all those rulers who have engineered the four-fold increase in the price of oil since October 1973.

It is Iranians as much as Arabs who are now recycling their new-found riches at Ladbrokes and the Playboy Club. That distinction, London Arabs complain, is rarely made. And still less, they say, do people distinguish between the Arabs themselves. On the contrary, they are arbitrarily lumped together.

'The British are completely obsessed with the Arabs,' says Naim Atallah. A Palestinian, he settled here in 1948 and, while retaining a deep but non-political interest in the Arab world, he is completely assimilated to his country of adoption, a highly successful publisher and film producer. And yet, he complains, whenever anyone writes about some new venture of his, such as his film *The Slipper and the Rose*, he has to link him with the contemporary Arab phenomenon under such titles as 'The Sheikh of Showbiz'.

Some 50,000 Egyptians visited Britain this year, and in many an Oriental cabaret or restaurant, Wimpy or Pizzaland, there are Egyptian waiters or dishwashers. You would hardly guess that there are serious Arabs as well as frivolous ones; some 8000 Arab university students live lives not very different from their British counterparts. Getaway Arabs as well as gregarious ones: 'Ten years ago, whenever I saw a compatriot,' said one, 'I used to go and talk to him. Now I run away.' Permanent residents as well as transients.

For every migration leaves a small deposit. The migrations have not only been touristic. It was a political upheaval, the creation of Israel, which brought Naim Atallah here. Since then,

19

London, like other capitals, has received its share of exiles.

Where the threat lies in all this, most Arabs fail to see. It is true that London is now absorbing more Arabs, of more kinds, than ever before – absorbing them, in fact, on a scale that could make it, in some yet unforeseeable degree, into an organic extension of the Arab world itself.

To the British the Arabs may be coming here as the conquerors, with money as their weapon, of their former imperial masters; but to many a discerning Arab it is a very different story; for him Arab London is the reflection not so much of a British, but of a far deeper, Arab sickness.

27 September, 1976   **David Hirst**

Those political mothers

The difference between American and British politicians is that the Americans have mothers and, in a tight corner, they take out their mothers and wave them about. Much like Bernard Shaw who threw his mother into the battle of life, or said he did because he knew it would shock the English.

The last time I saw Richard Nixon he was disclosing to the White House staff that his mother was a saint, while holding his pocket handkerchief before his streaming eyes like the Walrus.

You wouldn't think Mayor Daley of Chicago had a mother. Yet, surrounded by the braying press yesterday, he threw them the surprising sop that 'today's a better day, my mother used to say' – a gnomic rhyme which they accepted respectfully. President Ford had a mother because, unveiling a mural of peculiar awfulness covering his life's work, he appeared much moved. 'I owe everything to my father and Dorothy Ford, my mother,' he said and wept inconsolably.

President-elect Carter has a grey-haired but colourful mother known inexplicably as Miss Lillian. She was disclosed sitting in a rocking chair in front of an old cast-iron stove dismissing Washington: 'Heck no. I'm staying in Plains. I kin sit around and fish.'

Later, the election beyond doubt, she unbuttoned her jacket to show a Jimmy Won T-shirt, remarking it was the first time they had seen the President's mother do a striptease and she would be thrown out of the church. Meanwhile, she kept a good hold of Carter's convivial brother Billy who 'starts drinking a can of beer around 10.30 a.m. and stays with it,' according to ex-mayor Lindsay. As it was now 3 a.m., Billy's comments were largely unintelligible.

I enjoy these open-ended American elections more than anything else on television. Oh, the hurly-burly of NBC after the deep peace of the BBC. NBC has David Brinkley, whose great advantage is that he looks no worse after eight hours in the saddle than he does at the beginning, and John Chancellor who, quite early, was involved in explaining that when he said Democrats were poor and uneducated, he didn't mean they were poor and uneducated, he meant . . .

They also have women reporters who look beautiful, intelligent and dry-cleaned even at 3 a.m. on the White House lawn. It is, however, the imperceptible unbuttoning of the reporters in the small hours which makes this kind of programme so rewarding. The moment when they say 'as long as it's this hour in the morning' as if no one were listening and start to yarn about whether shrimp pickers work harder than nit pickers and about Baptists and Brother Billy Carter's vagaries.

I like the foreignness of it. 'It's almost like the bottom of the ninth innings with two outs,' said the reporter from Mondale's HQ, evidently feeling he had clarified the position. And the commercials which the BBC couldn't stop in time – 'Brought to you by Union Carbide. Today something we do will touch your life.'

And the names. There is hardly a President whose name could not be pronounced by an Anglo-Saxon with ease. But in the parallel senate elections there were Metzenbaum, Sarbanes and Beall, there were Pete du Pont, Riegle and Esch. And Zumwalt. Zumwalt complained that everything in Virginia – the airport, the avenues – was named after his opponent Byrd because the Byrds are an old Virginian family, and also because Zumwalt Airport takes some saying.

I also liked Amy Carter in the early morning waving and waving, and yawning and yawning.
5 November, 1976   **Nancy Banks-Smith**

The Squire of Plains

'You know, you English can probably understand Carter better than Americans can. He's gentry. He's the squire of Plains. He does not speak for the rural proletariat, but for the once impoverished gentry of the South.' I. F. 'Izzy' Stone has closed down his Weekly, but his incisive views are readily available.

He is appalled at the 'sentimental mush' which passes for serious comment on Carter even in hard-nosed publications like the *New York Review of Books* and impatient with the obsessive speculation about the personalities who will be involved in the succession – 'The likeliest man to follow Dr K,' etc., etc.

Stone has a keener instinct than many of the pundits downtown. He has not yet been to Carter's home town of Plains, Georgia, but has read enough to sense its economic and social structure more accurately than the authors of some of the frothy descriptive pieces in the American press. 'Carter owns the grocery store and the warehouse and the seed establishment, and most of the land. And sure, he's nice to the blacks. That's genuine, I believe. The gentry always were nicer to the blacks than the poor whites were. But that doesn't keep him from exploiting them as share croppers and tenant farmers and workers. I don't see that Carter likes to pay them more than the minimum wage. His attitude to labour is very much that of the rural capitalist.'

What does he think of Carter's team of senior advisers on foreign policy? 'Well there's a little group of corporation lawyers, bankers, and ex-military men around the Council on Foreign Relations in New York. They seem to crop up as the experts on foreign policy in every administration.

'They were the architects of the Vietnam war. Some of them very belatedly tried to get us out of there, but I don't think they represent anything new. They have so many Protean disguises –

the Trilateral Commission, the Council on Foreign Relations, and so on. They are really branches of the Bankers' Club in New York City. I'm not saying they're bad people or wicked or terribly benighted. But they're the core of American imperialism. Some are more intelligent than others; some are more flexible. I don't see them as very different from Kissinger.'

To those who wonder at the speed with which the country absorbed defeat in Vietnam, Stone replies that it was a small defeat and people learnt only a small lesson. But it was encouraging that the lesson came out briefly in the debate over Angola, and Congress's refusal to be stampeded into war.

Carter-watchers have spilled a good deal of ink on the answers Carter gives to this audience compared with that one, what he proclaims here, what he proclaims there. Izzy Stone draws attention to what Carter does not say. He rarely mentions Angola and does not say he heartedly approves of what Congress did. 'He might say, "If the Russians were fool enough to get involved in Africa, let them. They will be sorry later." What he actually says really implies a variant of Kissinger's machismo policy. If the other great power challenges you anywhere, you either pick up the chip or look like you've backed down. Carter says he would have used every means at his command, including an embargo on food, to force the Russians out. In other words he would have had a more complete confrontation.'

Stone is afraid that Carter 'may be another of those Democratic types that got us into war before. The Democrats tend to be more aggressive in office than the Republicans, for one thing because they're so sensitive to the charge of being soft on Communism. When the Republicans are in power, power sobers them.'

Stone also finds Carter's use of anti-government issues disturbing. It distracts attention from what he sees as the real issue which is the enormous power of the presidency that has grown throughout the Cold War under Democrats as well as Republicans. Just saying 'trust me' – well, Nixon said that.

Sometimes Stone may sound like a cynic. He would like to be an optimist and join the herd of wishful thinkers on Carter but his innate scepticism is too strong. Several times he comes back to the basic point that Democratic and Republican administrations are very similar, and that it would be foolish to expect much change either way. When he was a daily newspaperman, one of his bosses pointed out a saying which he has never forgotten. The Republicans give big business 100 per cent co-operation. The Democrats give them 95 per cent but get damned for the 5 per cent difference.

'The Democratic Party is a vehicle for social reform in periods of great unrest. But today there is no consensus for reform. When Roosevelt spoke he referred to a nation one third ill-clothed, ill-housed, ill-fed. Now it's one fifth. The forms of discontent are fragmented and contradictory but the coincidence of race and poverty is terribly bad for the country. To the extent that Carter offers some hope of overcoming the racial split, it's good but it's still largely emotional and cosmetic. I don't yet see how real it is.'

Stone is sadly convinced that many of the country's problems will continue under the Democrats. 'Tax reform was being blocked in Congress by the Democrats. They had a chance to outlaw the CIA and did not. No one really had the answer but it would be refreshing to have somebody speak with more candour instead of all that Sunday school stuff.'

Once again Stone repeats his refrain, 'Look, Carter may be all right, I don't know. It's a gamble. It's a pig in a poke. You can't have a campaign that costs millions of dollars without it setting limits. You can't stray very far off the path. All we can do is hope.'
4 November, 1976   **Jonathan Steele**

One hundred per center

With a knife at her throat Jessica Mitford once cooled a would-be rapist's ardour with a political lecture. 'I knew if I lost my nerve for one minute I'd be dead. So I tried to bore him stiff, which I succeeded in doing. He said he hadn't had a woman for a year, since serving in Korea. I said, that's why they send people to Korea, to make animals and brutes out of them. What you should do is join the Peace Committee. I'll give you the address of the local one.' Nonplussed, the attacker let her go, though not without first beating her badly.

She refused to report it to the police. 'He was black, you see. And the party line at the time was that there was no such thing as rape. Because that's how whites so often framed black men. And I would not have been able to identify the chap. So any black in the area would have been fair game for the notoriously racist Oakland police.'

That same political commitment plus excellent nerves helped 'Decca' – family nicknames are a Mitford mania – through the nightmare of McCarthyism in America. She relates her years in the Communist Party in a new book, *A Fine Old Conflict*, which takes up where Hons and Rebels ended, after her husband, the romantic ex-public school rebel (and Churchill's nephew) Esmond Romilly is killed in the war and she is left behind in America with an infant daughter.

What isn't in the book is that she got the telegram saying Esmond was missing in action on the very day she had arranged passage back to England. 'I left out some painful parts, like that. Anyway it was getting too long.'

A Fine Old Conflict does omit some of the uglier aspects of life as an American Communist, which I remember from my party days in Los Angeles during the same Cold War period. It's a breezy, fast but often poignant read which reflects the author's odd combination of qualities: perhaps *because* she was such a 'one-hundred-per center,' as we used to call hard-liners, she could afford to poke beastly fun at party bureaucrats and their stilted syntax.

Shortly before leaving the party she wrote – with the collaboration of her still extant 'Book Committee' of Communist friends – a classic satire on left-wing pompousness titled *'Lifeitselfmanship'* a take-off on her sister Nancy's essays in *'U'* and *'non-U'*. (This is an appendix to the book.)

For a while there we rank-and-filers thought her wickedly funny essay heralded a new dawn for inner-party democracy, but the Old Guard made a *putsch* so the good people left running 'in a thousand directions like schoolchildren when the dismissal bell rings,' she writes.

Talking to Jessica Mitford and her labour-lawyer husband Bob

Truehaft at her publishers in Bedford Square brought back a part of my life which until recently no 'ex' felt safe enough to ventilate freely in America. The Truman-McCarthy heresy hunt gave amnesia to a generation of liberals and radicals, which is why Decca Mitford's book has been so important there. She makes it all sound incredibly normal yet also risky and super-charged – which it was.

When I said how lucky the Truehafts were to do their party chores in a sophisticated radical town like San Francisco, they laughed. 'But my dear,' replied Decca in that crisp, assured upper-class accent which must have flummoxed many a class enemy, 'we lived in *Oakland*.' It was across the Bay, the provincial Hoboken or Jersey City to the metropolis Decca calls 'S.F.' An industrial backwater, Bob terms it. Crowded with whites and blacks brought up by the trainload from the deep south to man the wartime shipyards and factories in the Bay area.

'Every time we had black people at our parties and meetings – which was often – the local bully boys would black up our children's faces and send them home crying,' Decca recalls. 'The neighbours would shout at us, "We don't want the niggers around here". Or telephone Bob and call him a kike, and heave rocks through our window.' They were forced out of their first home in an all-white neighbourhood – but sold it to a black family.

In those pre-civil rights days people simply assumed that anyone who had black people to their homes were Communists. 'And in our case that was true, of course,' Decca smiles sweetly.

To Decca the struggle for black rights was simply the American form of that international anti-Fascist crusade she'd signed up for in the 1930s, when she saw Germany, then Spain (where she eloped with Romilly) and finally her own family succumb to the virus.

I find it easy to believe that protecting Oakland ghetto kids from the redneck police was her way of apologizing for the fact that Oswald Mosley was her brother-in-law and her sister Unity was 'Hitler's Nordic Goddess'. Except that apologies just aren't in Decca's character.

She still defends the party against accusations that it cynically 'exploited' the race issue, though candidly agrees that the

Communists used her organization, the Civil Rights Congress, to recruit blacks. 'Why not? The Communist Party was the only organization at that time that held interracial meetings.' True, I say. But didn't the party's own self-critical 'struggle against white chauvinism' go so wildly out of control that it drove out some very good people? 'Nonsense. I thought it was a very healthy thing. Why, I knew of one white party family who made blacks coming to a meeting pretend to be servants by going around to the back entrance because having blacks in your home was a sure way of attracting the FBI. People guilty of such outrageous conduct towards black comrades were called up on the carpet, and if they didn't grovel a bit they'd be expelled. Jolly good thing too.'

We reminisce about the bad old days when every other party member was suspected (sometimes correctly) of being an FBI agent. The paranoia was often justified, especially when Cold War liberals like Hubert Humphrey proposed putting American Reds into concentration camps. (As late as 1962, when Robert Kennedy was Attorney-General in charge of such matters, Decca learned that she was still liable to arrest under the government's 'Emergency Detention Program'.)

FBI pressure on blacks, many of them vulnerable public-service employees, caused them to drop out of the Civil Rights Congress, wrecking it. 'And what's more,' Decca says with a trace of angry bitterness, 'government harassment succeeded in turning a number of them into stoolpigeons.' Bob ruefully recalls how a close black friend, a carpenter who offered to do the wiring in their house, was revealed later to be an FBI informer.

Since this is a professional interview I don't push my view, based on talks with old comrades in America last year: that the more 'public' Red you were the less you suffered from the hysteria. Fear of exposure was the FBI's most lethal weapon, but what if you were already out in the open?

Though Decca still believes party policy on 'taking the Fifth' amendment against self-incrimination was correct, she admits that she and Bob already were so exposed – he as a militant lawyer in police harassment cases, she as a 'nigger lover' – there was little the FBI could do to them. And they'd deliberately adapted to a lower standard of living, 'so economic pressure couldn't be used

27

against us,' Bob says.

He implies that while self-imposed poverty for political reasons was a challenge to Decca the ex-aristo, he – who'd been raised in Jewish tenements in the Bronx – was less enchanted by it. 'Perhaps also,' Decca muses, 'I don't feel pressure as much as some people did. Having been through the Spanish Civil War and seen Esmond go through all that, one didn't really expect to live very long. Anyway,' she laughs, 'I always thought I'd be killed in a revolution.'

Despite Decca's 'cool', she admits there was a frightening moment or two in the Fifties when you never really knew whether America was going to turn into a German-style police state. The effect on kids could be traumatic, especially if the CP parents never told them anything. But the Truehafts made a conscious effort to involve Dinky and her younger brother Benjy, with interesting results.

Dinky – Constancia Romilly – was an impressionable eleven when Decca took her by the hand to witness with her own eyes her mother's House Un-American Activities Committee appearance. Now 36, Dinky is a registered nurse in one of New York's 'snakepit' hospitals; a Marxist, she helps organize radical taxi drivers and has two children by James Forman, a black hero of the sit-in struggles which she joined. Benjy, a mere toddler at the time of HUAC, is 29, a piano tuner and politically passive.

Like almost all my Los Angeles ex-comrades who survived what Dalton Trumbo called 'the time of the toad', the Truehafts no longer follow a political line. A latter-day lifeitselfmanship has no time for militants like-minded but single-issue oriented.'

Bob fights free speech cases in court, Decca's 'crucible of struggle' is 'life itself' (phrases she immortalized in her parody). Recently she led – and won – a huge, noisy fight at San Jose State College which had invited her to be a visiting professor of sociology and then insisted she submit to fingerprinting and a loyalty oath. She positively glows recounting the campus-wide battle.

Decca adores students, who have given her standing ovations, but is much less keen on American feminists. As someone who – on principle – did not cry copper after her own attempted rape, she has no time for militants like Susan Brownmiller whose book *Against Our Will* (Decca insists) suggested that the young southern black Emmett Till, lynched for whistling offensively at a white woman, had it coming to him.

She once risked her life by travelling into the heart of enemy country, Mississippi, to agitate for Willie McGee, a black due to die on a trumped-up rape charge, and she is not about to side with anyone, socialist feminist or not, who points the finger at a black man.

In England she offers few opinions about current American politics, except that 'Jimmy Carter is one more disgraceful President'. She is far more anxious to talk about the danger she sees here.

'What's happening to Phillip Agee and Mark Hosenball is an absolute, total shocker. To me it's reminiscent of the onset of McCarthyism in America – minus the sense of struggle against it.'

On a previous visit to London she was disgusted by the attitude of even Communist lawyers to the arrest and jailing of Pat Arrowsmith for distributing a leaflet about Northern Ireland. 'We said to our friends, "Why the devil aren't you making a huge demonstration in Piccadilly about her?" And they just shrugged and said, "Oh, that's just silly old Pat. She asked for it." Absolutely disgraceful.'

A Fine Old Conflict is published by Michael Joseph
17 May, 1977   Clancy Sigal

Farming out

The visit by Mr Carter to Washington (England) has been much publicised, and you might think that the name of the town and its historical associations were the reasons for the decision. In fact, County Durham was the third choice.

When Mr Carter first expressed a desire to get out of London, he said in fact that he would like to visit Mr Callaghan's farm and weekend retreat. He had assumed that Jim's farm was in Jim's constituency in Wales, and he also planned to visit the nearby birthplace of Dylan Thomas (being a great fan of the poet).

When he learned that the Callaghan farm was actually in Sussex, Mr Carter was undeterred. That'll do, he said. Oh no it won't, Mr Callaghan said, when he heard of the plan. If Mr Carter thinks that I'm going to have 150 secret servicemen tramping all over my wheat, he's got it all wrong, world economic revival or no world economic revival. Which is why Mr Carter is going north, rather than south, or west.

3 May, 1977   **Peter Hillmore**

A very English affair

On the mantelpiece in the room where Phillip Agee's case to be allowed to stay in Britain is being held stands a solitary Coca Cola bottle with a single flower in it. This curiously Anglicized piece of traditional Americana is an apt symbol of the whole Agee hearing, where three English gentlemen are listening to Mr Agee justify in great detail his revelations about the American CIA.

The hearing could hardly be in more English surroundings – the former United Services Club in Pall Mall, all polished wood, shining marble and glistening chandeliers (an equally apt symbol of England and empty because of the economic climate), while Mr Agee's language in his prepared statement could not be more American, peppered with words like 'neutralize' and 'spooks'.

The press and anyone else interested in watching British justice being seen to be done are excluded from the whole building, and there are at least a dozen policemen patrolling the ground floor and standing outside.

The room where the three-man panel – Sir Derek Hilton, Sir Richard Hayward and Sir Clifford Jarrett – are hearing the case, is on the first floor up the Grand Imperial staircase. On its huge double doors, incongruously, are the words Ladies Room. Now it is the Agee Room. Sir Derek, a former head of wartime intelligence, sits at a huge blue-covered table. In front of each member of the panel is a file containing the case put by the security services for Mr Agee's deportation.

Mr Agee has never been allowed access to the case for the prosecution, and the closest he has got to it is about ten feet, sitting at the table opposite the panel with his two 'friends', lawyers Lord Gifford and Mr Larry Grant. The Agee side is worried that the file is not particularly big, appearing to contain at most 30 or 40 pages.

Mr Agee's evidence on the other hand is much more copious and is strewn across his table. He has included in his statements everything that he thinks may be relevant and it is full of complicated sub-headings and detailed analysis without knowing if it is actually relevant. The panel listen impassively as Mr Agee reads his 500,000 words. They give little response. Yesterday morning they asked only three questions, one of which was a request for Mr Agee to repeat a sentence.

The panel gives no clue as to what information it is after, or what kind of case Mr Agee has to present. It doesn't even have all that much power, as it only exists to 'advise' the Home Secretary. Mr Agee and his friends cannot help feeling that it is all, plush room included, a public relations exercise without the public being present.

Because of the secrecy, every little clue that the panel might appear to throw out is seized upon. At lunchtime yesterday Mr Agee was convinced that his revelations about CIA involvement in Jamaica was at the core of the case against him. He could only justify this on the fact that the panel actually opened their files and took some more notes when he started to get on to that subject.

To add a note of bizarre informality, Mr Agee's family has been allowed to listen in on the hearing, sitting on a chintz-covered sofa beneath a huge ceiling-to-floor picture of some ancient dignitary. In spite of the secrecy and the somewhat formal informality there are certain reminders that the English Civil Service bureaucracy is at work: when coffee was brought in for the panel and Mr Agee, a man in a three-piece suit told his family that if they too wanted coffee they would have to bring their own in future (as there wasn't enough to go round).

13 January, 1977   **Peter Hillmore**

Group worship returns to Stonehenge

The summer solstice at Stonehenge is now celebrated by a grand company of policemen, trespassers, pot takers, coach drivers, pop bands, barking dogs and distraught farmers, none of whom, apparently, knows what is truly going on.

This year's first pop festival followers evidently broke into a National Trust field, half a mile from the stones, on Friday night. By yesterday there were well over a thousand, accommodated mostly in the now familiar tents, teepees and makeshift shelters, but occasionally in brand new polythene wigwams, like greenhouses.

The whole spectacle is now a kind of ramshackle ritual. The coaches on the way to the official car park opposite the stones pause so that the passengers can gaze at the 'hippies.' Policemen move about from control point to National Trust field, some on foot and some squashed in vehicles. The fans say 'yeah man,' – it sounds as old-fashioned now as 'yes sirree' – and the wood smoke cuts the pure air of Salisbury Plain like the scent of burnt chips.

'There's a lot of power round here, man,' one follower volunteers, indicating leylines and ancient barrows. One group tries to harness some of it by sitting silently, eyes closed, to encourage the sun to shine. The old symbols of alchemy and the zodiac flutter on flags and tent flaps, but the sky stays heavy.

A kind of rump parliament meets squatting on an ancient barrow, and decides against permitting a hot dog stand. It also passes a resolution against cutting down the farmers' trees for kindling, a practice which evidently disturbed the police over the weekend. 'It's like cutting somebody off at the knees, man,' one voice proclaimed, transforming wilful damage into ecological immorality in a sentence.

Cyclostyled handouts are issued from time to time, from sources as mysterious as the stones. 'Don't take any drugs off the site and if you get searched, tell Relief, whether you are busted or not,' one says. 'We should like to make it quite clear to the police that although we co-operate with reasonable requests we don't take kindly to groups of policemen heaving our friends in the woods.'

There is a threat that the Sex Pistols may come to perform, but no one knows when or why. The road outside is thick with the law, but what is to be done?

Beside the entrance to the field, a policeman notes the registration numbers of cars as they enter. A local milk roundsman in a grey smock who sold almost one thousand bottles before lunch says: 'They should organize it, and let the tradesmen in.' Union Jacks, a defiant innovation if ever there was one, fly high above the tents, among the soaring kites and the woodsmoke. There is much tramping about, sitting and strumming and waiting for the dawn.

'I mean, it's the way we live now, isn't it?' the milkman says totting up his takings. 'It's anarchy in action, man,' one of his customers says. Down the road the tourists from Europe and beyond retire to await the dawn between clean sheets.

21 June, 1977   **Dennis Johnson**

Shrinking feelings

People are feeling something happening to them, deep down, unexplained. There is a mysterious feeling that something is wrong; but they themselves, they know they are innocent . . . But somebody or something is hurting them . . .

I laid the book aside. It was gone opening time on a high blue-skied spring morning, all church bells and birdsong: Holy Week. The Holy Week in the three ale bar where my footsteps led was a crowded sacrilegious time and I was pulled, as by the force of gravity, to a table in the corner where several strangers sat.

One of them was a red- and purple-faced little man, like a garden gnome gone to drink. He was brooding over a newspaper, looking at the television page. What lives of quiet desperation people lead, I was preparing to say to myself when the little man said, 'There you are. What am I always saying?'

'What are you always saying?' one of the fellows asked. 'I never seen you before, I just came in here and sat down.'

33

'It says here that Vincenzo Labella, the producer of *Jesus of Nazareth*,' the little man bowed his head for a moment in respect, 'it says that while researching *Jesus of Nazareth*, starring Robert Powell and costing practically more than any TV production before and since, that they found the cross Jesus got nailed to weighed 580 lbs.'

'How much is that in stones?' one fellow asked.

'A lot,' the little man said. 'And so this TV producer says Jesus must have only carried the cross piece or patubulum which was made of roughly hewed oak and weighed 80 lbs and that he was nailed to that and then hauled up on a rope and the patubulum or crosspiece was then hooked on to the centrepost or splite. So there you have it, that's what I'm always saying.'

'What are you always saying?' another fellow asked.

'People are getting smaller. Go into any Catholic church and watch the stations of the cross. It always has Our Lord carrying the cross, don't it? Go into a museum and watch one of those old pictures, they always got Our Lord carrying the whole cross don't they? They couldn't all be wrong could they?'

'So here comes this TV producer and he learns the cross weighed 580 lbs and so he says Jesus couldn't have carried that. He says the cross must have come in sections. Rubbish, that. In them days people were bigger: 580 lbs being nothing to them in them days.'

'Crapite,' one of the fellows said. 'You can't tell me a man could carry 580 lbs up a hill after going 40 days with no food plus getting a crown of thorns hammered into his head. Besides, Our Lord was only 6ft tall. The nuns always told us that. Everyone knows that. He was the only man ever who was just exactly 6ft tall and if you don't believe me you can check the records in . . .' he paused. He didn't know where you could check the records. 'In Bethlehem,' he said. 'Or,' he added, 'call up the *Echo*.'

'And that, chief, only proves what I'm saying,' the little man said. 'It's the food. You could be only 6ft, which would be practically a midget for them days, and still carry 580 lbs up a hill because the grub they had in them days was real food and not all these chemicals.'

'Hold on, Billy,' another said. 'What about the suits of armour then?'

'I'm glad you asked that, Jim. That armour wasn't grown-ups' armour. It stands to reason, it was the kiddies' armour. The grown-ups' armour would have been all rusted and banged to buggery from jousting and all that carry on. The armour that survived is toys, what they give the kiddies to play around with. Some day they'll do the forensics on them suits of armour and I'll be proved.'

'What?'

'The forensics,' the little man said. 'It's a myth they put round to make people feel good that everyone is growing taller. All the time we're in actual fact growing smaller. Take a look at history. See what they ate in them days. Little men couldn't have ate them groaning boards, the tables loaded down with all that food like you got in those days. The world is getting more and more crowded and there is less and less food and room, so everyone is growing smaller. Mine's a pint of mild and bitter mixed.'

'What about them basketball players in Yankee land?' a fellow asked, returning from the bar with the ale.

'Watusis,' the little man said. 'You check the records, you'll find them seven foot six inch basketball players are direct descendants of Watusis. I'll show you something,' he said. 'Hey, chief,' he shouted.

There was a carpenter at the bar. The little man took the carpenter's measuring stick. He sat down and took off his shoe.

'What's this?' everyone giggled.

'A foot, right? An eight-inch foot. Where'd the other four inches go since a foot was a foot and 12 inches was a foot, answer me that? They didn't make up these names for nothing. A foot was a foot and a yard was a yard was – ' he got up, unfolded the carpenter's stick to three feet – 'and a yard was the length of your arm in them days. Look it up, you'll see.'

'Well,' one of the fellows said, 'if the world is getting crowded, it's a good thing we're getting smaller.'

'Is it?' the little man asked. 'What about the gravitational pull then? What about all them satellites spinning around the earth? There's hundreds. And they're just the known satellites. What about the unknown satellites? They're weakening the earth's

35

gravitational pull by slowing the rotation of the globe. Haven't you noticed how time seems to fly by these days?'

'I've noticed it's a long time between drinks,' one of the fellows said.

'It's my shout,' the little man said. 'I'll get them in.' He stood up, but not so you'd notice. 'Of course,' he said, 'they still tell you there's 24 hours in a day. They don't want you to know. It would cause a panic. Stands to reason that. But they know. And you can feel it.'

'Feel what?'

'The lessening of the earth's gravitational pull. I often feel light headed, sort of floating like I was going to float away.' The little man disappeared into the elbows of the crowd at the bar.

We waited. Pretty soon the landlord started ringing bells. The little man never returned: 'crushed to death under somebody's foot or he's floated away from the lack of gravity,' one of the fellows said.

'Personally,' another fellow said, 'I think there's a lot in the theory that Jesus,' he bowed his head, 'was a spaceman.'

'Time, gentlemen, please,' the landlord shouted, and not a moment too soon.

9 April, 1977 **Stanley Reynolds**

Lord Grade's Easter message

To take Lord Grade's Easter message, I went at breakfast time to his suite over ATV House. He'd already flexed his intercontinental muscle on the phone for three hours. As usual.

The coffee was freshened. As London got to work, Lord G entered his second phase. In no time I was owner of one of his custom-made, bowsprit cigars. Hands in pockets, the smoker could kick the ash off the end. Lord Grade says he is a great ham, and tries to live up to this idea of himself.

At Easter, he says, he likes a small English hotel with a number of lines open so he can get away from it all. When he calls them he feels people are delighted to waive their normal objections to weekend business. Relaxing this way, he'll have 20 scripts to read, and maybe in four days only get through half. He's plainly one of these fellows who gets very tense if they relax too much.

To relax him now, I noted that Italian critics had been enthusiastic about Zeffirelli's *Jesus of Nazareth*. He frowned. Apparently I'd hit a wrong note. Enthusiastic was useless, when in America they were unbelievable! The Times, toughest of all – man called O'Connor – had raved. Daily News was glowing. And the Wall Street Journal! Not forgetting 90 million amateurs in communion with them. He waved a bundle of cuttings at me as if to thump me with them. Ecstatic, he said firmly. That was the only word.

The film was more than Jesus; it said there should be a closer relationship between all people . . . black, white, green, yellow . . . Was ecstatic really the word then – wouldn't ecumenical be it? He said it was more than religion, it was people.

We talked about some people on the inside track, instruments in the divine purpose of setting up this $18 millions film. Seemingly the Pope played a vital role.

After Lord G finished Moses, the Italian Ambassador mooted a private audience with His Holiness. Not to mince words, being a Jew, it really meant nothing. 'Thanks,' he said. 'I've got so much work on but, you know, I'll think about it.'

His way of thinking about things is to tell Kathie, 35 years his unflagging connubial support, a *sans-pareil* at stalling on the phone, and a Catholic to boot. 'You must go,' she said, and went along too, though it's a wonder if she has a business trip once in two years.

The Pope is not the cold fish you imagine from television. Lord G was knocked out by his warmth. The Grades were alone in the Vatican when the Vicar of Christ walked in. He smiled. He sat down. Two Monsignors put on his robes and things. He moved his arms about, and beckoned. Lord G saw he was dealing with a wonderful human being. He was gone. He was almost paralysed with awe and warmth.

The Pope gave thanks for the Moses series and wanted to know about it. Lord G said it was meant to be an epic, but with a purpose, that being to remind people that there are Ten Commandments. The Pope thought that wonderful. He scattered blessings by proxy on the whole unit. Kathie got his permission to use the endorsement for publicity. From his youth as a Russian immigrant in the East End, Lew Grade always prided himself on his memory. He recalls that he won scholarships so often, which he couldn't take up on account of being Russian, that the London County Council convened a special meeting saying, 'That's five to date. It can't go on. We'd better pass a bylaw so the boy can win something more than half holidays for his school.' But now his memory failed him. What further was discussed went out of his head, except that the Pope thought it was great.

Kathie remembered. The Pope had said: 'Why not do The Footsteps of Jesus?' And it must have been in his subconscious too, because when he said to the Director of Italian State TV, 'How can we follow Moses?' and his co-producer said, 'What about Jesus?' his hand came up like a robot's to shake, and he said, 'You've got a deal.'

Well, he knew the tremendous risks, because Zeffirelli is a man who makes paintings come to life, and to do that you have to spend a lot of money. He had a lot of resistance from people who made the point that it would cost a lot of money. It did. They're a long way from getting it back. But he reckons it may be an annuity for ATV, maybe until the Second Coming, or he himself cashes his cheques in for the last time on July 29, AD 2000, when he is 93.

The great thing was not to offend anybody, Moslems, Catholics, Anabaptists . . . He reckons they've come up 98 per cent inoffensive. It would have to be 20 hours to cover the others.

He was not keen to talk about the 10 Commandments, though he felt that people keep 90 per cent of them. Oh, and which is the awkward 10 per cent? He would not like to embarrass people, but there are too many divorces, so that says which it is. Today you have to avoid saying 'Thou Shall Not Commit Adultery' for fear of knocking all those people who feel that times have changed.

But he felt freer talking about some of the 10 Things that Happened to Lew Grade. They included an apple store on the roof of a house in a village in the Crimea. And being sharp in Bethnal Green. And acute in the embroidery firm, and how to figure the additions in a flash for style 6781, button 3281,

38

material 6s 4d a yard.

And the Happening that set his course – when he won the Charleston Championship. And went partners with the man who always came second. And was double-crossed by him, when the fellow went behind his back to the manager and poached his dance on a table.

They were known as Grad and Gold, and then on the Continent in review, solo, Charleston and Eccentric dancing, and the great break of a billing at the Moulin Rouge, where this big poster misspelled his name, and he became Lew Grade. Today, he claims, he can still out-Charleston the next man.

He had flair for spotting an act, and became an agent himself. In 51 years in the industry, he says, he has been victim of no more than about 10 deals made in bad faith. He reckons to sum up people pretty well. If it takes two hours to explain a good idea, then it's no good. He has to get it in five minutes.

As an agent he booked everybody bookable. His first after the war was Bob Hope, paid £5500 a week for a fortnight at the Palladium. On a split commission with Hope's agent, that meant his cut was £550. He spent £700 on a party celebrating his achievement at the Embassy. A line of his superstars in similar frames stretch their cordial regard for him all across one long wall, like the world's most costly chorus line. There's hardly room there for Jesus Christ.

9 April, 1977   **Alex Hamilton**

And on the third day, the shares rose. According to yesterday's stock market report, Lord Grade's ATV shares 'put on 4p to 74p in recognition of the high acclaim awarded to Jesus of Nazareth.'
13 April, 1977   **Peter Hillmore**

Farewell state

This week being Milton Friedman Week – the Chicago charlatan is ennobled in Oslo tomorrow – it is appropriate to continue to

39

abuse his disciples and, who are far worse, those hypocrites who although intellectually unconvinced by monetarist nostrums are prepared to inflict them upon an unsuspecting populus.

There are some economists who hold Professor Friedman's work in professionally high esteem; others – it would seem a majority – do not. In any case the acclaim or obloquy of fellow professionals is no sure measure of achievement although, in this case, one is obliged to hope that posterity is not appointed jury. However elegant they may be on paper we must hope that the professor's theories are not put to the political test.

Sir Keith Joseph apart, I cannot think of a politician who is in combination clever and idiot enough to try. The intellectual fringes of the right flirt with Friedmanism, or their own modified versions of it, but retrogressive utopianism of that kind obtains little echo from the rank-and-file of the 'stupid party'.

Friedman, let us be clear, purveys an appealing-to-some, although nostalgic and unhistorical, concept of 'human nature' but is at best satirist, no sort of guru, when he engages in prescriptive clowning, whether as columnist or chat-show veteran. For example, as frequent and foolish a theme in his journalism and tele-punditry is about how Dicey was right in foreseeing, in 1913, that the rudimentary foundations of what we now call the Welfare State contained the seeds of liberty's destruction. Dicey of course was wrong, as was a mass chorus of nineteenth-century commentary which held that the franchise would bring the early destruction of democracy, equality the destruction of liberty, and progress the destruction of everything good.

Lloyd George for Dicey embodied the imminence of the extinction of liberty. The end was nigh. Thirty years later the end was Nye. And according to Friedman's pejorative framework of reference the inhabitants of the twentieth-century welfare society, enjoying *a combination of* liberty and material improvement undreamt of by their nineteenth-century ancestors, are incarcerated in some monstrous Gulag where not only are they forcibly deprived of the liberty which was available in Engels's Salford but cruelly brainwashed into the belief that human life might be so sweet as to, once in a while, allow the opportunity of 'such a thing as a free lunch'.

40

In case it should be thought I am engaged in parody listen to the professor speaking:

'We are standing on the shoulders of the nineteenth century, but there is no period in human history that I know of in which the ordinary man, the ordinary citizen of the world, improved his lot and his opportunities so greatly as he did during the course of the nineteenth century.'

Literally, as an historical observation, it is true, of course, but Friedman, who worries about the cost of everything, including 'free lunches', doesn't seem to worry about the cost of freedom when 'freedom', like lunch and everything else, is left to the allocation of the Market. And he is always pressing the analogy of an economic and political 'market' and, of course, preferring the former to the latter but never, of course, dealing with such points as how society shall coerce its members into perfect individualism. By anti-Combination Laws?

The tax collector (he doesn't deal with the police) is in his eyes a coercive agent and taxation itself, in the violence of his language, is a form of coercion. He proposes an 11th Commandment to the effect that 'everyone shall be free to do good at his own expense' but what he means is 'thou shalt not seek to do good at another's expense', that is to say, with tax payers' money.

This is his reasoning: 'If you are going to do good at somebody else's expense, you have to take the money away from him. So (sic) force, coercion, destruction of freedom (note the escalation of language) is at the very bottom, the very source, of the attempts to do good at somebody else's expense.'

The attitude of mind at work is familiar through being as old as the modern world. By purporting to hold Man in high esteem 'Economic Man' can be placed in correspondingly low esteem, betraying – one may suspect – a somewhat dismal view of 'human nature'. By this mode of thought – thriving to this very day in Chicago, and in Printing House Square – man's dignity remains intact in the face of all 'natural' assaults whether by pestilence, famine, earthquake, or control of the money supply but is somehow threatened by 'unnatural' forays of an improving kind by man himself whether led by Franklin D. Roosevelt, John Maynard Keynes, the Labour Party or any other – in Friedman's book – 'do-gooder.'

Why trouble, you may wonder, with the eccentric opinions of an economics professor whose serious reputation is thrown in doubt by the extravagance of his public statements on political matters? Because he has cast a kind of spell and is in danger of adding another 'ism' to our times. And to the extent that the people of this country are to be made the guinea pigs in an experimental application of Friedmanism they are entitled to ask of the experimenters 'How are you different, and in what way are you superior, to your predecessors who, as recently as the 1930s, exposed us to the law of markets in the belief that there was somewhere, written in "nature", a code of discipline more effective than any man could devise and voluntarily observe?'

9 December, 1976   **Peter Jenkins**

Today's civil servant is taken from the Book of Kings. After my revelation that the Treasury's counter-inflation man is called Mr Jeremiah, it appears that the assistant secretary at the Department of Prices on the counter-inflation side is a Mr Solomon. The fight against inflation is fast becoming a Holy War.
8 April, 1977   **Peter Hillmore**

The cost of taking the waiting out of wanting

It was 6.15 in the evening, wet and dark when the debt collector and I knocked at a door at the end of a council estate cul-de-sac. A tired-looking woman of about 30 answered the door and peered into the darkness. She saw who it was, smiled and asked us in. Her husband was asleep on the settee, a small child curled up beside him. 'Wake up!' she kept shouting at him, and he grunted. 'People to see you!' she shouted again, and eventually he sat up and stared at us.

They had four children under five. The colour television was blaring, but apart from a three-piece suite, the room was empty and bare. Two children were squealing and struggling on the stairs. She talked about her debts. 'He fell out of work, and he's only just got a job,' she said.

They were paying a total of £10 a week in debts. This collector was taking £2 a week for a oink unit. Someone else was taking for the three-piece suite, and there was money outstanding on 'the club', a mail order catalogue. They paid up calmly. The three-piece suite was made of plastic and already looked sad and old. I couldn't bring myself to ask what outrageous sum they had agreed to pay for it by instalment.

Debt collectors summon up images of broken-nosed heavies with alsatians straining at the leash. They are traditional villains. It's easy to see why British Debt Services, the biggest debt collecting and credit reference service in the country, employs a high-powered PR to take journalists like me out to an expensive lunch at the grand Arts Club. It's the kind of thing that makes the hackles of most journalists rise. What are they trying to cover up? What lies are they trying to peddle with the scallops mornay? Our prejudices against debt collectors run pretty deep (to say nothing of our prejudices against PR men).

So, that cold wet evening when the debt collector set off on his rounds, I went with him. I expected doors to be slammed in our faces, or no answer to our knockings, only the tell-tale flicker of a

'It's a very attractive scheme. After two years you can exchange your savings for ration books.'

lace curtain. But all the doors opened, and we were usually invited in. It was always the wives we spoke to, and they were friendly and smiling.

He didn't use strong-arm tactics – for one thing there's nothing he can threaten. What astonished me was the passivity of the people. They didn't attempt to resist, or deny the debt, and most of them paid up regularly, say 50 pence a week towards an average debt of around £80.

What the debtor doesn't know is that by the time a company has handed over a debt to a collecting agency, they have usually written it off as a bad debt. Overworked and understaffed court bailiffs can't begin to collect on all the thousands of court orders.

The agency takes on the debts, undertaking to pay 40 per cent of what they collect to the company, and 20 per cent to the collector, keeping a handsome 40 per cent for themselves. Collectors are part-timers, working in the evenings. This man worked for a big whisky firm in the day. There were teachers, clerks, a doctor's wife, also collecting in the area.

The agency has not paid for the right to collect the debts, nor have they paid the collectors, so they stand to lose nothing at all. A collector's only incentive is to collect as much as he can as quickly and as easily as possible. That means that if a debtor makes trouble, never pays or creates a scene, the collector will stop calling pretty rapidly, as he can't afford many unproductive visits for which he gets paid nothing.

Understandably, big companies don't like talking about this aspect of their business. For the astonishing fact is that if you live in an inner city or remote country area the chances are you will never be made to pay a debt. Debt collectors refuse to visit some areas, Brixton, for instance, where they are afraid to knock on doors. Court bailiffs in small towns may get round to distraining people's goods, but hardly ever in urban areas.

Most of the people we visited that evening had been in debt several times before, and yet they managed to obtain credit over and over again. Although credit reference services are widely used, the more disreputable firms, who charge high prices to cover bad debts, aren't fussy.

To most people who honestly pay their bills within a reasonable time of their first demand, the ease with which people get away with non-payment comes as a shock. The .5 per cent of debts not paid are fed straight back on to everyone else's bills. The PR man, though, shrugged cynically and said: 'Well, most big stores mark their goods up 100 per cent so it doesn't matter that much to them.' Certainly these losses are nothing but profit to him and his company, the bounty-hunters.

A man from the John Lewis Partnership said: 'A lot of people these days seem to think it's alright to "rip off" big companies. It is a lazy attitude people seem to fall into without questioning it. It's the same with shoplifting. I can't understand it.' And I had to agree – until I had a closer look at the debtors.

It is by no means only the poor who get into debt and stay that way. But it is certainly the poor who get caught and collected on. In a council house that we visited, the couple had three small children. Their colour television was on and they didn't turn it off. They appeared as they spoke to have become oblivious to its loud sounds and images. A fierce alsatian barked at us but was locked away.

'We owed £90,' said the woman, young and pretty. 'We ordered a tent and a whole kit, but when it arrived half of it was missing. It was supposed to have Li-los and sleeping bags and things with it, but only part of the tent came. We sent letters to complain and we refused to pay, but they never answered. We got bills and writs. It did go to court, but we let it slip. We hadn't any papers or anything, and we didn't know what day it was. Now we pay £1 a week. I wouldn't want my neighbours to know what you call here for.'

The collector was a little taken aback by this story. It turned out that he had no idea at all how any of the debts he was collecting had been incurred. 'Never mind,' said the woman, with a smile. 'We've only got a bit left to pay now.'

The next family couldn't remember what they were paying for. It was 'the club' again, a mail order catalogue. These catalogues are often much more expensive to buy from, but because they offer what look like very good terms, they encourage people to enter into heavier and heavier commitments. 'Oh I don't know what it was. Yes, we've been in debt a few times,' said this house-wife, a middle-aged woman. 'The trouble was that we wanted to pay, but they wouldn't send us the pay slips and envelopes, and then we fell behind.' Her husband was a school keeper, and was just leaving for work.

At the next house a thin and pained-looking woman in her early thirties with five children was sitting in a bare front room, with her black and white set showing Crossroads. 'I don't remember exactly what it was, but you can be sure it was no luxury. My husband's a roofer and this weather has put him out of work most of the time. I'm paying on the club. Once I bought a nightdress for Sharon which cost £3.95, and then I saw just the same one down in a warehouse for 99p.'

As we left the collector said: 'Yes, *you* may feel sorry for them, but they're still running a car. It's amazing what they can do on social security. These ones did a moonlight on me once, but I caught up with them.'

The collector had a curious mixture of attitudes towards his debtors. On the one hand he tried to stay completely removed, and to look at them only in terms of what money they would pay; and whether they were worth collecting on. He was friendly with them. On the other hand he accused many of them who were on and off the dole as skivers. 'I don't know how they do it. They have cars and colour tellies, *and* they're paying on other things they've bought.' He was so prudent himself, that he couldn't really understand fecklessness at all.

I asked him if he thought it wrong of companies to sell expensive shoddy produce so hard at these people who were clearly in no position to enter into credit agreements. Their husbands were only sporadically employed.

The rubbishy goods were grotesquely overpriced because the companies took into account the high rate of bad debts they were likely to incur. By the time they came to pay the goods had fallen apart, and the price had risen to include interest and collection costs. He shrugged. 'I don't understand why they do it. No one makes them,' he said

My round with the debt collector showed me that one of the ways poverty permeates every aspect of people's lives is that the poor get worse products at higher prices. Inability to travel and shop around, ignorance of anything outside their immediate environment and experience, makes them easy prey to catalogue companies offering pretty pictures, promises and golden images to gloss over the real tacky nature of their over-priced products.

Confronted with someone coming to the door, they would pay up without question, and apparently without resentment. There was something about this passivity which filled me with gloom. Why hadn't they realized they need not pay? They were not afraid of courts or gaol, but confronted with authority on their doorsteps, they paid up unquestioningly. It was not a matter of innate honesty getting the better of them.

I was tempted over and over again to tell them not to pay, that if they didn't pay, nothing would happen to them. But my privileged status prevented me. If none of them paid, eventually, the catalogue companies and other hucksters would stop plying them with goods and the whole shameful round would come to an end.

Of course the collector was keen to tell tales of drunken vicars, ladies with race horses, and other rich people he had occasionally collected from – but all of his 160 debtors on his list when I visited with him were living in council houses, and many of them were on social security.

14 March, 1977   **Polly Toynbee**

Loyal toastings in the City

Stockbrokers decked in red, white and blue yesterday paid homage to Britain's largest private invester – Her Majesty the Queen. It was the third day of jolly japes for the men buying and selling chunks of British industry and although little business was done, a good time was had by all with the champagne running even more freely than usual.

To give the Queen a little investment bonus for the jubilee, prices were marked higher with the *Financial Times* index closing 3.2 points up at 457.8. No one was quite sure how much value this put on the Royal investments because they still remain a secret following the recent exemption from the new companies Act.

The colourful scenes on the stockmarket floor encouraged the usually level-headed men from Exchange Telegraph, who collect together the day's share price activity, into waves of ecstasy. At 3 p.m. yesterday they reported: 'It was certainly a gay day in the London stock markets. However, the cheerful mood owed nothing to the unchanged minimum lending rate, which was expected anyway, but merely the combination of jubilee celebrating that has restrained business for the last three trading days. The Stock Exchange hadn't experienced such jubilant scenes for many a year, with colourful hats, bunting, umbrellas and rosettes all adding to the atmosphere. A raffle in which the prize was a Union Jack Consolidated Mines share certificate raised the sum of £50 which is to be sent to the Cheerful Sparrows Charity.'

If the stock market was giving the City its colour on the eve of the jubilee, it was the London insurance market in the form of Lloyds which was putting its hand in its pocket. The shrewd men of Lloyds, who each year boost our balance of payments with hundreds of millions of invisible earnings, have managed to find an ingenious way around the pay code.

Each of Lloyds' 2000 employees has been given an extra week's pay as a jubilee bonus – and the Department of Employment apparently gave its O.K. without a whimper. It's all a matter of precedent, explained the men at Lloyds. They paid similar bonuses at the time of George V's jubilee and George VI's coronation as well as at the coronation of Elizabeth II.

With the City so active in getting the spirit of the jubilee under way, it would be easy to forget that manufacturing industry is also doing its bit. At 5 p.m. yesterday afternoon came the momentous announcement: 'B. and A. Britton Ltd., the Tartan salad and delicatessen group, reports runaway demand for its high quality Jubilee Salad, introduced to cater for the "season" coinciding with the Royal celebrations.'

4 June, 1977   **Alex Brummer**

Jubilation

We will observe two minutes' silence for ITV which, when consulted, was showing Ladies' International Bowling from Worthing and wrestling between Kung Fu, known to his friends as Eddie, and Tally-ho Kaye, who had no friends. Lady bowlers, I was touched to see, actually kiss their opponents at the end of a match. Wrestlers don't.

All this gave the BBC a walkover and a very jubilant Jubilee indeed. Tom Fleming is not my favourite royal event commentator, being given to pomp and much circumstantial detail. He knows the State Coach weighs $4\frac{1}{2}$ tons and was delivered at five in the morning, and the names of all the horses: Budapest, Beaufort, Rio, Santiago, and so forth. So forth not being a horse, of course.

They are greys because it shows the red and gold harness so well and that must be one reason why London, grey in style and stone, lends itself so well to pageantry. When most truly moved, Fleming is barely rational: 'One wonders what the conversation will be in the stable tonight when these horses get home.'

However, let joy be unconfined and criticism minimal. The walkabout was a genuinely gay and pretty business with the Queen being handed a painting here, a posy there. I watched with close attention and fed my findings into a computer. The conclusion is that the Queen is likeliest to stop and talk to you if you are young, male foreigner in a funny hat sitting in a wheelchair near a Boy Scout; the Duke if you are a nun with a periscope.

Bearskins do not count as funny hats, though Prince Charles was committed to wearing one which rendered him unrecognizable.

The best way to see St Paul's is to be a bat. The remarkable aerial shots from the dome were as round as a gunsight with the crimson carpet crossing exactly where the Queen knelt. Her vulnerability throughout the procession was both a worry and yet a defence in itself. Her face in church and perhaps off-guard seems to fall into lines for which grief would hardly be too strong a word.

However, the Archbishop of Canterbury is always good for a laugh. He quoted Jesus, adding with episcopal emphasis: 'How right He was!' I cannot explain even to myself why I find that so funny.

The drive back was a relaxed affair with boys in jeans running to keep up with the laundau, pigeons suprised by the joy, and not a car in sight except on sufferance. The whole heart of London was what planners are pleased to call a pedestrian precinct. Just people, how pleasant.

8 June, 1977   **Nancy Banks-Smith**

A royal progress to 'dirty Deptford'

The Queen walks into dockland during her river progress this morning through a gate on Deptford Steps, where tradition says that Raleigh (or Drake) spread his cloak for Elizabeth I. Some of her loyal subjects were hoping last night that the civic authorities can remember how to open it.

The gate is not known to have been opened for much of the last 25 years – although it is the only possible access to the Thames for the Pepys council estate of 3000 people and for all Deptford to the south of the estate. The town sailing club doesn't use it. Members have to winch their boats fifteen feet down a flood wall. And it remains locked to the middle-aged, redundant dockers and merchant sailors who often come to Deptford Steps to watch the dwindling traffic on what – in Raleigh's time – was the greatest marine thoroughfare in the world.

The closed gate says much about what history has done to Deptford, especially since the Queen was crowned. It symbolizes the reasons why the working-class area is seizing on her visit to hold a carnival and to try to burst back into life.

The Thames is sealed off to protect children who live in the 22-storey towers and lower-density flats only feet away from the water. The dockers on Deptford Strand laugh at this, claiming that in their own youth they used high tide to float up to Tower Bridge and low tide to swim back again. And – to the horror of the authorities – a number of estate kids do desert their well-designed adventure playgrounds to get to the river. They climb broken walls into Deptford Wharf and the huge corpse of Surrey Docks, where they have an area the size of the City of London to vandalize.

In a chapter on Deptford, the south-east London historian, Mrs Joan Read, quotes a riverside child as saying: 'Just look at the place, Miss. Empty, derelict. The docks are closing down. Most of the houses are pulled down. The old (railway) tracks around Grove Street are going to be pulled up. There'll soon be nothing left around here.' She tries to interest him in the building of the tower blocks but he replies: 'You call that interesting. There's nothing left to do.'

Until well after the coronation it was possible to derive excitement, pride and prosperity from a connection with the river. Pepys called Deptford 'a navy-building town'. Successively, Henry VIII's Royal Dockyard, the Naval Victualling Yard and the foreign cattle market – along with many other riverside industries – such as timber yards – were founded there. But one by one these folded or moved. A network of railways, while bringing prosperity to other areas, cut essential lines of communication for communities and firms in Deptford. A savage blitz, indiscriminate redevelopment instead of restoration, and contraction of the docks before and after Devlin, deepened the spiral of decay. The Deptford totters, who introduced the rag and bottle trade to London, are now more likely to be found peddling second-hand televisions or fridges in the back streets of dying shopping centres. In themselves, some of the new estates with their free central heating and sensitive layouts are excellent machines for living. But they are so hemmed in by decay and isolated from each other that the juvenile gang warfare which attracted the Edwardian nickname, 'Dirty Deptford', is starting to creep back.

One hammerblow during the Queen's reign was the draining of Deptford Canal – now a stinking trench – and the pigeon-holing, for cash reasons, of a plan to re-open it as a service road for new light industries.

Deptford's people have enough spirit left to resent visiting sociologists. As the Queen will find, they throw some of the best parties in Britain when they do get together. But as Joan Read said: 'So many of them have just been uprooted and flung elsewhere. No one knows one another because they haven't lived together long enough. It desperately needs some industry to come back into it. But we haven't got anything to attract it. You can't sell a view of the Thames.'

9 June, 1977   **John Ezard**

Saying nuts to salvation

A British substitute butter mountain has been rotting for a month without a peep of public protest. Autumn picknickers have been sitting on it oblivious to its value; ramblers have been walking over it and never given it a second thought. Even some naturalists have forgotten the value of the beech nut. Two hundred years ago beechmast was widely used in Britain particularly in years such as this, when times were hard or the harvests unpromising. In France, the oil from the nut still is used for cooking and as a substitute for butter. But in Britain, with the exception of a few areas where the farmers feed it to pigs or pheasants, the nuts are left on the ground for squirrels, mice, jays, rooks and pigeons. Can we afford the loss, particularly this year when the beech trees have one of their heaviest harvests?

Even to raise the question runs the risk of the Society of Civil and Public Servants finding new ways of staving off the cuts to its membership. A national programme for harvesting beech nuts, the society might argue, could easily accommodate the 26,000 civil servants who are due to lose their jobs – and without any of them having to dirty their hands in the harvesting. Any civil servant worth his salt (or his nuts) should see the potential in such a scheme: growers will require subsidies, marketing rules, harvest regulations, and price controls. At the consumer end, there is even more potential: beech nuts could replace the child benefit allowances that were due, and are now cancelled, next April. To avoid a low take-up, the exceptional nut allowance will be paid to all families – but to increase the number of civil servants, some nuts will be clawed back, two-parent families losing more in this operation than one-parent families. Two consecutive nut allowances will require a re-adjustment to be made to family income supplement, free school meals, rent and rate rebates, and free prescription charges. If there are still some civil servants unemployed, then a beech nut coupon scheme for pensioners could be introduced.

For fear, therefore, of a glut of civil servants exceeding the crop of nuts, a national beech nut programme should be ruled out. But it still seems a pity that thousands of tons of nuts should go to waste. Instead of sitting on them, picnickers should pick them up. Inside the four-lobed husk they will find two triangular nuts which yield, after crushing, a non-drying oil equivalent to one-fifth of their weight. Good beech years occur at fairly long intervals. The thrifty should make oil while the nuts last.

3 November, 1976   **Leader**

53

Rock of rage

These are extraordinarily difficult times, even for a sugar boiler at a seaside rock factory. In the very act of creating pleasure for millions of children, such a man can be driven by frustration to, well, indiscretions, like putting rude words in the rock.

It is not the social contract, or inflation, or Margaret Thatcher, or even the sheer impossibility of acquiring and keeping together a first-class team of trainee rock makers, though all of these factors take their toll. It is just one damned thing after another, so that eventually a safety valve has to be found.

No use striking. Whoever heard of a striking sugar boiler? The only way in which such a man can let the world know that all is not as sweet as it seems is to sabotage the product, or, at least, enough of it to make an impact. That, certainly, is the method chosen by Mr Michael Leigh, chief sugar boiler and lettering artist to Mr Graham da Costa, rock maker, of Torquay.

He has just ruined, if that is the word, more than 1000 sticks or 'bars' of lovely rock by inserting not Torbay or Brixham or Bournemouth or Brighton, as would be his workaday wor t, but a five-letter word that embodies precisely his feelings about things in general and, on one particular day, rock making in particular.

It seems that Mr da Costa was not too upset, and recognized that sugar boilers are artists of temperament and are not, moreover, easily replaced. Most of the rock thus tarnished was given away to friends and acquaintances over the week-end and, such is the venality of modern life, may even appreciate in value.

Mr Leigh thinks that some of it will inevitably find its way into the hands of children, which will be quite a shock for some mums as they stroll through the palms of Torbay in the early spring.

Mr Leigh is a Lancastrian, from Cleveleys, and pursued his art in Blackpool and on the Yorkshire coast before moving south. He speaks directly, in the rounded way of the north. 'Well, you know how it is sometimes,' he said. 'We've just opened up for the year. We have to work up to about 16 boilings a day, with about 1200 bars in each boiling. You get new staff who don't know what to do,

54

and some who are brighter than others. Then a few boilings go wrong. Then the boss says he's coming in to help, and he doesn't come in.

'So I ses to myself "it's good, is this." I decided to get rid of my feelings in the rock. Actually I wanted to put another word in, slightly longer, but I found I hadn't enough colouring without spoiling the outer coating. In any case, you have to be a bit more careful. The funny thing is, everyone seems to want more of it.'

Mr Leigh's indiscretion is like the substantiation of an old folk myth. It was bound to happen, sooner or later. The word he wanted to insert consisted of eight letters, and is generally considered to be a slightly ruder version of the one he was forced to choose.

Perhaps, at a time when everyone feels much the same way, it is permissible to print the legend in the thousand sticks of rock. It is – BALLS.

15 February, 1977   **Dennis Johnson**

The two horses of democracy

In the main plaza of the village, named of course after Generalissimo Franco, stands a small Citroën 2-CV with two loudspeakers strapped on top. A youthful voice urges the villagers to come to a political meeting and after some trouble with the tape recorder, the strains of the Internationale fill the square.

A dozen old ladies dressed in sempiternal Spanish black, hurry across to evening mass. But before they reach the church door the loudspeakers at full volume have already begun to break into a medley of Popular Front tunes from the civil war. This is rural Spain in June, 1977, the area that is expected to provide an avalanche of votes for the right-wing parties.

The province of Cuenca, south-east of Madrid on the road to Valencia, is a dry, poor and hilly zone where innumerable forgotten villages exist outside the mainstream of national life. For many decades it has been controlled by powerful caciques – rural bosses – who often control the village mayor and the village priest as well as the land and the workers on it.

Industrial, urban Spain is a leftist stronghold, today as it was in the civil war, but rural Spain is still thought to be in the hands of the right. In the town of Cuenca election posters abound for Fuerza Nueva, the Fascist party, with its slogan of 'God, Fatherland and Justice'.

Every evening the young cadres of the Socialist Party (PSOE) drive out into the villages with the fervour of early Christians and the dedication of civil rights workers on a voter registration drive in the Deep South. There are about 80 villages round here, each with less than 350 voters, but the socialist gospel has to be taken to each one.

Meetings begin late, after nine in the evening. Earlier the potential audience is still out in the fields. The area was in Republican hands during the civil war and to the south west, in La Mancha, anarchist cooperatives were formed. But at the end of the war the Republican leaders were executed and the population terrorized by the victors. Acute repression returned again during the period up to 1948 when Communist guerrillas were active in the hills.

The earnest socialists involved in the election campaign were initially worried lest fear and depoliticization would make the campaign irrelevant. But in practice this has not proved to be so. Meetings have been well attended and it is by no means clear that the instructions of the village mayor to vote for the local right-wing candidates will be obeyed.

The mayor still has considerable powers of harassment and the socialists have found that their meetings have been forbidden in some villages. Tonight, however, all is well. They have been given what is grandly called the town hall – a large room off the main plaza – but there are no chairs.

The audience consists of about sixty peasants, brown faced and oldish, wearing sweaters and ragged jackets. There is one old lady, three teenage girls, and two small kids looking through the window. The women are all at home.

'We are proud to be here,' the socialist candidate for senator tells them. She is a teacher in her thirties. 'We have always defended the interests of the working class.' The peasants take off their berets in deference and stand there twisting them in their hands for an hour while the set speech goes on. It is didactic and paternalist in tone, befitting a teacher.

She carefully gives a lesson about the voting mechanism, and explains that the old socialist symbol of a clenched fist 'should not be regarded as aggressive'. The fist she tells the peasants, is shown grasping 'the rose of liberty'.

Then she goes on to analyse the economic situation. How unfortunate that Franco's Spain was not able to benefit from Marshall Aid after the Second World War like the rest of Western Europe. She describes the plight of the emigrant 'with his sad wooden suitcase made by the village carpenter', who is forced to travel from one country to another 'doing the lowest jobs that no one else will do'.

There is a murmur from the audience as though to indicate that they think that she knows what she's talking about. But for the most part the speech is received in respectful silence and given a dutiful clap at the end.

The candidate for deputy then speaks, a typical Spanish intellectual with gold-rimmed glasses. He has already given me a copy of his most recent article on Marxism and philosophy. He speaks plainly, runs through the economic problems of the province – too much latifundia, not enough water – and holds everyone's interest well.

But the solutions presented are moderate in the extreme. There will be a tax reform 'not very big to begin with', and the large landowners will be taxed, but not expropriated. 'We can't use the phrase "land reform",' he told me subsequently, 'because they think you're going to take their land away.' The PSOE cadres don't talk about divorce or abortion either, both popular socialist themes in the cities. 'They can fly the Republican flag in Asturias, but not here.'

Perhaps the socialists are right to arrive in these rural areas with such a low key message. But my impression was that the peasants would have accepted, indeed welcomed, a much more radical programme than the urban intellectuals were prepared to give them. To wait for forty years, to be summoned to a meeting with the music of the Internationale and then to be told that a minor tax reform is on the way is a quick route to disillusionment with politics and democracy.

Of course the socialist leadership in the towns has an under-standable fear of a right-wing backlash, though at present it looks exaggerated. But if change does not come quickly to Spain under the new government, fulfilling the expectations aroused by the collapse of the old regime and the holdings of elections, then these nervous peasants twisting their berets may come to feel that they were better off before.

7 June, 1977   **Richard Gott**

Show time

What Lillian Hellman calls Scoundrel Time in the US was, of course, the age of Senator Joe McCarthy, and the Un-American Activities investigations, as only too well Miss Hellman knows, having suffered under it in the fifties in company with many others, the guilty and innocent alike.

In Britain we never had a serious McCarthy interlude, nor an Un-British Activities Committee, which is not to say we may not have one in the future, nor indeed that somewhere or other some-one may be cooking one up right now. In fact it seems pretty clear that at least one and maybe a score or so of MPs would be glad to stage a revival of the McCarthy roadshow and have a go at the 'crypto-Communist fellow-travellers' who are, so the story goes, lurking in the wainscotting of the Labour Party like so many cockroaches.

I am glad to say that this circumstance is being taken seriously (the accusation, I mean, not the crimes) as evidenced in last week's Commons shemozzle over privilege. It was somewhat over-shadowed by the Home Office's ineffably crude and clumsy handling of the deportation of the two Americans Agee and Hosenball, but there is a funny smell of Star Chamber in the air, and Scoundrel Time, like happy days, may yet be here again.

The Social Democratic Alliance has, too, published its list of prominent Labour MPs alleged to be playing footsie with

The Fifth Column

Communist front organisations or Left-wing barbecues like the World Peace Congress, and so on. This cast of demon kings includes fully paid-up democrats like Michael Foot and Neil Kinnock and Tony Benn and Eric Heffer and Stan Orme who, since most of them are friends of mine, put me in some risk of guilt by association.

Chief of the allegations against these fiends in human form is that at unspecified times they have spoken for, associated with, or even read, the Morning Star.

This, if true, is a grave and solemn matter, and it is a perilous thing for anyone sharing any part of what I understand is now

59

called the Governance of Britain to examine the views of an organization to which they do not belong without being ensnared by it. But if accepting the existence of a CP paper is culpable, who shall 'scape whipping?

I shall tell you a story about the Morning Star, which was then called the Daily Worker, and as you will recall was banned for a while in the war. It was suddenly released from its ban so abruptly that it could raise no staff for its reappearance. Whereupon Fleet Street, in one of its uncommonly rare demonstrations of professional brotherhood, rallied round the red flag in the most extraordinary way, and the first evening saw senior men, editors, technicians, Tories and Trots from every paper from Left to Far Right, sitting shirt-sleeved as down-the-table subs and copy boys to get the edition out.

They were interested, you see, in the press as an abstraction. You would be surprised to know of some who were there. I fear they would not be there today, and nor, I think, would I. But I commend the allegory to the SDA, and to Mr Sproat, and indeed to whom it may concern.

For example, a day or two ago in *The Times* it pleased my learned leader Mr Ronald Butt to reprove the Guardian editorial for wholly missing the point of the SDA accusations. The charge, he said, is not that these named MPs are the 'slaves of King Street', but that they are blurring the lines between the Labour Party and the extremists.

I believe Mr Butt may well be right, but I am still puzzled. I believe it is this blurring of the lines – in both parties, in both attitudes of mind – that is now confusing everyone to the point of electoral paralysis.

Never having been in politics, it had always seemed to me that extremism was the name of the game, and that if you had no absolutes what were you doing in the business? In my innocence I held that if you were a Socialist you wanted socialism; if you were a Tory you rejected it; both were arguable aims; it was in the middle ground I found the quicksands, and I still do.

I remember years ago in San Francisco hearing Senator Barry Goldwater's famous: 'Extremism in the pursuit of virtue is no sin. Moderation to that end is no virtue.' He was of course speaking mirror-language; a rather engaging way-out reactionary, but he had a point. I fancy no marriage between Lord Palmerston and Lenin, but that's what the boyos want.

I am reminded of the old questionnaire that used in the past to be filled in by those requiring US visas. After the routine business about whether you were, had been, or might be persuaded to become a member of the Communist Party, somewhere down the page came the simple question: 'Do you intend to overthrow the United States Government by force?' It always struck me as an inquiry of almost lovable innocence and fatuity, since those who had that intention were the least likely to say so.

I was always able with a clear conscience to deny any serious intention of overthrowing the US Government by force, since as a one-man operation the difficulties seemed too great. I am pretty sure that the Labour Party members who by extremely nasty implication have similarly been accused here would say the same thing about us. So what is the SDA worried about?

That the Leader of the House is an extremist, hands itching to seize the Mace? Perhaps once but, most evidently, not now. That the dreaded Benn is in league with the incandescent Kinnock to raise the legions of the West? At a time like this, when not only our jobs but theirs depend on being good boys in the eyes of the IMF?

Long live the sensible guys of the Extreme Centre. We have nothing to lose but our dreams, and they fade in the morning.

22 November, 1976   **James Cameron**

Up she goes

The spectre of Mrs Thatcher is hovering over Downing Street. A subtle transformation – or ought we to say transfiguration? – is taking place as people begin to perceive her not simply as the leader of the Opposition, but as prospective Prime Minister. The shadow begins to take on substance.

This process begins when the first smell of death escapes through the crack in the door of the Cabinet Room. The opinion pollsters are not quite sure yet but some of their evidence suggests that the public started to count the Government out and count Mrs Thatcher in from the moment of the Lab-Lib 'pact'. To many, it looked like two beaten sides joining forces. But whether the Government is as good as dead or not (some shrewd judges on the Tory side say 'not', or 'not yet') the psychological moment may have arrived at which people begin to look at the Tory leader in a new way.

This happened to Mr Wilson during the protracted run-up to the 1964 election; it never happened to Mr Heath in 1970 although he went on to win it. The Conservative Party managers, sensing the changing public perception of their lady, are beginning to capitalize on it. For example, yesterday's *Times* echoed some interesting thinking-aloud about how she might organize things inside Number 10. (She is on the right lines, by the way, if she really is prepared to politicize Number 10 overtly, to create a proper continental-style *Cabinet* – although it is fearful to think whom she might have in it – and to turn Number 10 into something more like a real Prime Minister's Department.)

Encouraging people to think of Mrs Thatcher in Prime Ministerial terms is a sound tactic by her handlers which also adds to the smell of dead duck gathering around the Government. The corresponding danger for the Tory leader is that as people come to look at her in this fresh light they may not like what they more clearly see, may decide that she doesn't quite fit the part after all or that she is – as Mr Attlee used to put it tersely – 'not up to the job'.

There is the further risk that the sweet promise of success may go to her head, like sal volatile to a young girl's, and give release to her high-spirited instincts which lie naturally a good deal farther to the right than she cares to let on.

If her heart is on the right, her head remains in the centre, although a good deal of self-discipline is required for this contortion. Caution and ambition are the two reins of her passion. So far, it must be said, she has led her party and handled herself with great skill and circumspection. Ministers who go around saying that she is ' Labour's secret weapon' underestimate her as party leader and as a vote-snatcher. She has shown restraint especially in refraining from committing herself to policies. Her tactical objective, now that the election can be glimpsed over the horizon, is to remain as uncommitted as possible while deflecting as best she can accusations of Carter-like 'fuzziness' on the issues. (The coming election, by the way, is certain to be conducted with close reference to the American campaign last year just as the 1964 election took leaves from the Kennedy-Nixon book of 1970. Shall we have television debates?)

Mrs Thatcher's popularity rating has risen quite sharply and, according to Gallup, the proportion of respondents who thinks she is 'proving a good leader of the Conservative Party' has grown from 35 per cent in March to 45 per cent in May. Conservatives are also learning to love her a bit more. Men remain more undecided about her than women. In spite of strenuous effort, Mr Heath remained less popular in the country than the party he led and unbeloved by his own rank-and-file but from time to time he appeared on the verge of things only to be repulsed once more. It is too early to say whether Mrs Thatcher has made her breakthrough, but if she has, her softer tone and appearance on television may have been a contributing factor.

The prospect of Mrs Thatcher in Number 10 is concentrating many minds. She is reported to be prey to what are called 'Ted-like tendencies'. Some of her colleagues are plainly scared of her; even Mr William Whitelaw's equable flesh has been seen to quiver. Her rages are terrible to behold, quite in contrast to the high-pitched billing and cooing of her public demeanour. Anyone wishing to put this to the test is advised to engage her in conversation about the merits of proportional representation. 'She goes absolutely bonkers,' said one who tried and lived to tell the tale.

The reasons for this are obscure. A tempting explanation is that her aversion derives from the experience of Mr John Pardoe standing against her in Finchley; more probable it is because she sees no reason for rescuing the Liberal Party from history's graveyard, where, in her opinion, it belongs and to which she now believes it to be well on its way.

Mrs Thatcher's most observed Ted-like tendency is to lecture industrialists on how to conduct their businesses, especially their labour relations. When in full flight on this latter aspect of management she has been heard to adopt a somewhat Churchillian

63

manner of speech, although not tone of voice; the talk is of fighting here, fighting there, and fighting there as well. She has been heard also to wonder out loud whether referenda might not be a way of discovering who rules Britain, the Government or the unions. Some of the industrialists and others who hear her wonder what kind of Prime Minister she will turn out to be. Sometimes they wonder whether she scares the unions as much as she scares them.

25 May, 1977   **Peter Jenkins**

Antipathy

Sir, – The University of Exeter is alive with red ants. They infest the library and run races up one's sleeve. When I was at the University of Southampton they were a perfect plague. At home in Tottenham we only get those grubby and ungainly black ants. Have the red ants some curious affinity for the middle classes? – Yours, etc,

W. Meyer

Department of Economic History,
University of Exeter.
9 June, 1977

No trouble in store

Never **has** a nation of shopkeepers had a better chance to keep shop profitably. With the pound at an almost unmentionable depth the customers come flocking in. Mr Healey may grieve but Harrods rejoices. Let no one complain that they cannot cross Bond Street because of the press of Sheikhs. They are there for the bargains, to help to make Britain's balance of payments less awful than it would otherwise have been, and to clothe their wives, their children, and their retainers in the best clothing that Britain can offer.

Everyone from Harrods downwards ought now to be looking for ways to exploit the bright side of the falling pound. Tourism, for example, needs more outlets outside London. Tintagel, Stonehenge, and Stratford-on-Avon are not enough. They cannot possibly absorb the army of visitors that a $1.60 pound (or whatever it is) will attract to Britain. Much more attention will have to be paid to the individual requirements of individual visitors. When it comes to Communists, Highgate Cemetery is an underexploited asset. Why cannot tourists from the East buy plastic replicas of Marx's tomb? Why can they not find it more easily?

For the Americans there could be easier (but much more expensive) access to the parish records in the Public Record Office where they are fond of looking up their ancestors. They could also be offered suitably expensive package tours to Whitehaven which John Paul Jones captured briefly in 1778. French visitors could be offered a similar tour of Fishguard which the French navy occupied, again briefly, in 1797 (causing, incidentally, an alarming run on the pound). Or they could be shown the ancient gun Winston Churchill fired at France in 1941, and missed. The Scandinavians, who are also immensely rich, could be tempted to visit the sites of the victories of King Canute (they range, expensively, from Sandwich to York) who is the only man who has conquered England twice before he was 21. This would not be exploitation so much as the intelligent use of a $1.60 pound seen as the one sort of asset it, dolefully, is.

2 November, 1976   **Leader**

When in Rome, do as the FO tells you

It was only after the first 100-strong advance guard of Liverpool's estimated 18,000 supporters for Wednesday's European Cup Final were in mid-flight yesterday that we were told that the pre-booked, too-good-to-be-true, plush hotel in snazzy, snappy Via Veneto had broken their contract and cancelled our accommodation. They had not been told, they said, that the booking was for English *football* supporters: they presumed it had been for a pious old-ducks party from the Liverpool Catholic Women's League for the big canonization in St Peter's at the weekend.

So there we were, differently pious, the very vanguard of the red-and-white army, all decked up but apparently with nowhere to go once we had landed. At the end of last week the directors of the five-star Beverly Hills Hotel held an emergency meeting and decided, 'no Liverpool'.

The London-based agent for the Phoenix travel firm, Michael Ross, had to travel to Rome at once. It seems that the Beverly Hills had washed their hands of possible mayhem and farmed out our party in little batches to outskirt boarding houses. He was lucky to find a new-brand central hotel 'which nobody had heard of because it had never had one guest yet'. It is their baptism. And there they all were when our three airport coaches pulled up, hymns, arias and Union Jacks flying through the window. You should have seen their faces.

Mr Ross explained the cancellation: 'There has been a terrific anti-British campaign building up in Rome for the match. On the television and in the press every day for a week there have been warnings of what to expect from Liverpudlians. They re-ran the film of the Leeds supporters breaking up Paris after the final a couple of years ago. They show pictures from any English Saturday.'

On our bus from the airport, Mr Ross solemnly read out a Foreign Office edict which had been sent to Anfield for every travelling supporter to sign: 'I, the undersigned, agree to (a) behave at all times in a responsible manner: (b) agree to occupy and never move from the seat provided for me at the match . . .' I later asked the embassy what the FO would do if their signed agreement was broken. Nobody there seemed to know.

Actually, I reckon it's a bit of a slander this time. For Liverpool, on the whole, are lovely supporters, for all the colourful warpaint and one or two too-early drinkers yesterday. Their wit, genuine exuberance and quietly smug enjoyment of their team is a warm pleasure to sit near. Meanwhile, Rome is not convinced. Already, they have announced that the Olympic Stadium will not be open tomorrow night for its capacity of 75,000, but for only 57,000. There is apparently going to be a lot of open space for the police to prowl in.

24 May, 1977   **Frank Keating**

'*He's already stopped me lying awake at night worrying about Rhodesia – two Mogadons with a cup of hot milk last thing at night . . .*'

Quelle diabolique liberté

Il n'est pas notre problème si les français refusent de parler notre langue, et nous seront damnés si nous sommes allant à apprendre français justement pour sauver les français le trouble. Il est ici que les inspecteurs d'écoles, dans leur regrettable rapport sur 'Modern Languages in Comprehensive Schools,' on fait leur grand erreur. Votre ordinaire enfant anglais a des plus importants choses à faire que de s'asseoir dans une chaise et passer le temps en essayant de parler une langue qui monstre toutes les signes, comme le Latin et le Grec, de mourant hors.

Il était bien entendu quand nous anglais ont joigné le marché commun quelques années derrière qu'anglais serait plus important que français. Sinon, comment expliquez-vous que le plupart du monde semble d'être assez content de conduire leurs affaires en anglais? Hein? Répondez à cela, s'il vous plait, MM les inspecteurs! Quelle sorte de monde supposez-vous que nos enfants sont aller à demeurer dans quand ils sont adultes? Si la reste du monde est allant à parler anglais obvieusement il n'y a pas beaucoup d'une future en apprenant français, et nos enfants sont mieux employés en faisant des choses utiles, telle que le sport et les 'handicrafts.' Les inspecteurs sont torts. Zut pour les!

18 March, 1977   Leader

New world, same old ways

'How can I sit down and eat with people from all the dictatorships?' The editor of a national daily newspaper had just boycotted a dinner for the non-aligned foreign ministers' meeting. It was just three weeks after India had regained its status as the world's biggest democracy. Lowering his voice, the editor continued: 'You know, I shall never again feel able to suppress anything in my newspaper on grounds of political caution.' Democratic breast-beating was still in vogue.

This particular editor had not, in fact, distinguished himself in the testing days of the emergency. He had taken no great risks, and had even offered some gratuitous support. The record of other editors had been far better.

Who resisted and who collaborated? It hardly mattered in a brave new world in which pride of achievement mingled with a wild hope that a new era had dawned.

'Look at my desk – it is clear of files,' said the new Minister of Commerce, Mr Mohan Dharia, fresh from an emergency prison cell. 'In the old days a Minister's desk was heaped with files – deliberately kept pending while money was collected for the party.'

'We shall have barefoot doctors,' anounced Mr Raj Narayan, the Minister of Health, the homely, oddly-dressed eccentric whose election petition sparked off the emergency and who finally defeated Mrs Gandhi at Rae Barelli.

The 'right to work' for 22 million unemployed, an end to destitution in ten years: this and much else the new Government had promised. Economists combining socialist with Gandhian ideas explained it could be done by decentralizing the economy and setting up agriculture-based cottage industries, generating at last the economic 'take-off' that big steel mills never did. The apparatus of the emergency was quickly dismantled. The Prime Minister's bloated office was pared down, the dreaded secret service cut down to size. The Home Minister promised to free the Naxalite revolutionaries who had been in prison without trial, or after mock trials, for decades, and to appoint inquiries into the abuses of the emergency.

The tone of politics changed. Ministers took scheduled flights instead of official helicopters. They actually invited the Leader of the Opposition to make a broadcast. To watch over the new order, the followers of Jayaprakash Narayan, the Gandhian whose revolt had started the chain of protest, were preparing to set up 'people's committees' in every village.

Even miracles were performed. Fifty veteran smugglers, wealthy men who had apparently financed both Government and Opposition in the old days, assembled in the sickroom of Jayaprakash, swore to renounce their trade, and even offered their skills in helping the customs authorities. Naxalite leaders conferred with Jayaprakash's followers, offering to 'renounce violence'.

Haunting this invigorating scene were some eerie survivals. As Mr Advani, the new Minister of Information, talked about the new order, his information officer, quietly taking notes behind his chair, was the same man who had served the last Minister – Mr Shukla, now denounced as one of the 'gang of four' who had terrorized India. The eeriest survival was Mrs Gandhi herself, still in her old official house, still attending and manipulating party meetings and still – uncannily – sending her 'special envoy', Mohammed Yunis (one of the emergency's most dreaded figures), on political missions to remote states. Her son Sanjay still lived in the house and went daily to his office at Maruti Ltd., the bogus firm for which he had allegedly subverted the financial administration of India.

Another three weeks have now passed and the euphoria is

beginning to evaporate. Attention from the newness of things was diverted by an old-style political crisis. Irked that, after its landslide victory in the northern states, congress state governments still ruled there, the Janata Party dissolved the assemblies and declared new state elections. The Congress resisted and, with much legal and constitutional rectitude on its side, appealed to the supreme court. It lost – a victim of its own past manipulations of the legal system. But the Janata Party had lost some of its magic too. Viable, elected state governments had been dissolved at the whim of the ruling party in Delhi. Embarrassingly like the old days.

With nine state elections upon them, Ministers now had less time to listen to the new economists. Committees were set up to put the new ideas into practice. The promised inquiry commissions failed to start work. It is whispered that ministers with skeletons in their own cupboards have lost enthusiasm. Mr Morarji Desai, too, has a son, and he, too, has been widely accused of misusing his father's influence for his own commercial gain. Mr Jagjivan Ram, the Minister of Defence, not so long ago declared he had 'forgotten' to pay his income tax two years running. Two other Ministers have been publicly involved in past corruption inquiries.

Naxalites were not after all let out in any significant numbers and it became apparent that the civil servants in West Bengal and Bihar – who had locked them up in the first place – were not giving the Home Minister much help in the matter.

Meanwhile coloured marquees have appeared outside the Ministers' houses to shelter people waiting for an audience. Few of the tents have proved big enough for the purpose. Power has been transferred, for the first time in the Indian federal centre, and the office seekers, the hard-luck cases, the relatives, and the true and false well-wishers have arrived for their share of the pickings.

12 May, 1977   **Walter Schwarz**

Bhutto's last orders for Murree's Lager

Receptions at Pakistani embassies across the world are pretty dull affairs these days, now that Mr Bhutto has proclaimed his Islamic Republic teetotal. Coke and Seven-Up are the order of the day in missions abroad and here, at such official parties as are thrown, one gets lime-soda till the limes run out, and then just soda. Pakistan under Prohibition can be, at times, a miserable place. The epicentre of that misery – for drinkers at least – is the country's only brewery: a splendidly Victorian relic, created by Whymper (of Matterhorn renown) and set in production for the express purpose of slaking the thirsts of tired British infantrymen, Murree's Brewery company of Rawalpindi, now grinding to a halt after 116 years of near continuous production.

Murree's London Lager, still served in magnificent two-pint bottles, is a welcome sight after a hard day's trek in the hills (or even an equally hard day's trek in the wake of some elusive bureaucrat) and is soon to vanish from the streets of Pakistan. The Prohibition Act 1977, passed in the National Assembly in Islamabad last week, makes 'the manufacture, sale, and use' of liquor totally forbidden 'without', as the *Pakistan Times* warned severely, 'exemption to anybody.'

Of course, like so much in the *Times*, it's not quite like that. Foreigners and non-Moslems can still persuade cadaverous-looking barmen to sell them a bottle of London Lager for 30 rupees or £2 – ten times the price Murree's sells it for – and if you care to have your identity card stamped 'chronic alcoholic' you can get the stuff almost, as it were, on the National Health. But in his efforts to knock the stuffing out of the Islamic zealots of the Opposition, Mr Bhutto's steady application of Swariat or Quranic law (Friday will be the Sabbath here, come next July) has been made extremely tough.

All of which is sad news for Murree's, for its German brew-master, Mr Heinz Kiel, and for its chief, Mr Minoo Bhandara, an Oxford-educated Parsee whose family bought the brewery from the British after partition thirty years ago. Mr Bhandara has made a considerable success of his brewery. He now markets two beers (London Lager and Murree's Export, the latter going on sale in Bradford next year).

There is one final irony, though. Mr Bhutto's official residence is but a stone's throw from the brewery and is, in fact, on the company's estate. The Prime Minister, it turns out, pays rent for his house to the Murree Brewery Company. If his landlord goes bust, Mr Bhutto will, to put it kindly, have been hoist by his own petard.

16 May, 1977   **Simon Winchester**

Pay-day for the Lebanon vultures

Today was pay-day for the gunmen who besieged and defeated this Palestinian refugee camp on the outskirts of Beirut, and even before the last of the snipers had been cleared from the wrecked buildings, they came to collect. From the rubble and out of the shacks of Tel al-Zaatar the gunmen hauled refrigerators, sewing machines, stoves, television sets, suites of furniture in red velvet, and piled them into lorries which they'd driven over corpses to get into position.

The camp is a macabre and sickening sight. It buzzes with flies who feed off the eyes and the wounds of the dead. Bodies litter the streets. I saw about 100, but gunmen who have been around the camp for several hours say 1500 are scattered about. In some dusty streets you don't notice the corpses until you have stepped on them. They have been squashed flat by cars and trucks and look as though they are made of straw. The smell is sickening and choking. Many of the looters wore breathing masks. I covered my nose and mouth with my shirt, which was soaked in sweat, and this acted as a filter.

The gunmen don't get paid in the normal way by the organizations for which they fight and sometimes die. They are given food, whisky, and cigarettes. Their families are sometimes provided with food. They believe they are fighting to save their country and they do it for ideology and not for cash. But when a prize like Tel al-Zaatar is gained, then the rules say they can

72

take what they find.

What is astonishing is that so much has survived the bombardments of the last weeks – not the buildings, because almost all of them are more full of holes than a Swiss cheese and many look as if one hefty push would send them crashing to the ground; but the personal possessions inside the concrete-walled, tin-roofed shacks. Tel al-Zaatar was an armed slum. Most of the inhabitants were labourers for the surrounding factories who over the years fitted out their miserable homes with middle-class Western comforts: the large refrigerator, the fancy stove, the three-piece suite. The Palestinian resistance who ran the camp provided massive fortifications, underground shelters, and tunnels which even today give snipers the ability suddenly to appear in an area which everyone thought had been cleared. A gunman belonging to the hard-line National Liberal Party died from a sniper's bullet shortly before a group of colleagues and I arrived at the camp, and while we were there the crackle of rifle and machine-gun fire was a constant background. At one point, just as we crossed into the camp, a bullet passed close enough over our heads for us to hear its high-pitched buzz.

The bodies begin right at the perimeter. And often the smell chokes you before you see them. Many have been dead for weeks, others were hit in the last day or two as they tried to flee to safety. They lie in groups, very often, families, including children, caught there in a close pack in the middle of a main road or hit as they tried to dodge down some narrow alleyway. They tried to escape with bundles of clothing. Because these are now open and scattered on the roads, the vehicles drive over them. There is much for looters to pick from the bones of Tel al-Zaatar before they need to turn their attention to a few bits of clothing.

The dirt roads of the camp are covered with a sticky, oily mud that sucks at your shoes with each step. There has presumably been a massive leakage of some fuel, because it has not rained in weeks and it was the lack of water that finally caused the defences to collapse. Fires have been started in several of the houses and the dense smoke mingles with the smell of death.

In one tin-roofed shack there's a photograph on the wall of a bride in a long white dress and a smiling groom. And today they're looking down on to a scene of chaos. All the possessions of a family – clothes, furniture, bedding, books – have been thrown on to the floor and you have to climb over them to get into the room. The photograph will not be there much longer. It has an ornate silver frame, and on pay-day that must be worth something.

With a National Liberal Party gunman as guide, we were taken to a clinic which had been operated by the militant Popular Front for the Liberation of Palestine: I had been there last March to hear from the Swedish doctors of the plans they were making for the coming battle. They were hoping to bring in blood bags and needles so the patients would no longer have to bleed to death; and to get in general anaesthetics so they would not have to perform operations on people who could not stop screaming. The clinic had not been badly damaged, but the medicine shelves were bare. Only a handful of white tablets lay scattered on a table. In one room, there was a pool of fresh blood on the floor, which meant a sniper had been at work nearby.

There is no doubt that the people of Tel al-Zaatar suffered dreadfully during the 52-day siege. They were desperately short of water and low on food. But that didn't stop the propagandists from trying to make things look even worse than they were, and the vehicle they chose was the issue of the wounded. In the three weeks I have been in Beirut, I have been constantly assured that medical supplies had run out in the camp and that all doctors would do for the injured was to bathe their wounds in a salt water solution. So it came as something of a surprise today to go into the main Palestine Liberation hospital in the camp and discover considerable quantities of medicines. It is highly unlikely they were planted there by the right-wingers, who have been too busy looting and trying to flush out snipers. Most of the medicines – and they included large, unopened boxes – were manufactured in Communist countries and were neatly packed away on shelves and in drawers.

I joined the looters myself, and brought out some random specimens of the lack of medicines: a bottle of aspirin, ten tetra-cycline capsules, and an injection ampoule of Decadron which is a painkiller. There was so much to choose from that if my

74

colleagues and I had loaded our arms full we could not have cleared even a room. It seems certain that the camp did run short of bandages, however. Some of those evacuated by the International Red Cross last week had their injuries covered with plastic bags, stuck on with tape. I was not able to discover what did happen to the wounded. They were not in the hospital nor were any bodies. A group of old people lay in the dust outside, but they were fully dressed, rather than being in pyjamas.

On the outskirts of the camp, we met the NLP militia leader, Dany Chamoun, whose group, 'the Tigers', played a leading part in the attack. He said they had discovered a factory in Tel al-Zaatar for making rocket-propelled grenades, but when we went to see it, gunmen turned us back. They said they were still checking for landmines. There was angry shouting between them and we followed the golden rule of always being nice to people with guns, and didn't insist.

Chamoun said: 'They made those gun grenades to NATO standards. Before they surrendered, they blew up most of the ammunition and the radio equipment. We found some destroyed Kalashnikovs.'

Chamoun – whose father Camille is the NLP president, and whose brother Dory runs a militia of his own – said he believed the fall of Tel al-Zaatar had broken the back of the Palestine resistance.

'Now they are beginning to get people from outside,' he said, 'There is a boat arriving at Sidon with 400 Algerians on it to fight alongside the Palestinians. But they will all die. They are receiving ammunition at the rate of 450 tons a week. I think the Palestinians will wait a bit before they attack. They have maybe 25,000 refugees over there which will keep them busy. Maybe we will attack before they do.'

'We would like to reunite this country. The idea of a religious war was not ours. It was forced on us. Partition will come to Lebanon unless we attack. My home-town is 42 kilometres from here and I intend to get to it.'

What about Tel al-Zaatar? Chamoun said: 'The next move is to bulldoze all this rubbish down.'

14 August, 1976   **Peter Niesewand**

The children of Israel

Israeli El Al stewardess: 'They think this is their airline. They get on in New York, make straight for the lavatories and I find them there, taking off their corsets, squeezing orange juice for their children . . .'

Professor in Jerusalem: 'When I was a girl in Romania, any social or political change made me ask one question – is it good for the Jews?'

American member of the United Jewish Appeal in Jerusalem (pointing to the American flags waving by the wall): 'Look, honey, our flag is everywhere.'

Golda Meir: 'Those . . . who have tried to opt out of their Jewishness have done so at the expense of their own basic identity. They have pitifully impoverished themselves.'

Englishman in Kent pub: 'I don't like Jews but I've got a lot of time for Israelis.'

Israel, by its very existence, has sharpened the old Jewish question. Once, the conundrum went thus: is Jewishness a race or a religion or both? Now there is an added ingredient, argued by many young Israelis: Jewishness is only a nationality and they quote the twelfth-century Rabbi Moses Maionides, who wrote: 'There is no Judaism without Israel.'

In England I am intermittently aware of Jews and when I am, I think in clichés – they are funnier, more sensitive, more melancholy, meaner, richer, cleverer, they never give you enough to drink, they get indigestion, they're too passive, they don't like the countryside, they don't like dogs, they go to shrinks, the women are always at the hairdressers, they live near other Jews, they are always professionals, never dustmen. And these, I might add, are the non-Orthodox, I do not know the Orthodox.

In Israel, after the initial outsider's shock – heavens, everyone here is Jewish, the politician and the charwoman, the bank manager and the dustman – consciousness of Jews ceased abruptly and never raised its head again. The relief was surprisingly powerful. For the first time I felt absolutely at home with Jews.

Here, they were ordinary members of the human race, in no more need of my best behaviour, my most careful sensitivity, than I was of theirs. For the first time they were fully a part of everything that was happening, good or bad, happy or sad, evil or honourable. For the first time, there were no corners of my mind I thought necessary to conceal. A small but definite reservation vanished. Politeness was exorcised and honesty could take its place.

But do the Israelis and the Diaspora Jews feel that distinction? How do they differ? Is the Israeli forming another identity, light years away from his grandparents in the ghettos of Eastern Europe?

Professor Rivka Bar-Josef, sociologist at the Hebrew University, Jerusalem, is a woman in her fifties, a long-time Zionist and now an Israeli, emigrated from Eastern Europe.

'The main change I've felt since coming to Israel is that here I'm responsible for what's happening, it's relevant to me. I hear American Jews complaining about American bureaucracy but, in the last analysis, they can say, ah, it is not mine. There is a possibility of detachment, they may feel "it is not my business". Here, we are constantly bombarded with responsibility, it invades all personal feelings, you cannot not be involved. I fought for a place where a specifically Jewish identity could develop to provide its own colour and image to the general picture of the world.'

In the beginning, the Israeli policy was to assimilate Jews from different backgrounds by ignoring the differences and stressing Israel, as the American founding fathers did. But it did not work.

'Real integration is only possible when background differences are recognized and incorporated. This was particularly true with Oriental Jews, now over 50 per cent of the nation. When they came from the Yemen, from Persia, from Morocco, from Iraq, they were insecure, they didn't try to hold on to their heritage because they thought it gave them a low status. But now we see the Israeli identity as a web of different colours and textures, a beautiful pattern in which you can trace one thread back to its origins.'

Professor Bar-Josef describes how each ethnic group is now contributing its own special saga of modern Jewish heroes from Morocco, Hungary, Iraq, Lithuania.

'By doing this, each group can feel it is contributing to the whole, to Israel, and yet can identify with the particular hero. We are introducing into school books these folk-heroes who reflect all the cultural heritages and the Oriental Jew has a special gift to give. The Western Israeli composer, for instance, is turning to the Oriental for something original, something that, together with Western influences, will emerge as purely Israeli.' Most important of all, Professor Bar-Josef feels that 'fate-control' is the great Israeli advantage over the Diaspora Jew. 'None of us have it totally but, within certain limits, Israelis feel they have something to say in the control of their fate. Jews have always felt that, in war, control of their fate is out of their hands. Whatever they did, nothing really changed. Here, we have more control and we can change some things.'

The professor points out that a knowledge of equality is vital for harmony, not only between Jew and Jew but between Arab and Jew. 'You offer friendship,' she says, 'if you are prepared to give but it is almost more necessary to need to receive. Dependency makes you over-compensate in some way. Recently I talked to some Egyptian scholars and I got the impression that they felt like Jews feel towards Gentiles. One Egyptian explained that they all feel the problem of equality. Because their society is less developed, they have a terrible sensitivity. If we got together, he said to me, 'what would you expect to *receive*?'

The young Israeli, born in the Promised Land, already has certain definite characteristics of his own. He is a child of the Holocaust, determined that Jews shall never die in *that* way again. Masada, the great flat-topped mountain by the Dead Sea, where 900 Jews chose mass-suicide rather than become Roman slaves, is his totem and he wears T-shirts proclaiming 'Masada shall not fall again'. And though less 'ordinary' than his contemporaries in the West, more serious, more aware of life and death, he is also more 'ordinary' than his parents and grandparents.

He has a robust peasant humour without the sour sadness of traditional Jewish wit. He is taller, more muscular, he stands and walks and lounges with the expansiveness of a cowboy. He is, surprisingly often, very handsome, either in a blunt Robert Redford way or in an evocation of the old prophets, with fine

Semitic eagle-nose and glorious masses of blond-edged curls. He may be pale-complexioned, with grey eyes, or so dark that he could pass for an Arab because he comes from the Yemen and an Arab is what he is, but for him Israel is his country, the place where he was born, that is all and that is enough.

Many young Israelis are not religious and, as such, a cause of worry to some of their elders who see religion as the only welder. They resent the very Orthodox who refuse national service, who do not recognize the State of Israel because no one has proved to them that the new Messiah has come.

'Do you know,' they say, 'there are parts of Jerusalem where we cannot go because they will stone us on a Sabbath or if girls expose their arms or legs?' They make jokes about the Rabbinate, who control domestic law. 'If we don't want to marry in the synagogue we go to Cyprus for a civil wedding. And poor so-and-so, she's a girl from Brooklyn who married an Orthodox Jew. He makes her have a ritual bath when she has her period and won't take any plates from her hand or sleep in the same bed.'

They feel even more strongly about Diaspora Jews. When I was in Jerusalem, 5000 members of the American United Jewish Appeal paraded through the city to the Wailing Wall. With true American ebullience they embraced, here and there, the Israelis who watched them pass. The Israelis smiled and looked deeply embarrassed, they were obviously discomfited. 'They give us a lot of money,' they said. 'It's not money we need,' they said. 'If they'd stop giving us money and come here,' they said, 'we could do a year's national service instead of three and a half.' They said, 'Taking American money makes us a pawn to the Americans, they feel they can tell us what we can build in Jerusalem and when we should fight. We wish they would leave us alone.' The emotions may be unrealistic but they are powerful.

I talked, over a Sabra breakfast (stomach-heaving roll mops and goat cheese) with an 18-year-old Israeli in his green uniform, his gun slung behind his chair. He said he had been staying with friends in the Jewish community in London after the Yom Kippur War. 'I had a friend who was killed in that war and they kept on saying "we". In the end, I leapt on a chair, tears streaming down my face, and I shouted, "Stop saying *we*". What did *you* do? We, the Israelis, won that war, *you* were here in England, in comfort."'

I talked to another young Israeli who had had the same experience after the Six-Day War. 'After I'd yelled at them all, after I'd said don't say "we", say "you", I got a reputation. They said to each other, don't touch on the war, he gets very edgy. And I found another thing, in England. I felt only really comfortable with Jews who were completely assimilated or with kids of my own age, non-Jewish kids. I couldn't cope with the Orthodox scene, the next-year-in-Jerusalem scene. You know how Gentiles have always been accused of being anti-semitic if they say to Jews, "Why don't you go to Israel?" Well, that's what I feel. Our hope in Israel is anti-semitism. Best thing you could do for us is go home to England and write "Go Home, Jew" on the walls. Never mind money, we need more people. Never mind lip service, get packing. The only Jews I have respect for are those who come here or those who assimilate. That's because the whole Jewish religion, the dietary laws, the lot, were worked out to keep us together until we could get back to Israel. And if a Jew doesn't come back now, his religion doesn't make sense.'

I write these things because they were said to me. Emotions are not always practical, they do not necessarily mesh with reality, they are not always kind. Older, emigrant Jews do not always feel this way and nor do all the Israeli-born. But the proportion of Sabras who feel alienated from the Israeli-centred Diaspora Jew is increasing and, it seems to me, inevitably so. When we were fighting in the Second World War, we were forced to feel grateful for American bounty, but we actually felt angry because of American hesitancy. Get in there, we said, frequently. Stop sending food parcels and start building, digging, fighting. Thus the Israelis.

Arthur Koestler, long-time advocate of the 'go to Israel or assimilate' policy, is furiously attacked by American Leon Wieseltier, Jewish scholar, in a recent issue of a New York paper. Mr Wieseltier says Koestler's idea 'is a supremely vulgar Zionism – at once pro-Israeli and anti-Jewish'. He says: 'Zionism will release from their Jewishness only those Jews for whom it was already insufferable.' He says, most cruelly, about Mr Koestler, 'only a Jew would have taken so much trouble to come up with an alibi for his own self-effacement'. Or only an Israeli. It was an Israeli academic who said to me: 'The real test for Israeli nationhood will be acceptance of a Moslem Jew.'

22 November, 1976   **Jill Tweedie**

A sense of fraternity

'Nobody in his right mind would want to change our present rulers for a Sadat, Assad, Bakr, or the Gadafy they would probably get if they tried,' said Hassan Husseini, teacher, journalist and sharp observer, 'and you can quote me.' If there were any serious opposition to the House of Saud, it would most likely be found among such highly educated, widely travelled young.

They are increasingly plentiful and one day, perhaps, they will grow restive, but they do not show much sign of it at present. An important reason, of course, is the absence of external stimulus. The so-called 'revolutionary' regimes of the Arab world, seen as abject failures, can no longer furnish that. But there is another reason – the continuing vigour of the House of Saud itself.

The family of Abdul Aziz, founder of the Kingdom, is still imbued with a sense of its own legitimacy, of the privilege and obligation that goes with it. But his fertility was perhaps the key to his heirs' success. His marriages were designed to consolidate tribal loyalties in the newly forged state. He had 42 sons, the nucleus of a ruling caste which, grandchildren and other relatives included, embraces at least 5000 members. It is a very exclusive club; a few foreign wives apart, princes almost always marry princesses.

Size seems to militate against the emergence of individual tyrants. There are of course clans and rivalries. The most influential inner conclave is the 'Seven Sudeiris', sons of the same mother, who are the Crown Prince, Ministers of Defence, Interior, their deputies, and the governor of Riyadh.

Tradition has it that, before she died, their mother asked them to meet every day, in the house of one of their sisters, to discuss affairs of state. But the Sudeiris are careful to grant the rival clan headed by Prince Abdullah, the command of the National Guard, the internal security force. For big decisions, consensus is arrived at through larger family councils.

Size confers another, crucial advantage. It makes the family omnipresent, in government, the armed forces, business. Key ministries are theirs; the new generation provides pilots and staff officers. They have eyes and ears everywhere, and, as if their own were not enough, there are those of their 'Ikhwa' too. Anything up to fifty of 'Ikhwa' or brethren are attached to princely households. Even the Foreign Minister, Prince Saud, urbane son of the late King Faisal, maintains the tradition. Their quarters adjoin his own stylish establishment. They are retainers or companions, often sprung from the original entourage of Abdul Aziz, who, in addition to a variety of specific functions, help keep their masters in touch with the world.

Some princes spend hours every day with their Ikhwa, as well as keeping open board for anyone who cares to profit from their hospitality. Important princes also have a 'Majlis', or open court, before which any citizen with a grievance or a plea can present himself. The Minister of Interior devotes two or three hours a day to his Majlis. The best princes hold court with a dignified authority, intuitive judgement and remarkable familiarity with the issues laid before them. Their prestige is high. The ordinary man automatically looks to them, for redress, before any other quarter. He may come from far afield, and foreigners, illiterate Yemenis or Palestinian technicians, come too. The princes either settle the affair on the spot (and often at their own expense), hand it over to the appropriate court or ministry, or seek further enlightenment through their own means. Modern technology – newly installed Arabic telexes – now assist in ancient tradition. So does money.

It costs a lot to be a prince these days. Their official stipend – perhaps £25,000 a month for top princes – is a mere pittance. Some raise money by selling off land. It was worth almost nothing when their father presented it to them, tens of millions today. Princes in official service are not allowed to go into business. Others are encouraged to do so – and thereby help finance their needier brothers.

It is an archaic system, but Saudi Arabia is in many ways still an archaic country. Of course it is changing with incredible speed, and pressure for political changes to match educational, economic and technological progress will relentlessly build up.

It was announced after King Faisal's assassination that a consultative council would be set up. But nothing has happened. 'We don't want to set up such institutions,' said Prince Salman, governor of Riyadh, 'just so as to look good in the eyes of the world. Anyone with ideas only has to come and discuss them with us.'

But if they are the wrong ideas – such as the establishment of trade unions, political parties or anything deemed likely to 'divide and disturb' – they will be automatically rejected. Obviously, therefore, the legitimacy of the House of Saud will only endure as long as the general acceptance of its authoritarian, patriarchal ways.

In its own view, it certainly still enjoys that acceptance. 'The family founded the kingdom, united it, and preserved it from foreign dangers,' says Prince Naif, Minister of Interior. 'We are close to the people, and enjoy their respect and confidence. There has been plenty of evidence of that.'

It is a standard princely plea; but few commoners, it seems, would strenuously contest it. The evidence includes the claim that there are no political prisoners in Saudi Arabia today. 'We never had more than 250 at any time,' said Prince Naif, 'and we released the last 63 two years ago.' His Ministry does not deign to reply to the inquiries of Amnesty International, but the claim – which few Arab countries could make – appears valid. It is certainly a sign of royal self-confidence.

But perhaps the most impressive evidence is the intelligentsia which the regime has not been afraid to create. Education projects, costing £11.5 billion, run a close second, after defence, in the gargantuan five-year development programme. There are now six universities in the Kingdom, with over 20,000 full-time students. The University of Petroleum and Minerals, the pride of Saudi educationalists, is acquiring worldwide reputation. Education is free. Undergraduates get 'pocket money' of £1000 a year. High salaries attract foreign professors. There are some 6000 Saudi students in the United States – not to mention other Western countries – a figure that no other Arab country begins to match.

In the more advanced Arab countries there is a serious brain-drain. By contrast, an extraordinarily high proportion of foreign-educated Saudis return home. Neither the political system nor the constraints of the world's most conservative society seem to deter them. For the regime is self-assured enough to tolerate the emergence of a technocratic class in which merit, as much as political loyalty, earns reward. The Oil Minister, Sheikh Yamani, is the exemplary Saudi technocrat, but in the Cabinet there are no fewer than eight PhDs.

The technocrats cannot but make inroads into the decision-making monopoly of the royal family and, through the institutions which they staff, reduce the anarchy of rival princely fiefs. They cramp the princes' ability to take fat commissions on foreign contracts, even if they are not above reproach themselves. The princes sit in on committees which vet the tenders.

By natural evolutionary process, the technocrats are agents of change. And they can see from close quarters that – though there are no PhDs in the royal family – it is on the whole more receptive to change than the mass of the populace. At the same time, however, there is an inevitable distance between princes and technocrats. Both know that it is the educated who will spearhead any challenge to the legitimacy of the House of Saud. 'We can sense their uneasiness,' said a university professor. 'Prince Naif came and spoke to us for two hours and told us that if we had any complaints and criticisms we should not hesitate to convey them to him. I don't think any of us did.'

Yet those who harbour political ambitions are not going to unveil them now that their rulers are at the apogee of their power and importance. They have no encouragement from outside, where Saudi money is helping to prop up discredited regimes far beyond their natural life span. They have little from inside, where the people are kept busy digesting their share of the greatest jackpot in history. When the authorities released the last 63 political prisoners, they paid them, too. Some are already success-ful businessmen. And it could be said that, in effect if not intent, the House of Saud is buying off the entire population.

21 June, 1977   **David Hirst**

A touch of class

One place in this world where the lion lies down with the lamb is over afternoon tea at London's Hilton. Sales-weary Jewish matrons eating strawberry cream teas and dishy young Arabs sipping Coke are distracted from one another among the tiny close-packed tables by the pianist, Naomi Davidov. She is the granddaughter of a Russian emigré, born in Llanelli, who every day from four till seven pours live notes out of a baby grand like tea from a huge samovar, mixing Schubert, Chopin and Beethoven with standard hits like *My Way*, *San Francisco* and *Dr Zhivago*, or interspersing Mozart's 'Elvira Madigan' concerto with sudden difficult sections of a sonata for a coming recital.

The other day, for instance, she played the Fugue from Beethoven's Hammerklavier Sonata, a tortured movement that wins student pianists more eviction notices than prizes, and looked up expecting the room to have emptied. 'But they were still there, a lot of Arabs, talking.'

Naomi has played the Hammerklavier, one of the most difficult works in any repertory, at a Purcell Room recital. She practises morning and evening, before and after the Hilton, and on her one day off, Monday, all day. It's a work she has lived with since she learned it at 17 for the Liszt Prize at the Royal Academy, when she was heartbroken to come second, not first.

She played it on arrival in Vienna to study under a master. 'He hadn't had the letter and wasn't expecting me. I said: "My name is Joy Davies. (I changed it back to the original Davidov later. There are so many musicians called Davies.) I've come all the way from Llanelli to study with you and I'm not going away." He said: "Play something", and I played the Hammerklavier. He said I had real talent.'

Naomi was an infant prodigy who took her first steps towards the concert hall at Llanelli Grammar School. 'I'd been having lessons with Mr Evans, a local teacher, from three and a half and I was playing Bach and Mozart at six. My headmistress heard me play and said I should go to Harold Craxton. My parents made enormous sacrifices for me to go to London once a fortnight and Miss Theyer Jones changed all the school timetables so that I shouldn't miss anything.'

Before Vienna, Naomi studied for five years in Paris and before that at the Royal Academy. Now she is her own impresario, running Emperor Concerts with friends and, with other young up-and-coming musicians, the Emperor Ensemble.

Concerts are lucky to break even, and Naomi is still paying back a loan to cover one that made a loss. Life is tough and there are no holidays or even week-ends. She has a car now instead of an overcoat. But doesn't seem to mind.

The Hilton job is bread and scrape. She could earn more teaching but although she loved doing *Pirates of Penzance* with the ten-year-olds she found it draining. As it is, she is permanently tired, needs nine hours sleep a night. It takes two ounces to press one key and playing for three hours takes more strength than digging the road – quite apart from mental and emotional concentration.

Working in a hotel was Naomi's own idea. She wrote round. The Hilton thought classical music would add class. She thinks it is good rather than bad for her and though snobs may look down on her for doing it, she says: 'Real musicians are full of admiration for me because they know how difficult it is. Shura Cherkarsky came up one day and said the fact that I was communicating with an audience would help me. And I'm expanding my repertory all the time.'

When she first came to the Hilton, she had to learn a lot of German music. *Mack the Knife*, and *Eidelweiss* for the hotel's German fortnight. 'I turned up in a dirndl skirt and it all went down very well. Then we had a Scottish Baronial Fortnight, so I got out some tartan.'

She keeps a close eye on her audience, noting how it changes. The Jewish ladies are giving way to dinner-suited business men. A well-lipsticked blonde thumbs through a copy of Over 21 and scans the Arabs with cash-registered eyes. Naomi, a large glass of Perrier beside her, is playing Coquette from Schumann's Carnival – another item for the coming recital. She doesn't recognize all the famous guests. 'Mohammed Ali and his family came. I knew it must be someone terribly important because the place was packed and all the waiters were standing behind me, which I hate. I thought it was Sidney Poitier. He was so distinguished and polite. I just kept on playing and in the end he came up and said: "I want to tell you how much I enjoyed your beautiful music." '

Sometimes it is distinguished musicians. 'One day it was very hot and there were just a few Americans, so I thought I'd run through *Opus III* for my next recital. Then someone came up and said he was surprised to hear it at the Hilton. It was Peter Frankl.'

She gets propositioned too, of course. She was recently offered a concert tour of the Middle East by a prominent Arab and another day someone came up and said: 'How would you like to play at the Albert Hall in January? Menuhin will be there.' She is never sure what to make of it.

As we talk a young man comes up. 'Hello. You don't remember me.' Naomi looks up suspiciously, then leaps up and kisses him. Of course. The head tuner from Steinway. How could she forget.

4 January, 1977   **Nesta Wyn Ellis**

Shaw Country

Canada is full of surprises. A two-hour drive away from the Stratford Festival in Ontario lies the Shaw Festival in Niagara-on-the-Lake. Here in a beautiful little country town that resembles Chipping Camden with white clapboard houses one discovers a summer festival devoted to Shaw and his contemporaries. It fulfils the same kind of function as Malvern in the 1930s; and one can hardly do justice to one's astonishment at coming out of a matinée to find farmers making hay while the sun shines in the field next door to the theatre or at taking a stroll off the main street to gaze at the American coast.

Like most summer festivals, this one is the product of one man's unshakable enthusiasm. Chichester has its Leslie Evershed-Martin, Stratford Ontario its Tom Patterson, and Niagara-on-the-Lake a lawyer named Brian Doherty. In 1961 he conceived the idea of a Shaw Festival beginning with *Don Juan in Hell* staged in the old ivy-covered, nineteenth-century Court House.

Year by year the project grew until in 1971 a Toronto architect designed a new Shaw Festival Theatre. From the outside it has the touching, red-brick ugliness of the Royal Shakespeare Theatre in Stratford-upon-Avon. Inside it turns out to be a spacious, 822-seater with a nicely raked auditorium, glass-walled lobby, a stand selling Shaw mugs, T-shirts and bags and even a library. Clive Barnes has said he thinks it's the best new theatre to be built in North America and I see no reason to disagree.

That's the good news. The bad news is that a party of international journalists arrived in Niagara to see among other things, a full-length version of *Man and Superman* (complete with *Don Juan in Hell*) only to find that Ian Richardson who plays John Tanner was in hospital with gastro-enteritis. However there was instant compensation in a production by Michael Meacham of Ben Travers's *Thark* that had the audience baying with hysteria and Shakespeare-saturated critics all but rolling in the aisles.

Written in 1927, *Thark* was the third of the nine Aldwych farces. It was written in accordance with a diktat from Tom Walls that ran 'The next one has got to be about a haunted house,' and it shows all Travers's genius for combining farcical incident with spiralling verbal absurdity. It's hard to convey in cold print why a line like 'You're Mrs Frush and you've taken Thark' (spoken to a Mayfair butterfly who hasn't the faintest idea who or what Thark is) should reduce an audience to pulp: suffice to say that it does. Meacham's production, however, works precisely because it blends elaborate comic business with attention to language. Paxton Whitehead (the Festival's Artistic Director) plays the old Ralph Lynn part of Ronald Gamble and, with his accosting profile, giraffe-like neck and long, spidery limbs, he leaves behind a memorable physical image. Whether thrusting an unwanted amatory rival under a fringed lamp-shade or leaping on to chair-arms like a demented gazelle, he has the dangerous energy of a true farce actor.

The Shaw Festival does Travers proud. Ironically, it seemed less at ease with a production of Shaw's own *Widowers' Houses* staged in the rather cramped conditions of the Court House.

Paxton Whitehead's production got across the essential Shavian point that you will never destroy slum landlordism by getting rid of men like Sartorius, the devouring property-owner, but only by changing the social system. But although Ronald Bishop rightly played Sartorius from his own point of view as an efficient businessman trying to provide homes for the homeless, the production lacked much definition or drive.

The coming Shaw season, however, also includes revivals of *The Millionairess* (with Ian Richardson and Carole Shelley) and the rarely-seen Great Catherine. And as one wanders down the wide tree-lined main street of Niagara-on-the-Lake one can't help wondering why it is that one has to travel three thousand miles across the Atlantic to find a season devoted to the greatest British dramatist since Shakespeare. Malvern, please note.

20 June, 1977   **Michael Billington**

Looking back at Superman

Sir, – Michael Billington cannot have read the plays of George Bernard Shaw since his Oxford days. To call him 'the greatest British dramatist since Shakespeare' is close to having a critical brainstorm, as well as perpetuating an exam-crazy classroom myth. Having recently seen *Saint Joan* in London and *Caesar and Cleopatra* in Sydney, it is clearer to me than ever that Shaw is the most fraudulent, inept writer of Victorian melodramas ever to gull a timid critic or fool a dull public.

He writes like a Pakistani who had learned English when he was twelve years old in order to become a chartered accountant.

From childhood I have read these plays, watched them, indeed toured as an actor and stage manager in them on one-night stands. Apart from this experience, any fair-decent writer I know could put his finger on the crass, vulgar drivel in any of them.

Simply read the stage directions of *Candida* (opening this week). I had the misery of once playing Marchbanks in this ineffably feeble piece. This is Shaw's idea of a 'poet' (having no poetry in *him* at all). The poet, a ghastly little cissy, is bullied interminably

89

by an idiot, Muscular Christian Socialist, who, in turn, is mothered by an insufferably patronizing bully of a woman. As a ten-minute sketch on BBC2 in 1898 from South Shields it would do. But as a full-length stage play it is hard to think of anything more silly, apart from the rest of the so-called 'oeuvre'.

The one possible exception is *Pygmalion*, in which I toured the Welsh valleys in 1954 for the Arts Council. But the miners were still better than the play. I, however, was very funny as Freddy Eynesford-Hill, which does go to prove that you can't make bricks entirely without straw – something play reviewers can never grasp about plays or actors.

But 'the greatest British dramatist since Shakespeare(?)'. Ben Travers could have had GBS before breakfast in Australia watching the Test.

By the time I was 25 I had been in (admittedly bad, but no matter) productions of: *Arms and the Man, Candida, You Never Can Tell, Devil's Disciple, Caesar and Cleopatra, Saint Joan, Major Barbara* and, perhaps worst of all, Chekhov-for-philistines, *Heartbreak House*.

Try *learning* them, Mr Billington; they are posturing wind and rubbish. In fact, just the sort of play you would expect a critic to write. The difference is simply: he did it. – Yours faithfully,

John Osborne

Edenbridge,
Kent.
23 June, 1977

John Osborne's Major Barbarism

Sir, – Michael Billington needs no defence ordinarily – and, though one might quibble with his choice of Shaw as 'the greatest British dramatist since Shakespeare', that choice is obviously legitimate. John Osborne, however, deserves a brief dose of criticism for his attacks of Mr Billington and Shaw.

What's wrong with Mr Osborne shows clearly in what he says about Shaw: Mr Osborne has no wit about him, and thus he never sees anything as complex or funny.

And another thing: Shaw would never have been guilty of such a racial slur as Mr Osborne offhandedly commits. Shaw was a good and brilliant man, a humane and curiously noble artist. Had he created Mr Osborne, he would have relieved his heavy dullness with something lovable. – Yours faithfully,

(Prof.) Bert G. Hornback

33 Oakley Street,
London, SW3.

Sir, – What a marvellous attack on Shaw – and poor Mr Billington – by John Osborne. Shaw's own assault on Shakespeare was more shattering but nowhere near as funny. In any case, he was paid for writing it. You were lucky: you got Mr Osborne for free! – Yours faithfully,

Michael Croft,
Director.

Shaw Theatre,
100 Euston Road,
London, NW1.
25 June, 1977

Fun fair for the Queen

It is alleged that when Illtyd Harrington was told the date the Queen would be officially opening the National Theatre, he gathered his pin-striped and smiling minions around him and said: 'Never mind about the stuffed shirts in there, we will show them what a bit of People's Art can be like.'

True? I put it to him on the South Bank a few hours before Her Majesty was due to sweep past the steam organ in her limousine last night.

Harrington, deputy leader of the Greater London Council and shrewd political innovator and energizer behind the make-up of a stage Welshman, contemplated the organ, the bandstand, the big

91

wheel of the funfair, and the other populist delights that were to greet Her Majesty, a few thousand children from poor Lambeth and elsewhere, and rather fewer pickpockets.

'Well,' he said, 'normally Walter Ulbricht would have loved this place and Stalin would have been mad on it. It's Stalin Alley – there's no one else about.

'Yet,' said Harrington, ignoring the cautious cluckings of his officials, 'this is the place where Burbage used to come to *enjoy* himself. This was the part of London where the groundlings came. So when we got the official opening date three weeks ago, I and other people said, "This has got to be a popular thing."'

We had just walked past the Royal Festival Hall and then the National Film Theatre, where the cartoons were due to be shown alfresco under the arches of Waterloo Bridge, a fairly new experience for European children. 'See?' said Harrington. 'Since the 1951 Festival of Britain, the South Bank has become like pre-revolutionary Peking. Everyone in their own cantonment. One doesn't want the Kulturkamp approach to life, so I said what was wrong with people seeing it opened up? There's nothing wrong with vulgarity.' His officials looked as if they were about to lay eggs in their pin-stripes.

We contemplated the murals on the boarding around the National Car Park site at the back of the theatre which partly obscured Her Majesty's view of the funfair, including a thirty-foot-long picture of an enormous dragon breathing fire. 'There is a danger of a great institution like the National Theatre becoming a National Mausoleum,' said Harrington. 'We need to be garish in public. A lot of children are being brought up by either people who organize things in a professional-minded way, or never seeing anything at all.'

They had asked London Weekend Television if they could let off fireworks from their river terrace just downstream. 'Ironically, they weren't easy to communicate with,' said Harrington. 'People are absolutely terrified in big institutions. Their attitude is, "We are running our show, and please go away, do what you like in the streets and don't try it on us. Why can't it be all nicely organized and Her Majesty sit down at 6.55, pull a little flag and it's all over?" Let's be frank about it, London Weekend were a disappointment.

So we will be firing the fireworks from the river which will be better.'

Then Harrington pointed to where the London firemen were due to play their hoses from a boat on the Thames, as they did in the Blitz. 'Careful,' said an official, 'the fire brigade do not give displays. They are simply demonstrating the potential of their equipment.' 'That's right,' said Harrington gravely.

Would the buskers on the National Theatre terrace still be there when the Queen arrived? 'I think so,' said Harrington. 'It is the Fascist in us, but we have arranged for a military band to be playing, and when she actually arrives we will all show deference and all the buskers and Morris dancers and other fellows will stand around, their bells not jingling.'

Harrington was disappointed he could not give me a foretaste of the three searchlights which would converge over the theatre.

'I remember the East End slogan from the 1935 Jubilee of George V,' said Harrington. 'Lousy But Loyal. If we are in for a period of Populist Monarchy, then the British Queen must be allowed to see people as they are and I have no reason to think she doesn't want that to happen.' No, he wasn't one of those who would be presented to the Queen as she arrived, and he didn't mind.

Some more immaculate functionaries arrived with schedules and gold cuff links. One gingerly ventured to enquire, observing Harrington's I'm For Reds (the Cincinnati Reds) badge, what he would himself be wearing for the occasion.

'My dog suit, of course.'

'Oh, how lovely,' said the official, his pin-striped radiance quite restored.

26 October, 1976   **Dennis Barker**

Overheard in Washington

I heartily approve of the American way of leaving the microphone on. Waiting for Jimmy Carter to arrive for The President's Inauguration (live on BBC2) the assembled celebrities called to each other like moose meeting moose, not caring, or not knowing that they were being bugged by a live mike. This, I take it, is a form of open government.

'I hope you've got the thermal underwear on,' said Ford's voice. The temperature was zero. They all indicated that they had their thermal underwear on. 'The snappiest dresser in town,' said an unidentified voice. 'You look great there, I'll tell you. Great.' That sounded like Hubert Humphrey. How great men do go on about the way they look and what they wear. I would never have supposed they did, if I hadn't heard it with my own ears.

The band played *Be Kind To Your Webfooted Friends* as Vice-President-elect Mondale arrived. 'Crisp dresser. Looking great,' said a voice predictably. 'You've got a bed in there, I hope?' – 'Oh yes.' 'Have you ever slept in a hammock?' (I think it was 'hammock'. Eavesdropping is not easy work.) This was a reference to Mondale moving into a house only recently and reluctantly vacated by the Navy. Great men evidently think beds matter. The only thing Ford took into the White House and the only thing he took away was a double bed.

It wasn't conversation to change the world but it certainly beat the formal speeches for human insight. For those interested in the formalities, I should mention that the President said in his inaugural speech that he was agin sin.

Probably Gerald Ford's interest in warm underwear is due to the homely fact that he comes from a town that manufactures red flannel. And then, of course, there is the warning example of Benjamin Harrison, who made a 90-minute speech at his inauguration without an overcoat, caught a cold and was dead in a month. Which is why no one has heard of President Harrison.

The Kennedy Inauguration was heard in a snowstorm and an attempt was made to heat the stand. When Cardinal Cushing was invoking the blessing of God, his lectern caught fire. The perverse month in which Americans insist on holding inaugurations leads to much innocent merriment like that.

But it was colder for Ford than Carter. Charles I wore two shirts at his execution so that he should not be seen to shiver and seem afraid. One of those was thermal underwear. An outgoing President too must try to make a good death.

November, 1976   **Nancy Banks-Smith**

Cold comfort for Americans still shivering under the impact of the worst winter since whenever it was. The New England Journal of Medicine carries a learned piece by one Melvin Hershkovitz, MD, of the Jersey City Medical Center. It discusses a new and increasingly common phenomenon, and is entitled 'Penile Frostbite: An Unforeseen Hazard of Jogging.'
16 February, 1977   **John Torode**

A Country Diary: Keswick

Perhaps the weather will have settled down by the time this is being read, perhaps not, but in any part of January one of the most comfortable places to be is in a cow byre – unless you are responsible for the mucking-out and so on. But it needs to be a traditional one, no cow palace with a high roof and echoing space but a place where the cows are still in wooden stalls with hay-racks and quite close to one another with the hay-mew low overhead. Here the

95

warmth of the cow's breath, the soft shift from foot to foot and the quiet munching of hay make one forget the cold outside. The middle of this byre is a cobbled passage way with a door at either end giving access to two yards but whether the wind is north or east it never seems to get in here – the men who built these fell farms and their sheltering barns surrounded by, mostly, ash or sycamore trees knew what they were about. This morning the farmer was carrying armfuls of hay to his stalled cows, the lad loading bales on the tractor to take to the young cattle in the fields, so it was no time for idle chatter but he did say that it looked as if it would last until spring and, as I crossed the slippery yard, 'Tek care' and added that he (no small bulk) had been down twice already but was not as yet, 'kessen' – cast on one's back like a sheep, unable to get up. The young cattle had almost finished their hay when I went back down the lane, it had been thrown over the wall but some had fallen at the wall foot, so I picked it up to hand it back and – all at once – held summer in my hands. There were soft heads of timothy and fescue, the papery pods of yellow rattle, red clover bobs and even the roundels of dog daisies and their sweet smell hung on the cold air – July in January.

25 January, 1977   **Enid J. Wilson**

Nuns keep Snowfire habit

The prayers of barefoot nuns at the Convent of Poor Clares, York, have been answered. Snowfire, the soothing tablet for rubbing on chapped hands and on chilblains, has been saved.

For those too young to remember, Snowfire was one of the great advertising names of pre-war days, alongside Parkinson's Pills for pale people, Beecham's Pills 'worth a guinea a box', and Force breakfast cereal ('High o'er the fence leaps Sunny Jim; Force is the stuff that raises him'). Recently Snowfire has been difficult to obtain and was in danger of being taken off the market. The barefoot nuns began to pray for its survival. As the Mother Abbess, Sister Mary Bernard, explained: 'We never wear anything on our feet, and in winter, although we wear boots for gardening, many of us get vicious cracks in our skin. We all agree that its healing powers are fantastic. Our only anxiety is that it might go off the market.'

Cynics would suggest that it was not so much the power of prayer as the sharp commercial instincts of a firm at Knaresborough, North Yorkshire, that saved Snowfire ('One touch of Snowfire soothes the whole world's skin'). The firm is now making and marketing it under licence from its owners, who found that Snowfire did not fit in with the pattern of their production.

The nuns belong to an enclosed order, and have no contact with the outside world. About twelve years ago they opened their doors to the press. One reporter found that they were still praying for the safety of men serving in warships that had long since gone to the breaker's yard. Nobody had bothered to tell the Poor Clares, and they had no way of finding out.

10 November, 1976   **Michael Parkin**

Sunshine and Best

George Best exhibited another riveting little cameo for Fulham on Saturday, yet to the pedantic mandarins of Lytham St Anne's he is still on trial. Not until his probationary three-month period is up in two weeks time, say these astonishing bureaucrats, will they give their decision on whether the Irish wizard will be allowed to stay and earn his crust in League football.

Just what can they be up to, when here we all are grasping and begging for the veriest crumb of quality? Even now, George Best remains one of the very, very few players with the ability to let the sunshine blaze through the dowdy, grey skies of our national professional game. Indeed, there is a case for the Lancashire pinstripes to flop on to their knees and plead with George to stay among us. We need him more than he needs us, this Huckleberry who really seems to have found his Mississippi down at the lazy, lovely old Thames.

On Saturday against Oldham – just as he had done the week before at Blackpool apparently – Best not only chased and harried with single-minded fervour on a skid-pan pitch, but warmed the very cockles with a collection of outrageously silky doodles that all the swank art galleries should have been falling over themselves to buy. He had some sort of hand in all Fulham's five goals, and in scoring the fourth himself, he put his signature to a glorious day with an exquisite flourish.

Twenty yards from goal, and dead in front, he fastened on to a loose ball; no one to pass to, two pals ahead of him were offside. He lazily beat a man, sensed the goalkeeper straying from his line, so he chipped the thing over his head in the gentlest parabola. Like Nicklaus caressing his way out of the wickedest sand trap. The ball kissed the crossbar on the way, fell over the line and dropped dead, with the poor goalie on his backside and all of us beside ourselves with the marvel of it.

If that was the virtuoso's solo, the goal before it was, collectively, almost as thrilling. This time Best, deep inside his own half, sold some slithering hatchetman a dummy de-luxe, released Mitchell with a stunning 40-yard pass and Maybank's forehead thundered home the centre. Maybank had already scored the second and Mitchell got the first and last. They both played very well, strapping enthusiasts each. Who will make room for Marsh when that worthy's pirouetting ankle mends? Neither of them on this form.

Oldham, by the way, contributed a sturdy fairness to the afternoon. If their promotion ambitions are to be considered seriously though, they really must start getting some visiting form together. Not that anyone could do much about Fulham and Best on Saturday, mind you.

6 December, 1976   **Frank Keating**

How it looked from Bay 13

Today is to the day the 100th anniversary of the first day of the first Test match ever played, which was here in Melbourne in 1877. Here, too, the Centenary Test has been conducted these last few days – on the field, in the pavilion, in bay 13, and at the

Hilton Hotel which happens to be just across the road.

The day starts at the Hilton, where they are not only running a beauty contest for the Princess of the Pacific, which has just been won by Miss Hawaii, but where they are also putting up most of the 219 cricketers of the past, from Fender to Cowdrey, who have been invited here. In the lobby, Harold Larwood, a short and slight man for a giant, says Lillee is a great, but, as to the England batting, they'd have done better with Eddie, even now. Eddie, standing next to him, is Eddie Paynter. Then a man walks up to you and says: 'I'm one of the has-beens, you won't have heard of me. My name's Gil Langly.' He once took nine catches in a Test.

In the morning, though, the main business at the Hilton is at its bottle shop. 'Drop into our wine treasure chest,' says the sign. A large crowd of young Australians, who are probably not staying at the Hilton, are carting in their Eskies and ordering not wine but 27 tins of Foster's lager. An Eskie is a polystyrene refrigerating box, full of ice and cans of beer. Some Super Eskies hold 200 cans. Most are smaller and, towards the end of the day, after the beer cans have been emptied and squashed, are themselves trampled into bits of polystyrene foam. Anyway, in the morning the filled Eskies are carted off to bay 13, of which more later.

The pavilion has almost the tone of Lord's, though the Long Room has, alas, been carpeted. There are prints of English public schools – Clifton, Charterhouse, Tonbridge – and sheet music of many years ago; *The Cricket Bat Polka* dedicated by permission to Dr Grace the champion; *The I Zingari Gallop*; and *The Eton And Harrow Valse*. Members must wear ties. They drink beer from those tiny Australian six ounce glasses which look as if they ought to hold whisky. This match is really ritual. Wherever on the ground there are plain walls they are covered with the names in white letters of the heroes of 100 years of cricket – Noble, Barnes, Spofforth, Trumper (who died young), and Massie (who had his one match of glory).

This is an Australian cricket ground, which means a ground used also for Australian rules football. It holds 120,000. On the second day, the Sunday, it looked full, but the attendance was only 62,505, a long way short of the 90,800 who came here to see the West Indies in 1961. Still, the place looks full because of all the space the Eskies take up, and 62,505 is still about three times what The Oval will hold. The public seating is divided into 26 bays, of which bay 13 is inhabited by the Australian equivalent of Manchester United fans. 'Don't go there with your tie on,' a member told me. 'And don't speak pommy.'

From bay 13, as the game progressed, came the odd tin can thrown at a fielder in greeting, some amiable abuse, and a rabbit let loose on the outfield. At three o'clock, when they were supposed to be liquored up, I took off my tie and strayed into bay 13, snarling a courteous greeting in Australian at a man who courteously snarled one at me. I was instantly taken for a pom. 'I'm one-eyed,' said a very big man. He evidently had two. He carefully explained that his temperament was such that he would be constitutionally unable to see any good in any Englishman. A companion of his, also friendly, said: 'Me, I wouldn't bash a pom, even if I was crawling drunk.' It was true. He was crawling drunk.

Larwood and Voce came on to the square at tea, announced by loudspeakers. Bay 13 didn't seem to have heard of them, not to know they were the bodyline poms of 1932-3, or even poms at all. The bay was awash with beer, and rolling underfoot with cans and smashed bottles. They gave me a Foster's, which is good beer, and we drank to Lillee, which any pom would be happy to do, unless he's Amiss.

This has been an autumn game. The seasons here are such that it is as if it were played in England in mid-September. By 5.30 the field is more than half covered in dark shadow. The players' shadows stretch twice their length. Flocks of birds wheel round the outfield – seagulls and not pigeons as at The Oval, and hundreds of them. For the First Test, and in the early days, they used to set the pitch East-West, and the glare of the sun must have been intolerable most of the day. Now the pitch is North-South, and the shadows are intolerable by just before six. On two days they have stopped play a few minutes early. Bay 13 is awash with Foster's. In the pavilion, never can there have been such a gathering of cricketers. The field is full of shades.

15 March, 1977   **Terry Coleman**

Arnold Bennett left here

Stoke was well named. Once, they used to say, it was the smokiest city in the world – an awful boast, if proud in its way. It was already better when I saw it last in the mid-fifties, though you could still see what they meant. Now you can go its full ten-mile length under a sky as blue as classic Wedgwood and breathe nothing worse than petrol fumes. The transformation is out of this world, or into it – as though hell had surfaced and changed over to smokeless fuel.

Would it have lured back Arnold Bennett? Improbable. If ever cool was a possible word to use for this furnace of a town, that was its attitude to its only (unless you count Mrs Craik) great writer. I once knew a journalist who asked Bennett why he never went back to his Five Towns, since he and they had made each other so famous. 'Because,' he answered, 'they n-n-never asked me.'

He did go back in the end, and in a way that a little earlier would have delighted him as potential copy – on the luggage rack of a third-class carriage, which was by no means the sort of travel Bennett was accustomed to. He had little choice, since his brother was conveying his ashes from Golder's Green to be buried in his mother's grave at Burslem. And there I ran him to earth – with the wrong date on his inscription: 'Enoch Arnold Bennett, author, born May 27, 1867; died March 29, 1931.' Actually he died on the evening of March 27 – in London, of course, which made the second date that much less important as far as Stoke was concerned.

The mistake would have overjoyed the novelist, whether or not it piqued the pride of the son of Stoke. Anyway, he asked for it, with those unflattering remarks such as the one he recorded about speeding through his Potteries on the train and shuddering as he looked out of the window. You don't forge home-town links with lines like that.

I spent six hours wandering about the Bennett country – the right number, since the Five Towns are really six though they maintain seven town halls. Burslem was so addicted to them that it has two, and was providing itself with a third in anticipation (wrong as it turned out) of being the administrative centre when the towns joined up. The result was a considerable unemployment problem among town halls, particularly in Burslem. In fact the federation of 1910 never really succeeded in creating much unity even if it worked demonstrably better than the later experiment of Rhodesia and Nyasaland. The towns coexist peaceably enough, and a man from Tunstall will always see eye to eye with a man from Hanley about the iniquities of that other and alien smoke 150 miles to the south.

Not so much a city, you have to admit, as a long urban contusion, an industrial varicose vein, still far from pretty to look at and baffling to strangers. But as I was duly informed, amiably enough, it wasn't built for strangers.

Certainly it would need the witch said to be buried in Burslem churchyard to articulate the constituent parts of the neck from Tunstall down to Longton's grim base; and things are not made easier by the local habit of calling Longton 'Neck End', which seems to put the entire geography in a base-over-apex situation.

How much would Bennett remember? He would be quickly lost in Stoke itself, its throat torn out by massive road works. The North Stafford Hotel still quietly flaunts the most handsome façade in the business: you'd never walk in there with clay on your boots. Josiah Wedgwood stands nonchalantly outside, toying with one of his pots. The ceremonious station itself looks as though it might have come off the top shelf of some giant dresser. The rest is broken into a thousand pieces.

Asking his way to Hanley, Bennett would blink at what he saw there, more in surprise than disapproval. This has become the sharp end of the city, with X-films, 'Britain's most famous discotheque', and disloyal street names like Piccadilly and Pall Mall. It was quite a surprise to see a youth eating fish and chips out of a newspaper, though encouraging to know he could afford them both. What, I couldn't help wondering, would Bennett make of the sculptural feature outside a huge department store, resembling a lightning conductor severely damaged by lightning?

More astonishing is how much would strike organ chords of memory. With the best or worst will in the world, the most dedicated replanners can't wipe anything like the whole tape clean.

The spine of Bennett's early life and fictional work remains. Roughly this is the Waterloo Road, running from Hanley up to Burslem – uncannily recognizable, though the sound is pitched higher now. He was born near the bottom end, lived later in a posher house (now a modest showplace) half-way up, and is buried near the top end. That wrong date on the gravestone seems appropriate, somehow. After all, Bennett got Burslem wrong. He called it Bursley.

And didn't he call the Waterloo Road Trafalgar Road? By any name it remains, identifiable and evidently indestructible. Horse trams, steam trams, electric trams, buses, juggernauts, subsidence, demolition men, it has survived them all. Even the corner shops are still there. Down at the more worldly Hanley end, you find continental grocers, Gentle John the Tattoo Artist, books extolling Doberman pinschers as pets, a shop offering electric organs (You Only Need Three Fingers).

Move to the introverted north, where they show little sign of such sophistication, and it's boiled sweets in glass jars and sudden vistas up side streets of slaggy, green-brown hills. I even found a bottle oven. Once the dominant feature of Stoke's farouche skyline, these are now rare and the survivors look like being suitably cherished. This one suggested not so much Arnold Bennett as Hans Andersen; I half expected to find it inhabited by gnomes with prestigious trademarks on their bottoms.

Out of this black clay they moulded grandeur, and still do. However, the popular trade, judging from the town's pottery display centre, goes in a lot for horses and carts and faithful doggies as well as the inevitable Jubilee stuff. Up at Burslem, Royal Doulton's headquarters look as proud and purple as a Georgian grandee, though humanized by the assurance to be read on the show case fronting the road: 'Royal Doulton are happy to tell you that the Bunnykins Family can now come out to play.'

How very nice to know that. It still doesn't, on the face of it, look much of a place for playing, and more serious burrowing than any the Royal Doulton Bunnykins are likely to do undermined whole sectors of the town in the past. Houses and churches would crack, adding to the hazards of life that must always have been high, even by the standards of the earlier industrial England. Those who escaped lead poisoning or silicosis were always liable to be carried away by the subsidence.

The older citizens still tend to look precarious, as though they could all tell a story about how they were snatched back just in time. They have learned to trust the buses, which appear to ply with a frequency uncommon in modern Britain. 'Anybody lost a hearing aid?' my conductor called. Nobody looked surprised. Come to think of it, there was no possible answer to a question like that.

27 June, 1977   **Norman Shrapnel**

San Serriffe — a very special report

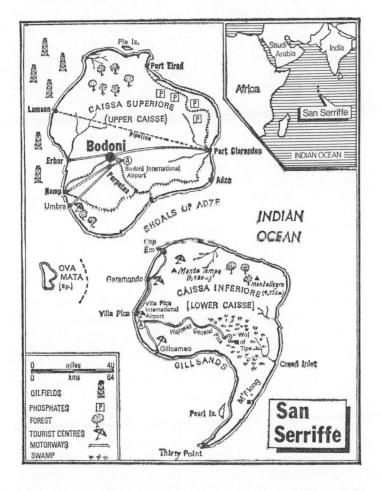

To those who have not followed its development at close hand, San Serriffe may be remembered only as a small archipelago, its main islands grouped roughly in the shape of a semi-colon, in the Indian Ocean. Until recently, that would have been an adequate description: a punctuation mark, as it were, in a long chapter of oceanic exploration. But fifteen years ago came the phosphate industry, ten years ago the first tourist packages, and five years ago the resource which has added bounteously to its riches: oil.

San Serriffe's currency, the Corona, is linked to its oil, making it one of the hardest in the world. It seems to appreciate, to the concern of foreign bankers, with every barrel that flows down the pipeline from the west coast to Port Clarendon. The people, likewise, are linked to the life of island insouciance which they once enjoyed and from which the Government, under General M. J. Pica, is trying hard to advance them.

Although it is true that the resulting social tensions are evident even to the most transient visitor he will also find a kindly and tolerant people: tolerant, in the eyes of people who cherish parliamentary institutions, to a fault. President Pica's emphasis on economic development, which he rightly sees as the best way to enrich the islands, has led to practices which some observers describe as authoritarian and which the Opposition, under the ageing Mr Ralph Baskerville, believes are only temporary.

From a diet of mutton, goat cheese, and damson wine it is a far cry to the international cuisine offered at many of the big hotels. The thatched huts still occupied by the irrepressible Flongs, an indigenous people at the tip of the southern island, are generations away from the two international airports at Bodoni, the capital, and Villa Pica. Yet something of the old tradition remains and not all that has gone was worth preserving.

Like his predecessors, General Pica inherited the old antagonisms between descendants of the original Spanish and Portuguese *colons* and those of the later English arrivals, sometimes humorously derided as the *semicolons*. Under the inspiration of his regime those feuds are forgotten.

Wealth has made it possible to solve, for the time being, San Serriffe's most acute physical problem. Early explorers placed the islands as much as three hundred miles farther west, and recent research has shown that they were almost correct.

The constant erosion of the western coasts, with corresponding accumulation on the east, is a process which, unless arrested, will bring the Republic into collision with Sri Lanka. (Bodoni, now in the centre of the north island, Upper Caisse, was originally a port.) As an expedient, lighters make the daily journey from the new wharf at Port Clarendon, built by Costains, to take shingle from the eastern coasts and put it back where it belongs.

Wealth – and again it is the key word to anyone interested in San Serriffe – is itself creating more wealth for the islanders, particularly for those highly placed in the administration. By making the islands a tax haven and creating duty-free zones around Port Clarendon and Bodoni all governments since that of Colonel Hispalis, which took office soon after independence, have attracted much hot and some questionable money to the islands. Once there, it has tended to stay. A number of large British companies are known to be interested in exploiting this aspect of San Serriffe's financial profile.

In almost all the social and public services San Serriffe is much in advance of comparable countries, with three geriatric teaching hospitals and a pioneer pre-school psychiatric unit attached to the university at Perpetua.

The university itself has begun to acquire an international reputation for its work on thermonuclear fusion and other alternative energy sources. And the schools are attempting a unique synthesis of the old and new so that in addition to mainstream subjects a San Serriffe teenager may well be offered pearl-diving as an 'A' level choice.

British policy towards the Republic is described by the Embassy as 'basically letting the chums get on with the show'. General Pica's Government is firmly allied with the West, to which his surprisingly powerful air force is a source of comfort in a potentially difficult area of operation. He has been known to ask, however, whether the West is firmly allied with him.

Western governments are aware of the fragile nature of previous administrations and, while obviously avoiding any overt involvement in local politics, would not be disinclined to do business with a successor, should General Pica wish to lay down the mantle of office. Of that, however, there is no sign.

1 April, 1977   **Geoffrey Taylor**

The leader's rise to power

For the last six years San Serriffe has enjoyed stable government, rising prosperity and freedom from strikes of any kind. This happy state of affairs is justly and widely attributed to the personality of the President, Maria-Jesu Pica.

Born 37 years ago of poor but honest sisal grinders in a hovel on the outskirts of Bodoni, he is now generally regarded – despite his relative youth – as the father of the San Serriffian people. From an early age he took a keen interest in politics, and before he was ten, had recruited a faithful band of companions who quickly became known for their skill in robbing the rich in order to reward the poor – which all of them were.

Conscripted into the army at the age of sixteen, Maria-Jesu Pica was an apt pupil at the Bodoni machine-gun academy and quickly rose through the ranks to become a sergeant before he was twenty and, by exceptional promotion, a general by the time he was 29.

A romantic at heart, his feelings hidden by a bluff exterior, he married Miss Elizabeth Baskerville, the daughter of an impoverished English planter (now Leader of the Opposition), after a whirlwind romance in 1960, by whom he has 8 children. Sustained by his wife's unfailing encouragement he studied long and hard, despite his military duties, to lay the foundations for San Serriffe's present prosperity.

But he freely admits that the main lines of the Pica Plan – as it is called – were derived from British economists. 'San Serriffe and I owe much to Maynard,' he often says privately. (Maynard, in this context, is the English economist John Maynard Keynes, decd.) Soldier, economist, and statesman, Maria-Jesu Pica is, however, above all a family man, a quality reflected in his choice of Ministers.

The Government of General Pica, elected for life in 1971, consists of Prime Minister Angelico Pica; Minister of the Interior Rudolfo Pica; Foreign Secretary Martin Pica; Minister for Oil Phosphates and Foreign Trade, Arnoldo Pica; and Minister of Education, Public Enlightenment, Woman's Affairs, Minorities and Culture, Esmeralda Pica. There is no Minister of Finance. Martin and Arnoldo Pica are the President's two eldest sons. Rudolfo is his first cousin. Esmeralda Pica is his aunt. Three other members of the Pica family – Giuseppe, Adolf, and Luigi – are serving life sentences for treason.

The Government was formed following a coup on 11 May, 1971, when seven regiments of dismounted cavalry, loyal to General Pica, overthrew the Government led by General Minion, of part Malaysian extraction.

The coup was not altogether bloodless. Although reports vary the casualty list was considerable, with many Malaysian immigrants reported dead while resisting arrest outside the presidential palace. For seventeen days Radio San Serriffe broadcast nothing but martial music interspersed with appeals for calm.

In his subsequent presidential address President Pica promised his people stability, two chickens in every pot, rigorous prosecution of General Minion and other enemies of the State, the abolition of Minionite newspapers, the establishment of a Government-controlled press and broadcasting service which would tell nothing but the truth, freedom of speech, and freedom of assembly subject to licences to be issued by the Ministry of the Interior. General Minion's funeral was attended by only a handful of mourners, all of whom were later found dead.

No restrictions are placed on foreign visitors except that their mail is censored.

General Pica, a comparative recluse, makes an annual public appearance on San Serriffian National Day, the anniversary of the coup of 1971. Traditionally he appears surrounded by the mounted cavalry and protected from the adoring crowds by bullet-proof glass.

1 April, 1977   **Mark Arnold-Forster**

A haven of industrial peace

Since the establishment of the San Serriffian TUC in 1943 – under the guidance of seconded officials from Britain's Congress House – the trade union movement has evolved naturally, in tune with Third World realities, and today labour indiscipline is almost unknown.

This is in sharp contrast to the situation which pertained in 1972 when Antonio 'Che' Pica, second cousin of the President, was elected TUC general secretary with 97.3 per cent of the votes cast after a closely contested first ballot which government scrutineers declared invalid. Then, there were 143 conflicting unions and wildcat stoppages were endemic. Today, a dozen tightly knit unions straddle the industrial scene and union-management co-operation is close.

A former military man, Che, who saw his future with what he describes affectionately as 'the shirtless ones', devoted several years to studying the most advanced industrial relations techniques abroad. He was a 'management intern' with an American-owned multi-national in Latin America and later switched to take a course in trade union organisation at Moscow's Patrice Lumbumba University. His experience stood him in good stead and, only three months after entering the phosphate mines as a day labourer, he found himself TUC general secretary.

It was on Che's initiative that all collective agreements on the island now expire on the same date each year and are personally renegotiated by him in what he describes as 'tough, pragmatic bargaining sessions' with the Chamber of Commerce. Under a unique experiment in worker democracy, management has surrendered all control of industrial discipline to the TUC in return for a closed shop with union dues deducted at source by management and paid direct to Che's office. The TUC is additionally financed by a ten per cent 'job placement' levy on all earnings. Workers seeking employment approach the TUC which guarantees to find them jobs in return for what is in effect a modest service charge.

The system works well. Che points proudly to the fact that there have been no unofficial strikes (or, indeed, official strikes) since 'mindless militants' who had been intimidating loyal union members, were expelled from the TUC three years back. And the fact that no union elections have been contested since 1972 is widely accepted as an indication of the democratic and popular nature of TUC leadership.

Che's substantial personal investment in the major multi-nationals operating in San Serriffe is welcomed in managerial circles as an indication of his confidence in the stability of the system he has fought to create.

1 April, 1977   **John Torode**

Transposed by the tides

The extraordinary eastward movement of the San Serriffe island group was first observed, accidentelly, by Sir Charles Clarendon, after whom the port is named, during an exploration of the Indian Ocean in 1796. Sailing north in his schooner *Excelsior*, he became stranded on a sand-pit east of the islands on March 13 – a date which he underlined in his log. Since only two years earlier Captain Meriwether Lewis, one of Cook's original crew (who later became Governor of Louisiana and was one of the most able cartographers of his time), had recorded that the waters east of the islands offered a clear passage, Sir Charles decided to anchor and investigate as soon as *Excelsior* lifted off with the tide.

It happened that Sir Charles, although a botanist and mineralogist, was also the author of the empirical hypothesis which explains why large pebbles rise and successively finer particles fall in sedimentary systems. He had arrived at his explanation (which proved on further investigation to be false) through direct observation of erosion of the Channel coast near Rye. He was therefore able to study the San Serriffe phenomenon in a comparative way and his diary for 1796, now at the Geographical Society at Kensington Gore, contains the first description of the extraordinary scouring and deposition pattern which continually shapes and reshapes the island group.

Sir Charles, however, saw only a part of the process when, during the spring tides, the spit of sand on which he was stranded and which was visible at its western extremity as a sandbank between the islands, was swept away. Sir Charles believed that this reformed further offshore, creating an ever-extending underwater hazard, and it is clear from his notes that he realized that the material was somehow accreting from the western shores. 'The land is being eaten by the sea,' he wrote, 'and raising hazardes to the Island Easte. In these wateres keep the islands to starboard when heading northe.'

Almost a century passed before this simple explanation was challenged and corrected. An expedition from the Royal Society – one of the earliest in the series of which the present Aldabra Expedition is the most recent – landed in 1886 to study the habitat. The loss of one of the expedition's two huts, set up on the western shore of the S. Island as a laboratory and store, drew sharp attention to the erosion problem. Systematic studies were made and the expedition brought back the first description of the complete repetitive cycle of erosion and deposition.

Linked intimately with the multiple tide system of the double island formation, with the biennial reversal of the main current flowing parallel to the east coast, and with an effect not understood by the Royal Society expedition but now known as a 'double Coanda', the scouring and deposition has two alternating major phases. In one, during the neap tides, material is carried from the western shores of both islands, and deposited in the form of a sandbank and spit which almost closes the strait between the islands, known as the Shoals of Adze, at low water and which reaches out eastward for about 1000 metres. Deposition in this position depends on the existence of the remnants of an earlier spit, and on the fingers of material reaching out from both islands into the strait which result from the reverse flow patterns during neaps. With the spring tides the reduced channel width between the islands leads to very high flow rates. Since the main water flow during these phases is southward the material now being scoured rapidly from the bank and spit is deposited in different ways on the north and south islands.

Deposition on the northern island falls uniformly on the eastward semicircular shore, while the stronger southerly movement draws out the deposition pattern on the southern island and accounts for the curious 'tail' which has developed over the centuries. But the phenomenon unique to San Serriffe, as far as is known, is that as the bank and spit erodes two or three 'herring bone' fingers are left reaching out partially across the strait. These are undoubtedly due to the creation of standing waves during the fast erosion phase, but if they did not occur accretion on the eastern shore could not take place and the islands would have disappeared long ago. As it is, the islands are in a quasi-stable state but moving steadily eastward. Because the scour and deposition rate changes as the cube of current velocity, the islands will accelerate at first gently and then more rapidly as they approach Sri Lanka. Simple calculations based on the present movement of 1400 metres a year and an exponential acceleration rate, suggest that the island group will hit the coast of Sri Lanka at a velocity of 940 km an hour on 3 January, 2011.

In spite of the difficulty of the waters around the islands, and the shifting hazards, a British gravel dredging company last year put forward the proposition that, by normal dredging procedures, it should be possible to stabilize the land masses long enough for proper surveys to be carried out. This proposal is believed to be under serious study by both the Department of Industry and the so-called Rockall Group at the Foreign Office.

In the meantime, basing his calculations on the most recent observations at San Serriffe and on the Institute of Marine Sciences computer model of the Channel, Dr John Funditor, of Imperial College, has put forward a daring scheme. This is to create a double Coanda island group in the English Channel where, according to Dr Funditor, the current patterns would lead not to an island movement, but to the gradual building up of a Channel barrage. This would have immediate and obvious benefits. There would be a direct road and rail link between Britain and the EEC mainland; the barrage would become the major Europort, accepting traffic from either east or west and would entirely eliminate the present Channel shipping traffic problems; the argument about the Channel would be silenced, and there would be a permanent reduction in the sea level of the North Sea. This last effect would be most important because it would reduce the costs of North Sea coast protection, reduce the risk of flooding, eliminate the need for a Thames barrage and make the arduous task of oil production a little easier.

It may well turn out that advantages such as these, likely to be ignored by Britain, will be grasped by the Asian countries towards which San Serriffe is moving. One fear, already being expressed in Karachi, is that as soon as the islands enter an economic zone as defined by the Law of the Sea, then its unique water flow pattern will be deliberately disrupted by an annexing state to prevent it moving out again. Since this could, however, destroy the islands completely, the view in both London and Washington is that this remarkable natural phenomenon should be allowed to run its full course.

1 April, 1977   **Anthony Tucker**

Spiking the cultural roots

Tourists fortunate enough to be permitted to visit the Flong settlements of San Serriffe during the summer solstice will be rewarded by the colourful spectacle of the Gallee sect stamping and shrieking in unison in the Dance of the Pied Slugs. This traditional ritual (so unforgetfully filmed by Hans Hasselblad in his seminal documentary of the thirties) is the subject of bitter anthropological dispute. Crabtree (1967) argues that the genesis of the dance transparently lies in East African gastropod fetishism. Jonas Hoe, the Utrecht ethnomusicologist, counters this thesis with the assertion that the accompanying instrument, the Grot (it looks rather like a slide bagpipe), is clearly of Pacific origin. The maverick Australian ethnographer, Mervyn Bluey, has publicly speculated that the Pied Slugs may well be vague folk memory of witchetty grubs . . .

But this, according to Lino Flatbäd of the University of Uppsala in Sweden, who has made a lifelong study of the components of the distinctive San Serriffe culture, is to carry comparative ethnology too far. 'I could, for instance, compare the Grot to the Tongan nose-flute, but what would that prove?' he asked as we sipped bitter-sweet *swarfegas* (a local liqueur scented with mangrove blossom) under the shade of the frangipanis on the western beach. 'But to speculate upon the origin of the Flongs is to miss the central fascination of San Serriffe culture. These people – all of them, colonists and indigenous, townsmen and peasants – have developed to a fine pitch the Cult of the Sonorous Enigma. Did you know that Mr Khrushchev (they don't really know anything about him here, of course) has become a folk hero here? Solely on the basis of saying "You can't make an omelette without breaking eggs". These people have a grave passion for phrases in which euphony and banality are perfectly matched: how else do you explain the Festival of the Well Made Play?'

Flatbäd sipped another *swarfegas* sadly. 'The festival probably existed in some other form in earlier times, but everybody seems to have forgotten what it was. I believe in the early sixties a liner stopped here to take aboard water and a British Council rep company on their way to Bombay gave an impromptu performance of *The Reluctant Peer*. It was received in puzzlement until after the final curtain went down and one of the passengers in the audience suddenly said loudly: "That's what I call a Well Made Play."

'A group of Flongs in the audience immediately burst into applause and went about for days repeating the phrase . . . The longer I stay here the less I understand these people. Do you know that if an islander wants to make it clear that he will *never* do something he says: "I will do it when the sociologists go away."'

The Festival of the Well Made Play is indeed a unique event. Every second Mayday, local committees of Flongs and islanders of European extraction combine enthusiastically to mount the complete cycle of plays by William Douglas-Home in English, Caslon, and Ki-flong. The festival begins at dawn on Mayday with a procession and a battle of flowers, the cycle begins at noon prompt and ends thirty-six hours later with dancing in the streets. But during that thirty-six hours the cycle is watched with a discerning intensity unmatched even by the Japanese connoisseurs of Kabuki.

It is not certain that the context of the plays is properly understood: the enthusiasm seems to be for ritual aspects of the cycle –
the Flongs, for instance, applaud widely whenever an actor
appears wearing a Harris tweed hacking jacket with a centre vent
and cavalry twill trousers *and* a paisley cravat.

'I sometimes think,' Flatbäd told me, 'that if a play didn't open
with French windows and a maid dusting the sideboard it wouldn't
be regarded as a play at all. There are some odd mistakes – somebody once performed the first scene of Ibsen's *Ghosts* during the
cycle and all were quite taken in.'

Nobody can offer a convincing explanation for the popularity of
the festival. Hamish McMurtrie is not concerned to try. 'These
island communities, they always distort and misunderstand
mainland cultures because they see them out of context,' he said
cheerfully. McMurtrie is chairman of the islands' Committee
with Responsibilities for the Arts. He is the son-in-law of His
Excellency General Pica, but was in fact born in Orkney. A
youngish, energetic polymath he has during the past four years
built up a series of fringe events to accompany the Festival.

He has developed the islanders' taste for the Sonorous Enigma
(on the wall of his office is a superbly crafted plaque bearing the
pokerwork motto 'There's nowt so queer as folk') but there are
evidences of his concern for his work. His office is decorated by
posters for the islands' first and only locally made film: a drama-
tized documentary about the control of infectious disease, it is
called *Yaws*.

McMurtrie is concerned to use the festival as a key to wider
access to European culture. Thus the foyer of the Cap Em opera
house has been host to an exhibition by the Peruvian minimalist
artist Felix de Garcia, and my visit coincided with tours by the
Bodoni Brass Ensemble and the Ampersand String Quartet.
Neither visit was a commercial success: the two together consumed almost half of the Ministry's modest annual budget, plus a
small grant from Unesco and a larger subvention from the CIA.

McMurtrie confessed himself disappointed but perhaps, he
speculates, the Home cycle itself might provide the answer. 'The
English culture is in some respects the dominant one. If I can
persuade the CIA to help further I may arrange for translations of

Agatha Christie, Arthur Wing Pinero, and Hugh and Margaret Williams. If those are a success we could try something really daring, the sort of bold experiment you use in your own National Theatre. What would you say about a performance of *Look Back in Anger* in modern dress?'

Outside on a whitewashed wall opposite McMurtrie's office, someone had neatly charcoaled: 'It never rains but it pours.' In the seductive climate of the San Serriffe June, it seemed answer enough.

1 April, 1977   **Tim Radford**

British and not proud of it

I cannot recall any television programme which in any way involved me that produced anything like the extraordinary public impact of the documentary made by Jenny Barraclough called *Go Tell it to the Judge*, shown on BBC the other day. For some reason – well, obvious reason – this hit viewers on the raw more keenly, and more immediately, than anything else in my own experience.

I am knee-deep in mail; Jenny Barraclough, whose sole concept it was, must be up to the eyes. Amazingly, not a nut-case in the lot, so far. On the contrary, letters from Leamington, missives from Malvern, cheques from Cheltenham. And all of them saying, in a startling coincidence of phrase: I had never believed it possible that I could be ashamed of being British. I had always trusted in British justice. I am aghast to learn for the first time of the cruelties being done in my name. I am a loyal middle-aged colonel, retired, and I am dishonoured. *What can we do now?*

The show that stirred up all this furore was, of course, an account of the British colonial and commercial record in Ocean Island, a minute speck of what used to be idyllic habitable land in the Pacific, which is now a wasteland, whose inhabitants have been wantonly and wickedly deported into exile and poverty, in the name of big business supported and sponsored by HM Government – which is to say, in your name, and mine.

Now it goes without saying that the programme was couched in my customary temperate and measured terms, straying no way from total objectivity. But total objectivity was quite enough to make it very clear indeed that for years HMG and its mining interests have tricked, deceived, threatened, conned, and mocked these peaceful Pacific simpletons with an avarice so naked it shocked even the judge. Not that it did the islanders much good, shocking the judge. Maybe, now, shocking the people may help.

It is far from a new story; indeed it culminated not long ago in the longest and costliest civil action ever heard in London. Still, from the rumpus caused by the documentary, it seemed that great numbers of decent Englishmen were startled to realize that officers of the Crown on the other side of the world were operating like a colonial Mafia. *And after all this time, have still not been brought to book. Nor, by all the indications, ever will be.*

It is a hard tale to synthesize, as it has been going on a long time. At the start of the century a smart New Zealand businessman stumbled on the fact that this Ocean Island, which is only $3\frac{1}{4}$ kilometres across, was practically solid phosphate – guano, from centuries of bird-droppings, an immensely valuable fertilizer. Albert Ellis, as he was called, moved in like a shot.

The Ocean Islanders were called Banabans. They were affectionate, welcoming, and illiterate. On the first day Ellis conned them into surrendering the mining rights for ninety-nine years, for £50 a year. It was too good to be true, at least for Mr Ellis. However, to consolidate the bonanza, the British Government was persuaded, without difficulty, to *annexe* Ocean Island into the Empire. In 1901 the baffled Banabans found themselves a colony, and the Colonial Office a conspirator.

Over the years the skulduggery went on. Every so often the Banabans had put their marks to legal documents they had no earthly means of understanding. The company's bulldozers tore the land away and shipped it to Australia. They destroyed the coconut trees, the main source of the Banabans' food. They promised to restore the ravaged soil; they never did. Ocean Island began to disappear.

In 1920 the Governments of Britain, Australia, and New Zealand bought up the phosphate company. The Colonial Office was now a prime party in this rapacious and squalid swindle. When the Banabans protested at anything now they could be, and were, officially threatened with *punishment*.

The Banabans pleaded for and offered to pay for, legal advice in these mysterious negotiations. *They were allowed no legal advice.*

There is much to be said for cutting this squalid story short, though it gets worse as it goes on. Finally the Banabans' two spokesmen and father-figures, Rotan Tito and his son Tebuke, came to seek help in the place where they knew justice was infallible: London. They had never been anywhere before, they knew nobody and nothing. Yet somehow or other their two prodigious cases came to court – and lasted 221 days, used seven million spoken words, and cost £¾ million.

Judge Megarry took four months to write an enormous judgement that said almost nothing. In the first case: yes, the phosphate people had reneged on their promise to replant the land, and the Banabans should get damages – but how much, he couldn't bring himself to say. Something neither too small nor too big; let them work it out. In the case against the British Government: the Banabans had no case at all.

Yet with an extraordinary rider. 'The question is not whether the Banabans should succeed in fairness, or ethics. I cannot make an award just because I conclude they have had a raw deal. Yet a judge must direct attention to a wrong he cannot right. I leave it to the Crown to do what it considers proper.'

Thus one of the most equivocal judicial statements on record. They won, but they lost; they were right, but they were wrong.

Tebuke Tito accepted this for the Banabans with an almost super-human generosity and consideration. 'They are good men I am sure,' he said, 'but I think I shall never understand the law. They mean well, but now we have nothing left, not even our home.'

The Crown is the fountainhead of a justice that, they say, must manifestly be seen to be done. Thus must be reflecting Philip Agee, facing the Home Office committee that proposes to deport him and won't say why. Said Sir Derek Hilton, the chairman: 'It is decided this is the system. Take it or leave it.'

Thus the two fugitive Indian monks Ram Roy and Namedeshwar Prasad, to be sent back to Nepal without a hearing. Says Mr Merlyn Rees, doubtless an authority on the Ananda Marga movement: 'You can't go letting people in just because they are monks.'

Thus Rotan and Tebuke Tito of Ocean Island, who went and told it to the judge, and were told in return : You are entitled to damages but I don't know what. You have had a raw deal from the Government, but judges aren't in business for raw deals. Go thou and sin no more.

And if possible, fellows, be British. It clearly helps.

17 January, 1977   **James Cameron**

Post Restante

It appears that the Post Office has a duty to provide postal and telegraph services but the public has no right to use them. The duty is laid down in the Act (the Post Office Act, 1969) but the right is not, and must be presumed, therefore, not to exist. This was one of the more unexpected arguments advanced during this week's Court of Appeal hearing by Mr Mark Saville, QC, on behalf of the two Post Office unions concerned, and he seemed to be saying that since no right existed nobody could complain that it was being taken away. Sir William Ryland has obviously scrutinized the Act more carefully than the rest of us, and the point made by Mr Saville may explain much that has been puzzling about the conduct of the Post Office.

The submission is, however, one of grave constitutional importance and calls to mind the case in which the Queen's Proctor, appearing both as *parens patriae* and *amicus curiae*, sought during interlocutory proceedings before the Senior Master, *ex parte* the Sheriff of Chancery, to enter a *nolle prosequi* on the grounds that the *ratio descidendi* was *circulus in probando*. Refusing leave, the Court found that, although *ex abusu non arguitur ad usum* still held, in a case where *certiorari* had not been granted by the Queen's Bench Division *quia timet* proceedings were, in the absence of a special locus on the part of the respondent, generally more appropriate, and that although *sint ut sunt aut non sint* remained open to challenge as a principle of English jurisprudence it was not for the Court to depart from R. v. The Tunbridge Wells Gas Light and Coke Company, *ex parte* the First Sea Lord, without more cogent arguments than had been advanced. The decision was never appealed.

22 January, 1977   **Leader**

Mrs Stokes the medium

Mrs Stokes, the medium, lives in an old soldier's flat, in a large charitable block in Fulham, London. The outside is engraved with the names of famous battles, and messages to the valiant from a grateful empire.

I went in through the arched doorway, past a wheelchair and a drowsing old soldier wearing a cowboy hat: the place seemed somehow fitting for a séance. As I went up the stairs I tried to puzzle out why I was so frightened. I am by nature sceptical of such things, but also eager to be convinced, and avid for supernatural stories. I hadn't wanted a private sitting. I'd only wanted to observe a group and I was a bit alarmed at suddenly being projected into it.

For the sceptics, I shall explain how I came to see Mrs Stokes. I called the editor of *Psychic News*, explained that I wanted to attend a séance in order to write about it. He gave me Mrs Stokes's name and number and told me to say I was a friend of his, to give her a false name, and not say I was a journalist. 'Don't say who you are, or you won't believe what you get. You'll think she checked on you.'

So I made an appointment in my married name. Now, in the twenty-four hours between calling her and my arrival for a sitting, she could have checked on me. She could have called back the *Psychic News* editor, found out that I was a journalist, and what my professional name was. Or she could at least have known that anyone sent by him was a journalist. But that seemed unlikely.

She was a friendly, cosy woman in late middle age with dazzling bright blue eyes. We sat in two armchairs round her gas fire, with a big ginger cat purring at our feet. There was nothing odd about her, or the room. We smoked and chatted for a minute or two. I was careful to give nothing away at all about my life.

She was clearly used to people coming to her in great distress so she started by saying: 'I see a great light around your solar plexus. I know that means you have a lot of trouble, everything in knots. Is it in your personal life? Yes, I see great conflict and unhappiness.'

I looked a little vague. I didn't know what to say, except, 'Well
. . .' She went on, 'You needn't worry about me, dear, you know
nothing goes beyond these four walls.' But she still got no out-
pouring from me. I suppose had I to come to her in distress, this
would have been a cue for me to respond in some helpful way,
that would provide hints for her to work on. At this point all my
scepticism was reaffirmed. I thought I understood her technique,
a system of shots in the dark, hoping for a response. I didn't,
though, think that she realized that she had a technique. She said
she was 'clairaudiant': she heard the voices of those who had
'passed over'.

The atmosphere was quite relaxed. She didn't go into a trance,
or do anything dramatic. She chatted, sometimes to me, sometimes to the spirit world, and sounded as if she was talking to
friends on the telephone. She began on names.

'Is there someone still living in your family called John? Is it
John? No, it's Joan! Is there a Joan?' I said that was my mother-
in-law's name. It made me jump.

'Yes, I think there are some people belonging to her talking to
me.' She tried a number of other names, Leslie, Joyce, then
Eileen, my mother-in-law's sister. Was it lucky guessing? Once
she'd got the names she didn't have much to say to or about them.
She tried a few more names. In any family with all its branches,
there are a great many names around; a lucky hit is fairly likely
among cousins and ancestors.

'Who's that?' she'd say. 'I didn't quite get it, dear, try again. It
sounds like Eric? Is it Eric, or Derek?' I said that didn't mean
anything to me. 'Scrub it, dear, I missed that one,' she said to the
spirits, and began to search again for a reason for my visit.

'Your mother, is she called Annie, or Anne?' I said she was,
again nearly jumping out of my chair. 'Is she sick, or in hospital?'
I said no, she was well. 'Then it's just that she's had a lot of
trouble in her life. Have you a grandmother on the other side?
Yes, I think you have.'

I said I had. 'She's never been contacted before, nor have any
of these people around you who want to talk to you, so they aren't
very good at it. Your grandmother, you say, it's your mother's

mother? I'm trying to get her name. No, I can't. There's someone here called Tony. Does that mean anything to you?'

I said it did. He was an uncle who died before I was born. 'He says he's watching you. Excuse me asking, but did he do away with himself?' I said he did. 'Yes, I asked him how he got to the other side, and he said he took himself across.' I was amazed.

She went on. 'Your grandmother. I can hear a bit stronger now. Is her name Barbie, or Barbara, perhaps?' I said it was. 'She died of a cerebral haemorrhage, a stroke? Yes, that's right. She's very nicely spoken. But she doesn't like me at all. She only wants to talk to you. She's very polite. They want you to know they watch over you.'

She tried a lot more names – Keith, Alice, Mary, Doreen, and an Alan, very strong. I said none of those names meant anything to me. Then she said, 'Is there a Jason somewhere close to you?'

I said, again with astonishment, that I had a brother of that name. 'He has reddish hair, auburnish?' I said yes, he had bright red hair. That was the only physical description she gave of anyone, and it was absolutely right.

She fumbled around again for a reason for my coming. 'Someone is very sick?' I said no. 'You and your husband are not getting on too well?' I said no. 'You are having trouble in your work? I see someone thrusting a notebook and a bunch of pencils at you, saying get on with it. Get writing. Are you a writer, a journalist maybe?'

I don't know how she came to that conclusion. Maybe the editor of *Psychic News* often sent journalists to her. Maybe it was the obvious answer, since I had produced no good reason for wanting a sitting urgently.

She said: 'Your grandmother, Barbara, says your husband is a nice man, not handsome in the ordinary way, but good at heart. Has he got something twisted, a toe perhaps? She says why doesn't he get it fixed?'

I said he had a funny tooth. 'Oh, a tooth, that's it. Well, she thinks he should have it straightened.' She tried a few more names. 'Freda, Frederick, Francis? No? Then scrub it. Try again, dears? I didn't hear that one.'

In condensing an hour-long sitting I have probably done her

more than justice. There were a good many more false starts and names I didn't know. She tried a lot of blind alleys about my life. The number of children, she got right, the sex wrong. If I gave her the slightest hint she seized it, and magnified it, often wrongly, going just on my yeses and nos. It was hard not to collude with her, to lead her on by almost giving her answers. She told me nothing I didn't know. But to pick my brother's unusual name and looks, to pronounce on my uncle's death, to find my mother and grandmother's names was really astonishing. I suppose it was telepathy. But as far as I knew, I was not thinking at all about those people, especially not about an uncle who died before I was born.

I would like very much to believe that these were really messages from the other side. Who wouldn't? The spiritualist message is one of hope and joy. Everyone there is happy, and they all want to tell us not to worry, death is lovely.

But I find it very hard to believe that Mrs Stokes was really talking to the dead. For one thing, why didn't they say anything interesting? Apparently the dead rarely do. Why don't they tell *exactly* what it's like over there? Or give some useful information?

My grandmother, Barbara, said I should be careful not to drift away from my husband, we should talk more and she told us we were both talented writers. Later, talking about something else, the medium asked if I had a George on the other side. I said that was my grandfather's name.

'Well, your grandmother wants you to know that she and George are together and happy.' Can death so transform people and relationships? If so, the people on the other side just aren't the same people we knew.

'Is there a Lawrence or a Larry anywhere in your life?' asked Mrs Stokes. I said that was my uncle's name. She must have assumed that Lawrence was Barbara's son as she said straight away: 'Barbara wants to send lots of love to him.'

This absurdity made me giggle and nearly guffaw, since Lawrence is an uncle on my father's side, and can have scarcely known his brother's mother-in-law.

It was not a question of trickery or cheating. I am sure she really believed she could hear voices. Perhaps she did speak to the dead, but I find it hard to believe that it is possible for some people at some times to come back and not for all people all the time.

I called back the editor of *Psychic News* to thank him for putting me in touch with Mrs Stokes. He said he hadn't spoken to her about me. 'Sounds as if you've had a good sitting, for a first time. No, I rule out the view that it's all telepathy, as she can't tell what you're thinking if you ask her. She tells what she's told from the other side. If it was telepathy, she'd respond to tests, which she doesn't.'

Whatever it was, it was dramatic and exciting, an excellent £5 worth, but it hasn't changed my view of the world. But let the last word go to Mrs Stokes: 'These people belonging to you on the other side, they're saying one more thing to me. They're saying "tell her to write more about the spirit-world and psychic things. Psychic things are in now, an up subject, and she'll do well in her career if she writes a lot about it." '

23 May, 1977   **Polly Toynbee**

After King Cotton

The first person I saw I really felt I knew was Queen Victoria. She still looked remarkably well, and only moderately disapproving, and it struck me anew – as it had the first time I saw her a quarter of a century earlier – what a constitution it must take to sit out like that by the Piccadilly Gardens, decade after decade, in all kinds of weather. And not getting any younger. Waiting for what? Wanderers to return, perhaps, as they so often do. Stepping out of Piccadilly Station gave an unexpected lift to the spirits, due I suspect to the intensely dreary atmosphere of the station surrounds in the days when we called it London Road. Almost anything would have been better than that, and this was much better.

Also a release to leave the station, any station. They are now virtually interchangeable: all equipped with sophisticated time-saving aids most difficult to locate or read, devoid of seats or exits, and populated by well-dressed, worried-looking men with wafer-thin brief cases. Only the rich go by train and the rich are worried. I didn't remember such Manchester men before. The people in the streets looked different too. So I was delighted to see familiar faces – old Wellington still looking spry though the graffiti merchants had been at him, and Peel none the worse except for a few pigeon-droppings streaking his waistcoat, and Victoria holding her orb with an air that boded ill for any vandals who might venture to get too bold.

An early hand grenade, Her Majesty might have been clutching. That was one thing I could now identify: there was a new aggression, a harder edge – especially on the skyline, with those huge new shapes behind the gardens, the super-hotel for the worried-looking men, the soaring office block rasping the world with the rough side of God's tongue, the Eagle Star building with its eccentric roof like a giant eagle with a broken wing.

None of that I found impossible to take. Manchester always had a gift for fantasy, a tendency to astonish. But there was Market Street to digest too, and here was something else.

I recalled the great warehouses with their elaborate and exotic gestures – Palazzo, Mercantile, Lancashire Venetian, and all those churches and public buildings in demented variations of Victorian Gothic. Nor was sheer size anything new: the Watts Warehouse in Portland Street would have awed King Kong.

The horror of Market Street was something different. It was not the excess but the monstrous decorum of the new tile mountain; and now they were speaking of an addition to Manchester architectural style, the Market Street Lavatorial.

It is all too true that former Mancunians often return to spit on their own doorsteps without even bothering to walk inside. Their reactions must be treated with reserve. They are out of touch with local affairs and riddled with nostalgia if not worse diseases. Sometimes they contradict themselves absurdly. One visit sees them reviling the town for its ugliness and grime and its primitive eating habits. A few years later they will be complaining that it has grown unnaturally clean and too sophisticated to maintain its tripe shops and other tokens of a healthy regional life.

Wrong as I could doubtless be, it did not seem to me, watching the shoppers scuttling about like disturbed ants, that they were going to enjoy their brave new world. Market Street never had pretensions to beauty or distinction but at least it related to people – their needs, their somewhat morose pleasures, above all their size. It seems a rum way of getting to heaven, though the prospect was offered for years in the chapels. Is there even any pie in this sky, now they've made it?

Desperately struggling to keep my feet on the ground, I hunted for surviving relics of the Manchester I knew. No easy matter at all. The Manchester I remembered, or thought I remembered, was full of dark alleys hiding fragrant delicatessen shops, chophouses where you sat at cracked marble-topped tables, pub philosophers who went on about life until you bought them bitter. Fantasy abounded. 'No Jacobites served here,' one pub warned. A golden arm would thrust itself through a wall, and I once saw a back street lined with fire escapes, all ending a good fifteen feet short of the ground. Nothing was ever explained.

Useless to look for these, or the book-barrows where you could find marvellous things for a shilling, or the medieval fishing-tackle shop with a floor like the waves of the sea. They did say that the old black-and-white Wellington Inn was being preserved although, carried away by the high-rise frenzy, it had nervously jumped several feet into the air and was too shaken at present to receive visitors. I fervently hoped it would recover.

The Royal Exchange was there, looking astonished to survive, and so was St Anne's Square, well-preserved as ever and growing a handsome set of shrubs. Apart from having lost one of its sides Albert Square was doing better still, with real trees and a rejuvenated town hall. I hardly recognized it. Clearly, if you can take it at all, a good scrub-down will take years off. But there was poor Albert in the middle of the square. It seemed doubtful whether he could stand such treatment. Unlike the dear queen, Albert was looking very poorly indeed, in spite of his protective canopy. But this was falling apart, and there was naturally great concern about the whole situation. With all those millions being spent just over the road, it seemed only right that a modest sum was being proposed to keep a roof over the Prince Consort's head.

Well, Manchester was a pioneer in the clean air campaign, and if it had happened earlier, poor Albert and a lot of humbler folk would have been the healthier. Now Mancunians have their clean air and grope about in it blindly. King Cotton was a bit of a monster, but he knew what he was after. He ruled a black town much given to fogs. The fog is now uncertainty or worse, a total cluelessness as to what the city is about or where it is going.

THINGS WILL BE LOOKING UP, a property company poster boasts; they can write that again. The brutality of the approach to the cathedral up Deansgate is underlined by a concrete bridge not nearly as pretty as the iron one masking St Paul's, an effect it seems to emulate.

But there, up against the cathedral's flank, the scene softened into the only island of man-sized relaxation I found in a day's concrete march – big shady trees, people on benches, cats. Here was a charming corner of Manchester they had forgotten to develop. Or had the bishop put in a strong word?

1 November, 1976   **Norman Shrapnel**

A Country Diary: Kent

Kent Hatch stands at the gateway of the county where the sandy ridge of charts and commons stretches westwards into Surrey. The Victorians made it fashionable, dotting the hillside with their villas. In one square stone house tucked away in the beech woods Constance Garnett wrestled with the subtleties of Chekhov and Turgenev. In this most English of landscapes the line of birches, still leafless, at the edge of the terraced garden suddenly appear as silver memories of the great Russian spaces. They must have brought cheer to at least one of the regular visitors to the House, Prince Kropotkin, dreaming of better worlds. Ranks of larch and pine on the hill reinforce the exotic image with heather staining the clearings with purple. Walking the shadowed tracks above the house now, one imagines the brilliant conversations of those literary giants who strode them a lifetime ago, Joseph Conrad with thoughts of darker forests, Henry James evolving an elaborate turn of phrase. As they explored the jungles of birch and holly, wild rhododendron and oak bursting with the restlessness of a new season, there was Edward Thomas on hand to give them the entirely native view pointing to celandine opening as bright as new paint, the golden rosette of coltsfoot, a great red-tailed bumble bee humming into the last of the yellow crocuses. Yet the larch just breaking out with clusters of green needles, now 300 years a native, seems as exotic as the guests this sun-trapped hillside once welcomed.

25 March, 1977   John T. White

The Black Ghost walks again

I had often wondered how it was that Lancaster's city centre presents such a Georgian façade to the world. Although historically it was the county town, little of its medieval core remains – unlike, say, Chester or York – except for the gaol. On the other hand, the town largely missed out on the industrial revolution which took place to the south of the county, so even the back street terraces are of eighteenth-century grey granite rather than Victorian red brick.

A clue to the city's dark secret emerges in a new play by Philip Martin which opens at the Duke's Playhouse in Lancaster on Friday. The play is called *Sambo*, and it reveals that Lancaster's golden age, when it reached a peak of prosperity in the middle of the eighteenth century, was based on the slave trade.

Philip Martin now lives just outside Lancaster at Quernmore in the Trough of Bowland. He was intrigued by a sketch in one of the Duke's community roadshows about the local legends of Sambo's grave – the burial place, out at Sunderland Point on the marshy estuary of the Lune, of a Negro slave. One version has it that Sambo was the fourteen-year-old houseboy of a Lancaster slaving captain, who pined and died when his master left him behind and was buried at Sunderland Point because he was denied consecrated ground. Another simply says he was an old, white-haired slave who was drowned and washed up on the beach. Either way it's odd to find a Negro buried on a lonely tidal peninsula on the north Lancashire coast in 1736. And there's not much explanation from the sentimental verses inscribed as his epitaph: 'Full many a summer's sunbeam warms the clod, And many a teeming cloud upon him drips . . .'

But it is the material which Mr Martin and the company exhumed while they were researching the play which is going to rattle a few of Lancaster's skeletons. Like the discovery that the family which owned the land on which the theatre (a converted church) stands made its money in the slave trade . . . or the fact that three lord mayors of Lancaster were slave captains. 'It's been kept pretty quiet,' Mr Martin says. 'But there are some documents – inventories and so on – which show that the trade was very lucrative.'

When Defoe's tour took him to Lancaster in the 1730s he was unimpressed – the town was dying on its feet. Within thirty years, according to the play's director, John Blackmore, Lancaster was the third largest slaving port after Liverpool and Bristol. By 1771, Lancaster's trade was about one sixth of Liverpool's, which would put it at just over £1 million (at contemporary prices) when the population of the town was little more than 10,000.

One incident, which Mr Martin uses in the play, demonstrates the sort of attitudes behind these profits. A Lancaster slave ship was becalmed in the Sea of Thunder, on the notorious middle passage from West Africa to the United States. One of the slaves was found to have smallpox, but the captain would not sacrifice him and throw away the £20 he was worth at the auctions. Inevitably the disease spread, and all 200 slaves were eventually tossed overboard as supplies, especially drinking water, became short. On his return to Lancaster the captain claimed the insurance money on his 'cargo', and the local jury found that it was a 'just jettison'. It was only when the insurance company appealed to the House of Lords – on the ground that the slaves were not insured against disease – that it was written into English law that people could not be jettisoned like horses.

The Lancaster trade eventually died out, Mr Martin says, towards the end of the eighteenth century when the African kings refused to deal with the Lancaster slave captains because they were 'untrustworthy'. They managed to slip in one last trip in 1806, just before the trade was abolished. But the Lune was already silting up, putting an end to Lancaster's hopes as a port, and when Glasson dock was built across the estuary at the end of the eighteenth century Sunderland Point became known locally as Cape Famine. The town went into decline again until linoleum came to its rescue and eventually, in the 1960s, the university became the biggest employer.

There isn't much of a race problem in Lancaster today, but only because the place is so depressed there is hardly any coloured immigration. 'There is a very minute ghetto,' Mr Martin says. So the question the play asks is what would be the reaction to a black man coming to Lancaster now?

Philip Martin knows the answer. He went for a drink with Paul Barber, the black actor from *Gangsters* who plays a black actor coming to Lancaster to play Sambo, and he says: 'The manageress started saying things like "It's a black day today, isn't it?" to the other customers. Paul didn't even notice.'

Isn't there a danger that the play, by confronting Lancaster with its own submerged guilt, will only make the situation worse? 'I don't see how it can make it worse,' Mr Martin said. 'It might save them five years.'

28 February, 1977   **Robin Thornber**

When in Singapore

Sir Stamford Raffles (1781-1826) was a clerk with the East India Company who founded both the London Zoo and the city of Singapore. The name means literally Lion City. He was an English gentleman. 'Let it still be the boast of Britain,' he said, 'to write her name in characters of light . . . If the time should come when her empire shall have passed away, her monuments will endure when her triumphs shall have become an empty name.'

Well, Raffles has two fine statues in the city, one just across from the cricket club, and another down by the north boat quay in front of a lot of grotty sampans. The second has a plaque saying that with genius and perception he changed the destiny of Singapore from an obscure fishing village to a great seaport and a modern metropolis. But one of his greatest monuments is certainly the Raffles Hotel, which started as a tiffin house, became a sort of hostel for itinerant sailors, and in 1896, the year before Victoria's Diamond Jubilee, became a grand hotel named after the founder of the city.

It is one of the few hotels I know which take you back in time. Grand Duke Cyril of Russia was here, of course. So were Mary Pickford and Haile Selassie, Rudyard Kipling, Joseph Conrad, and Somerset Maugham. Kipling said: ' When in Singapore, feed at Raffles.' Conrad is supposed to have leaned over a verandah and conceived the idea for *Lord Jim*. Maugham wrote *The Moon and Sixpence* in the palm court where I am writing this, both of us sipping Singapore gin slings.

The palm court is in an open courtyard. The Livingstone palms are 90 feet tall. Frangipani and hibiscus bloom. Maugham said this garden stood for all the fables of the exotic East. The gin sling was invented in 1915 by Ngian Tong Boon, who concocted it of tanqueray gin, cherry brandy, fruit juices, Benedictine, and Cointreau. The honourable job of barman is here hereditary. Members of the Ngian family still sling gin in a long bar off a corridor known as Cad's Alley.

There is a tiffin room, for tiffin. There are 127 bedrooms, all made to accommodate the likes of Grand Duke Cyril. Maugham's is preserved, though not the library of his books, which got stolen. I am ashamed to say my room, which is 27ft by 45ft, appears to be larger than Maugham's. It has canopied beds, a dressing room, sofas, tables, height, and space, space, space. It costs rather less than the Hilton.

When the last war came, and when in 1941 the city was bombed every night, the clients continued to dance in the ballroom till midnight. Were they not English gentlemen and ladies? When the Japanese came, their generals took one look at the place and decided to live there. Were they not Japanese gentlemen?

In 1945 the English returned again, one not having had a bath for three years. He took one at the Raffles, saying it was the most beautiful experience of his life. When the hotel reopened, the waiters dug up the silver beef-trolley which they had buried in the palm court. Japanese gentlemen were given to looting.

This most British of hotels was founded by three brothers named Sarkies, who were Armenian. It is built in a style which is distinctly white French renaissance, and is at present run by Roberto Pregarz, who used to be a *maître d'hôtel* on Lloyd Triestino liners. Mr Pregarz cherishes the history of the place. Two years ago he met the man he believed to be the hotel's oldest guest. He came, in very old age, on a cruise ship. He had been born in 1886, and first came to the Raffles in 1905 when he was in the Royal Navy. Mr Pregarz refuses to have jazz in the hotel, saying it is not a night club. String trios play *I'll See You Again* in the palm court. Huge, slow propellers move under the high ceilings. Noel Coward, who came here often, never could stand air conditioning.

As he shows you round his hotel, Mr Pregarz refers to a prepared script. Into the long bar. 'Anecdote,' he says. 'An old writer fondly recollected a certain Dutch anthropologist who used to consume eight to ten bottles of gin for breakfast every morning.' Is that so?

The Billiard Room. The Raffles used to have four tables. Now it has only one. Back in the 1920s a tiger came in for a game, and sat waiting under a table. It was shot by Mr C. M. Philips, a headmaster. Not, surely, before it was first asked to leave? No Englishman would shoot a sitting tiger. After all this is Raffles, you know.

8 March, 1977   **Terry Coleman**

Last of the Summer Wine

Over the tops, through Honley and Austonly, Upperthong and Netherthong, to Holmfirth, flattening itself against its black, slimy hills, cuddling into itself in the keening, slicing November wind. Straight into the Shoulder of Mutton, then, for a couple of pints and a portion of potato pie swimming in pea pûrée.

A Compo enters – sixtyish, woolly hat, wellies, Park Drive cupped protectively. The landlord and I have been chatting about the BBC series, *Last of the Summer Wine*, which is filmed in

Holmfirth. 'What do you think of last week's episode?' the new-comer is asked. 'I think it were bloody trash,' he says. 'It were rubbish.'

All the same, Roy Clarke's creation does reflect one aspect of Holmfirth: a kind of gay, abandoned melancholy. A humorous, rueful, deadpan pessimism. Before the series really put Holmfirth on the map, the town was famous for its saucy seaside postcard factory and the flood of 1852, when eighty-one people drowned. 'And don't leave out the Great Plague,' says George Taylor, play-wright and local historian. 'It arrived in infected clothing from London.'

In the Shoulder of Mutton, just a few doors from the emporium of C. A. and E. Battye, Specialists in Gloves, Hosiery and Corsets, the man in the woolly hat grows expansive as the gas fire takes the chill out of his wellied feet. 'There's nowt funny about Holmfirth,' he says. 'Why a woman threw herself into t' millpond t' other neet. She were a widow and happen she was tired of life. And a bloke up t'road gassed himself because his missus left him. My missus left me, but I didn't gas myself, did I? I'd like to gas her, mind.'

Look upwards from Holmfirth's main shopping street, where a Dayglo poster announces that Derek, Dorothy and Nadine Elliott will entertain at the Civic Hall on Thursday, and the butcher boasts that he stocks Sutcliffe's Tripe, Cowheels, and Trotters, and the town teeters above you almost impossibly.

Every now and then, the BBC's denimed darlings swoop down on this bleak scene; the shops are rated for quaintness quotient by camera crews, the pubs rhubarb with actors' gossip, and the streets ring to cries of 'Marvellous', and 'Wonderful', and 'This place is so bloody true it's not *true*'.

Holmfirth views these carryings-on with the same stoical gloom they display when they watch the end result on their television screens a few weeks later. 'I'll tell you the only reason we watch *Last of the Summer Wine*,' says the landlord of the Shoulder of Mutton. It's simply because we like to recognize the locations. We can't stand the actual programmes. Most of the blokes in it can no more put on a Yorkshire accent than I could put on an Oxford accent. And everybody in it seems so soft. We're a lot harder in real Holmfirth – although we have us fair share of idiots, naturally.'

Although the series never mentions Holmfirth by name, it seems common knowledge all over the country that it is filmed in the Yorkshire town. So thousands of visitors are attracted to Holmfirth every summer, eagerly scanning the streets for originals of the three elderly, whimsical dropouts portrayed by Bill Owen, Peter Sallis, and Brian Wilde. Local resentment may run high, in a passive kind of way, but there are still enough people, like Compo in the pub, willing to fit the image.

Just outside the town, right on the tops, there is a pig farm with a big notice outside: 'Genuine (naturally reared) Home Fed Pork. Half Pigs, Single Joints. We Sell Owt Baa Squeak.' (Trans: We sell anything except the characteristic pig noise.)

And it's true: they will sell owt in Yorkshire. Times are hard, and they're laying workers off at Bamforth's the postcard factory (after all, these days it costs more to buy a stamp than a postcard) so, in spite of their inner reservations, perhaps before too long we'll see a statue of Compo in the centre of Holmfirth, alongside the great Flood Memorial.

22 November, 1976   **Stephen Dixon**

Quiet quads raise revenue

Cambridge people – who, as Rupert Brooke found, 'rarely smile, being urban, squat and packed with guile' – believe they have found a typically cunning answer to the tourist problem – a visa system.

In recent years tourism has been doing very well for Cambridge, if you are one of the shopkeepers sharing in the £18 millions annual revenue, or very badly if you happen to live in one of the colleges which generates it. Hugely increasing numbers of visitors drawn by the fallen pound and the restoration of King's College chapel, are getting bolder. More and more of them are nipping into empty fellows' rooms, taking crested college teaspoons as souvenirs and trying on doctoral gowns.

The better-behaved tourists congregate in Queen's Cloisters or

Trinity Great Court in groups of fifty to sixty, 'which means that if there is just one guide he has to address them in a very loud voice,' Mrs Honour Ridout, the city's tourist officer, said yesterday. 'When a student in an adjacent room hears a detailed description of the college wafting through his window it doesn't help the concentration. It is threatening to disrupt working and living conditions.'

So, from Friday week, organized parties will need a pass to get into the university, limiting the maximum size of each group to twenty-five. Porters will man the lodges and patrol the grounds, counting heads and watching for conduct likely to bring the good names of the colleges into disrepute. Group passes will cost £1 each, to cover administration.

It won't stop the Germans, who will find that the park area around the college Backs and the River Cam offer an unpluggable breach in the defences of St John's Trinity, King's, Clare and Queen's. But it is expected to curb the more docile Americans and there are hopes that the young Swedes will be reasonable.

Coach firms and tour operators will be asked to give at least two weeks' notice of their visit. The city trusts that the fee will not alienate the 2.5 million tourists who spend an average of £7 each in the precincts, some of it on the precincts, some of it on plastic-wrapped honey at Brooke's Grantchester.

Travel agencies may be tempted to retaliate, however, by including in their brochures the advice given in Baedeker's 1878 *Guide to Great Britain*: 'Oxford is on the whole more attractive than Cambridge to the ordinary visitor; and the visitor is therefore recommended to visit Cambridge first, or to omit it altogether if he cannot visit both.'

31 March, 1977   John Ezard

Bad ones

'When Desman comes to slep with my mum I ave to go in the bath in a bed wot my mum puts there. When I fall asleep it's OK but I don't like Desman he comes ever such a lot of nites to slep and the tap drips.' Leila Berg quotes this fragment from a child

137

taught by Beryl Gilroy in a working class London infant school.

My eye roves over Mrs Berg's accomplished prose* but stops, startled as a child breaks in again: 'I went to Hampstead Heath. I sor a man sitting on a seet – He sed come ere boy – When I went ner him he had his willie out – I ran becos me mum sed never stop ner a man with his willie danglin don.' And – I really shouldn't loiter over the fifty or so such extracts embedded here – but there's time for just one: 'God is very old. He has been livin in the skies sins the Dinosaurs was livin. His cloes is all torn becos the angles stopt mend in them up. God has a wife and some kids. The bad one is the devil.'

The bad one of course is often the ordinary working class child in school, and later blazoning defiance at the Stretford End. What I admire about Leila Berg's work (to which this small book is a reflective, telling, but too indulgent annexe) is this readiness to listen to the voices of ordinary children and to accept that working class culture which enfolds most of them.

You might be surprised at how determined our media and our schools can be to turn a shocked blind eye. Her delightful *Little Pete* stories were taken off *Listen With Mother* because Pete went downstairs backwards and argued with busy adults. Her early publishers ('the gentlemen at Oxford') insisted that no child in her stories should say – forgive me – 'bottom'. They must whisper 'behind'. Her main classroom contribution – the series of Nippers readers – let loose all headmasterly hell. One protested against a fictional child murmuring 'I wish my mum was here', because it reinforced 'repeated errors with the subjunctive', and waxed wroth at another child who laughed 'Now it's *me*' – instead of (of course!) 'Now it is I'.

The sad class divide is all captured in the protests from teachers who complained about the mention of football pools, beer or fish and chips in her school readers. As one said: 'there are no fish and chip shops in my district, and neither I nor my children have ever seen one.' Where do you come from? asks Mrs Berg. 'Clapham,' said the teacher.

13 January, 1977   **Brian Jackson**

Reading and Loving by Leila Berg (*Routledge*).

138

Ealing touch

The run of old Ealing films on BBC2 has been saying some extraordinarily interesting things about accents, proving that fashion changes in them just as in other forms of personal decoration, and that these changes are remarkably wide and general.

In *Dead of Night*, made in 1945, the admired middle-upper-class speech was a kind of costive inarticulacy. The characters quacked their lines out in short, staccato bursts, as if the divine gift of speech was a faculty like a bowel movement. Without the evidence of this film the gorgeous Googie Withers, then about to burst into her flowering as a mature actress, might refuse to believe she had ever quacked the line 'Petah! You must be maed!' to Ralph Michael, but here she was doing it. So were they all, and quite naturally too; nobody was telling them how to speak. Today she and the other survivors of this film speak the standard, unaffected educated English that is now admired; probably without any conscious knowledge of having changed. As for the old quack speech, you hear it now only as an object of parody – and on the lips of some expatriates who left England many years ago.

Another curious thing: you must have noticed that today only exceptional young actors can manage the good, clear English needed to play, let us say, the Princes in the Tower. Most of them can't produce a vowel without two or three unwanted diphthongs in it or get their tongues and teeth round consonants. Bad teaching, you say, and blame the drama schools. But in Ealing's *Passport To Pimlico* the middle-class actresses who were supposed to be Cockneys were ludicrously incapable of producing the flat vowels and consonants. I cannot explain this except by asking if since changes in speech fashion are some measure of class change, some accents become so fashionably detestable at various times that they become virtually unlearnable by anyone to whom they are not natural.

The films' attitude to their characters was as hierarchic as Shakespeare's. In *Dead Of Night* all the stories were about southern middle-class people. Even in *San Demetrio, London*, a film about a true merchant-navy exploit, the only permitted accents for the officers were educated southern. The seamen spoke the acceptable variations: stage American, Cockney, Scottish, Welsh, and the southern pseudo-rustic tone called Mummerset.

The much-praised *Passport To Pimlico* was filled with stereo-typed impersonations of policemen, bank managers, civil servants, barrowboys, all shoved along as it seems now, without a spark of true observation of life. (I noticed that the policemen's helmets looked too big for them, just as they always did in Hollywood pictures about London. Perhaps the things *were* too big.)

The real uneducated southern class existed as clowns and groundlings, whose role was to demonstrate such dog-like virtues as trust, loyalty, obedience, and tail-wagging under difficulties. As for the Midlands and the North, they might as well not have been on the map. Yet these films were all made for national distribution, and did good national business, as though the area north of Watford took it for granted that entertainment films would be about those glittering people down south.

Basil Dean was the only producer of his time to wonder if there might be real people out there. Before the war he rescued Gracie Fields from producers who wanted to Londonize her. The films he made with her, allowing her to be the unabashable Rochdale lass, proved unshowable in London and caused box-office stampedes everywhere else. But for ten years after the war the only films I remember seeing in the south made in the north were some Old Mother Riley comedies with Frank Randle and Kitty McShane.

The Castors, a French trio of acrobats, lie on their backs and use their feet to juggle with log-shaped objects. The Bulgarian Boichanovi troupe form a five-person-based pyramid and then fire two more persons on to the shoulders of the top pair. They do such things flawlessly, time after time after time. It is as if the Ballesteros troupe of golfers always drove 280 yards, always hit their second shot to within a yard of the flag, and always holed the putt. Yet the Boichanovis carry begging bowls compared to what the Ballesteroses are going to pick up for skill that is by comparison riddled with fallibility. The moral for parents is, if your child shows outstanding athletic ability, make sure there is some kind of bat and ball involved.

4 June, 1977   **Peter Black**

Fair tigress of the courts

Through the early 1970s a long-running West End drawing-room comedy contained the line 'I hear Virginia's doing very well at Wimbledon.' For eleven months it was just a bit of dialogue in a weary, dreary play. But for every night of July, it was received by the whole house with a groaning sort of titter, a tittering sort of groan. Even the Yanks got the point. For in July the knowledge was still heavy in our breast that Virginia had flunked the big one yet again.

For almost a decade now, Miss Wade's Wimbledon woe has seemed the longest-running tragedy of our whole drama season. She's been going to win the thing, no doubt about it, every year since 1967. This spectacular annual failure – especially those times when such comparative nonentities as Christine Sandberg or Ceri Martinez have put her out – has unfairly clouded appreciation and gratitude for her in this country, where eight out of ten people, I fancy, reckon top tennis is only played seriously for the last two weeks of June in SW19. But in the year-long and wickedly tough international circuit, Virginia Wade has been one of the leading five woman players in the world for a long, long time now. Sure, she's made a lot of money flying the flag. Profit, certainly, but not much honour in her own country.

Now watch her win the Wightman. But, dearie me, we are guaranteed a few palpitations on the way. That goes without saying when our Sarah Virginia comes home to play – remember that time at Nottingham a couple of years back when she was one set, 9-8 and 40-love up on her own serve to Evonne Goolagong – and still blew the thing?

Take last weekend: on Friday night at the Albert Hall she played the perky little whizz-bang merchant, Sue Barker, in the

141

Dewar Cup semi-finals. The press had set it all up as for the British Women's championship. So what happens? Miss Barker, totally unconcerned, goes out and swipes away merrily; Miss Wade, a dozen years the senior and winner of Forest Hills the year after Sue had passed her 11-plus, is a bag of nerves, grunting and groaning like an overacting wrestler, scowling like an over-reacting dowager, her cheeks blotchily-purple.

Somehow she muddles through in the end, thanks mostly to Miss Barker's late flush of generosity. 'Yes, it's ludicrous to get so nervous. But I do, and it seems there's nothing I can do about it,' she admits afterwards.

But Friday's tetchy spinster is Saturday's blooming bombshell. Away with the twitch and in with the sunshine. Against the incomparable Chris Evert there's not a nerve end to be seen. The world's No. 1, who hadn't lost a match in thirty since April, is swept from the court by a performance of bold, bracing beauty. 'I have honestly never played better. I have tried so many times to out-think Chrissie, but this time I just decided to go out and out-play her,' Miss Wade said.

She plays Miss Evert again tonight. But Saturday's win has already put her team in splendid heart. At the Crystal Palace yesterday, there was a hale and healthy confidence about the British side. Virginia is very much chief monitor, head girl. The juniors, as well as the opposition, delight in talking about her. Behind her back of course. Confided one: 'We're taught and taught that the whole game today depends on percentage play, and being fully aware of the decisive points in a match, the ones you absolutely must win. Not Virginia: she'd rather lose spectacularly than win ordinarily, prefer to lose a brilliant rally than win a point by an unforced error.'

Miss Wade's philosophy appeals to more than me. She has a sizeable fan club around the world. For those who like their dame to be more haughty than hearty, as bright as buttons yet as black as thunder, ever arrogant yet ever vulnerable, nice-nasty, beauty-beast, she is a veritable Miss World of any year.

Imagine Princess Anne playing Mrs Robinson in the Benenden production of *The Graduate* and you're getting the picture. In 1973 the American poet, Galway Kinnell, sent over a profile of praise and devotion. He had fallen for Miss Wade's 'incredible lionlike beauty' at Forest Hills. 'She was,' he wrote, 'the last amateur in the big time, the last utterly human player . . . She not only ignores, but appears to despise, what one might call the second-rate virtues: precision, steadiness, patience and cunning. She pursues absolute tennis, tennis by which its inner necessity will not only do that gross thing, win, but will also be recorded and remembered, stroke by stroke, much as a great championship chess match is remembered.'

Christopher Brasher (who else?) once wrote that 'there was someone somewhere who could do for Virginia Wade what Franz Stampfl did for Roger Bannister' and make her the best in the world every day.

For my money, I think we should all praise the Lord and pass the motion that Virginia stays just as she is. Miss Barker's coming along fine, to be sure, but except for those who sit on horses, Miss Wade is surely our only world-class sportsgirl worth writing home about. Only two reservations: I wish she wouldn't squat with such straining Arabian determination when she waits to receive service, or be quite so shirty sullen with meek little linesmen.

11 November, 1976   **Frank Keating**

Virginia Wade is the Wimbledon champion at last – and it didn't matter one jot that it was one of the worst finals in memory. The day will be long recalled for the ecstatic scenes at the very end when the Queen gave her the trophy and even starchy All England men and matrons relaxed upper lips and thunderously let go with 'For she's a jolly good fellow'. Whether the anthem was addressed to the Queen or Miss Wade they cared not a fig. And nor did England.

But, by jove, Miss Wade made the nation sweat as ever. She has been trying to win the thing for 16 years now and it was not until well into the afternoon that nails stopped being bitten. She beat the mountainous Dutch girl, Betty Stove, 4-6, 6-3, 6-1.

Miss Wade's first year at Wimbledon was in 1962 and coincided with the Queen's first visit. Afterwards Virginia said it had been so joyously noisy that she had not heard all the Queen had said to her at the end. 'It didn't matter, it was just great to see her lips moving.'

Rampant patriotism apart, it must be said that it was an awfully dank, dull match full of terrible unforced bloomers by both girls. The Queen's long-known aversion to lawn tennis cannot have been changed. Indeed she had pulled on her white gloves, was straightening her skirt, glancing at the clock and looking to get away to the tea-time racing results mid-way through the third set.

From the start both players were as nervous as field mice at harvesting, the Dutch girl seemingly the less so, for she won the first set – at the end of which you could probably hear the silence a mile away. It looked as if we were in for the biggest anti-climax since the Titanic similarly came across something large and unexpected all those years ago.

It was 3-3 in the second set before the despairing, muttered prayers of 14,000 people got through to their girl in the cathedral. It worked! Virginia reeled off seven games on the trot to take the second set and squat, unassailable, on a 4-0 lead in the last.

The power of prayer! Miss Wade's father, a retired archdeacon, also did his stuff. 'Yes,' he admitted before the match, 'I did pray for Virginia this morning.' Though he added after some meditative thought: 'But then I always pray for everyone each morning.'

2 July, 1977   **Frank Keating**

Pages from a Peruvian diary

Araucana, our daughter, has brought her Paddington bear back to darkest Peru. We wanted to call her Loyola, but the Chilean magistrate wouldn't allow it. He said it was a boy's name. So we called her after the southern tribes of Chile, where she comes from, the fierce Araucanians – sometimes called the Mapuches – who were never defeated by the Incas, nor by the Spaniards. They only succumbed at the end of the nineteenth century to Chilean repression (who says that Chile was a democratic paradise before General Pinochet came on the scene?).

Araucana was born in Melipilla, a small Chilean town between Santiago and the sea. She was picked up in the street at the age of one week by the Carabineros, the Chilean paramilitary police, a byword then for neighbourhood friendliness, like the British bobby. Times have changed. We acquired her when she was nearly two. She had been farmed out by the children's home to a family in a shanty-town on the outskirts of Santiago. She got much love and not much food, and is still small for her age. Then everything seemed calm in Chile. It was honeymoon time for the Allende government.

Now it is the turn of the soldiers all over Latin America, and Araucana is nearly seven and has a broad Yorkshire accent. We have brought her back to visit South America, and Inti as well, so that they can have a look at the continent they came from – and not have too many illusions about it.

Inti, our son, is already nine. He comes from Cochabamba, in the middle of Bolivia, the poorest country in Latin America. We found him in an orange-box by a Pepsi-Cola stand outside the zoo. He had no known father, and his mother had too many children to feed. Now an English schoolboy, he remains an addict of the music of the South American Indians. He tends to identify with the shepherd boy on the record sleeve, sitting on the mountainside playing the quena and looking after his flock of llamas.

That often seems a more attractive prospect than the fogs of Humberside. Quite right too. But South America is not all shepherd boys with llamas any more than Indo-China is ragged urchins on water buffalo – romantic though the photographs are. Somehow a little reality needs to break in. How do you explain to optimistic children that there is a great wide world outside where there is no colour television, and no central heating, and no baked beans for supper? Probably this is only a lesson that can be learnt over time. Meanwhile, there is, for some, the possibility of travel – while the children are old enough to take things in, and young enough to ride at half price.

So, with an outlay of £2500 (£1300 on the return fare from London to Lima by British Caledonian, two adults, two children; plus £1200 (maximum foreign currency allowance for four permitted by the British Government) for food and travel and

lodging) we have arrived in darkest Peru, together with Paddington bear, for a month's exploration of the South American hinter-
land.

In the past few years, Latin America has become synonymous
with military dictatorship, fierce repression, terror squads, torture,
and political prisoners. It has become almost impossible to write
about the continent without listing a catalogue of horrors in every
article. What is more, there is not much light at the end of the
tunnel: the soldiers are corrupt and ignorant, confident in their
firepower; the civilian politicians are impotent and discredited;
the intellectuals are uneasy and uncertain, devoid of fresh ideas;
the guerrillas are weak and on the defensive.

In the vast Americanized urban conglomerations that pass for
capital cities in this part of the world, there is an atmosphere of
foreboding. If, by some miracle, the soldiers were to retire from
politics tomorrow, what would take their place? There are few
fresh hints available.

So it seems sensible to escape from politics for a while, and to
travel inland, into the past, to see what remains in the provincial
towns and villages of Latin America's former way of life.

In the tracks of Mr Meiggs

Peru's Central Railway, which leads from the coast to the high
Andean plateau, starts at the Desamparados station in the middle
of Lima. A stately classical building, located next to the presidential palace beside the river Rimac, it is guarded at present by a
large armoured car – symbol of military rule and a reminder that
a state of emergency is still in force in Peru as in much of the rest
of South America.

The military government that has controlled Peru since 1968
has recently entered a more complex and turbulent period, and its
actions have been increasingly questioned, first by the Right, now
by the Left. Growing social tensions, an unusual level of inflation,
and successive devaluations of the sol, have led the government of
General Francisco Morales Bermudez to seek allies on the Right.

The revolutionary rhetoric of the early period has been abandoned and many of the reforms are gradually being reversed. But by the current standards of Latin America, Peru remains a beacon of enlightenment. Repression is at a minimum, and the atmosphere is now sufficiently relaxed for the Government to abandon the nightly curfew which kept the citizens of Lima shut up in their houses from two till five in the morning.

We were up and about at that hour in order to get to the Desamparados station in time to catch the 7.30 train up into the Andes. The station is built on three levels, the train itself departing from the basement. The building has a vaulted glass roof supported by stout Doric columns.

On the pediment above, the legend 'Ferrocarril Central' is inscribed in elegant lettering, and a large clock face announces proudly that it was made by 'Johnston of Croydon'. The timetable, printed in 1971, still refers to 'The Peruvian Corporation Ltd.' – the British company that used to run the railway   and in the booking office there is a bust of Henry Meiggs, the famous American 'concessionario-constructor' who built the line in the nineteenth century.

It was built to service the great mines at Cerro de Pasco high in the Andes and the smelter at La Oroya. Minerals still provide half of Peru's export earnings – the rest coming from the sale of fish-meal, cotton and sugar. The wagons bring down copper, zinc and lead to Callao, Lima's principal port on the Pacific. Once a powerful American mining company, the Cerro de Pasco Corporation was nationalized by the military and has now been renamed 'Centromin'. For decades it was an object of hostility and criticism by the Peruvian Left, but it took a military government to place it in the hands of the State.

The railway which climbs almost vertically to nearly 16,000ft., was designed to carry minerals down to the sea, but it has become something of a national institution, bringing immigrant peasants from the sierra to the big city, and providing a reasonably cheap and convenient method of maintaining contact between two very different zones of Peru. Now, too, it carries the impoverished tourists of the late twentieth century, long-haired and long-legged American and European students, the men indistinguishable from

147

the women, all seeking an escape from the modern world.

Henry Meiggs did not see his railway in these terms, however. At the ceremony at the start of the project, on New Year's day 1870, he said that 'a great social revolution' was to be wrought by the locomotive, 'that irresistible battering ram of modern civilization'. Its whistle, he declared 'will awaken the native race from the lethargy in which its dominators have kept it for so many centuries'. Steam, he underlined, 'is the most rapid and secure means of introducing life and material development to the backward Amazonian regions'.

Nowadays the engine is powered by diesel, not steam. The railway has been brought up to date. The carriages too are new – made in Sheffield – with green plastic-covered seats, formica-topped tables and aluminium luggage racks.

At the same hour every morning, the one passenger train of the day speeds off from Desamparados station with much ringing of the bell. It wanders through the grey and ochre shanty towns, through the eucalyptus and maize of the Rimac valley, and then begins its painful zigzag course up into the Andes.

After three hours of steady progress it has already climbed 10,000 ft., and the steward operating from a tiny corner of the carriage, begins producing food and drink. There is no Inca Kola, Peru's nationalistic response to the American soft-drink invasion, but we are offered Kola Inglesa instead, perhaps in deference to our or the railway company's origins.

At Calera station, around midday, the railway line reaches its highest point, 15,686 ft. An anxious white-coated man speeds through the carriages with a triangular leather bag from which he dispenses oxygen to those in need. The altitude affects people in different ways. Some go red, others white, some just fall asleep.

After La Oroya, a narrow rock valley dominated by the chimneys of Centromin's smelter, the train emerges in mid-afternoon on to a broad plateau of great beauty and considerable prosperity. It clatters through a landscape of varying shades of green, through fields of maize and barley, until it reaches its evening destination of Huancayo, two miles up in the sky.

Beyond Huancayo, a large market town which services a wealthy wheat-growing valley, the Andes fall away into the tropical jungle.

Just north of here is Santa Rosa de Ocopa, where the Franciscans set up a training college in the early eighteenth century to send out missionaries to convert the jungle Indians in the basin of the Amazon.

I have a copy of the map of the area, made by Friar Manuel Sobreviela in 1790, and marked with different signs for the villages of the faithful, the converted and the infidel. Beyond the reach of the friars, peppering the fringes of the map, are the initials NB, standing for 'Nacion Barbara'. In recent years, worried by the possibility of a resurgence of the guerrilla movements of the 1960s, the Government has pushed new roads rather than missionaries into this impenetrable terrain . . .

Maoism above the snow line

We had lunch here with a cheerful lady from the San Cristobal University who had just collected the latest copy of *Peking Review* from her pigeon-hole. The Maoists are the largest political group in Ayacucho, she says, and they dominate the university.

More magazines from China arrive in Ayacucho than in the whole of Peru, and the pavement booksellers in the old colonial square, the Parque Sucre, do a brisk sale in the latest pronouncements of 'Chairman Jua' and the doings of the 'Banda de los Cuatro'.

The San Cristobal University has 6000 students. The town's other university is not functioning properly at the moment because of certain 'problems' – apparently another left-wing group is contesting the authority of the Maoists.

After lunch we were introduced to a young and busty Peruvian woman who had spent ten years in Rome and now was living with an Australian who melted down silver coins to make jewellery. 'Ayacucho is a very conservative place,' she said. 'It lives in the eighteenth century.' Asked to elaborate, she said that her parents were very old-fashioned and insisted that she should be at home by 9 p.m.

Ayacucho, 8000 feet up in the Andes, was the scene of the last great battle fought by the Spaniards in South America. In December 1824 at La Quinua, a plateau not far from here, Bolivia's lieutenant, Jose Antonio de Sucre, defeated the Spanish army, effectively putting an end to colonial rule in Peru and what was to become Bolivia. Near here too, at Huari, was the headquarters of the great pre-Inca Huari civilization, which survived from 600 to 1100 AD.

The ruins, virtually untouched by archaeologists, stretch over a vast area of nearly a thousand acres. Now they are almost completely overgrown with cactus plants and it is quite difficult even to imagine what the city was once like.

A few peasants snatch a living from the stony fields between the ruined walls, and where the wooden plough has turned the soil it is possible to recover a rich hoard of broken pottery.

We came to Ayacucho across the mountains from Huancavelica, a day's journey. We were up at 5 a.m. to catch the early Oropesa bus to Santa Ines, a village on the road from the coast to the sierra.

In the dark at our hotel door, an old Indian cargador waited to carry our luggage and seemed disappointed when we declined his offer. We only have two suitcases, and a leather grip, and the children have a rucksack each, so we are not too heavily loaded.

We reached Santa Ines in about three hours, over a spectacular pass above the snow line, with herds of llamas grazing beside the Choclococha lagoon. The village proved to be a huddle of houses on the road junction and little else.

We got off the bus, which continued its journey on to Pisco on the coast, and stood forlornly by the roadside waiting for transport to come the other way. The sun was up, but at 12,000 feet the temperature is cold.

A woman sitting by the roadside, knitting with a baby on her back, said that she had been there for two days, waiting for transport. We had travelled with a Brazilian couple on the bus, and after a while a German couple turned up who had spent a chilly night in the village.

Hours passed and no wheeled traffic came by. Rumour had it that there had been an avalanche beyond Castrovirreyna on the

Pisco road and that this was why no buses or lorries were getting through.

With eight 'gringos' waiting, we began investigating the possibility of chartering a lorry to Ayacucho.

Eventually, just after the German couple had gone to look for a lorry driver, a bus appeared on the horizon, shrouded in evil-smelling smoke. It was already full, but never mind. We threw our cases on to the roof and piled in.

On the outskirts of Ayacucho was a police roadblock, a control which exists near all the large towns in the mountains. Our passports were checked, and the identity cards of the Peruvians. The police officer was white and efficient.

The Indian peasants on the bus looked worried. Two young ones were taken into the police hut for questioning, but were eventually allowed to rejoin the bus. We drove into the town just before dusk . . .

19-24 May, 1977   **Richard Gott**

Last waltz with the Czar

I mean no discourtesy when I say that the first surprise was to learn that she was still alive; but Princess Viktoria Luise, the Kaiser's daughter, daughter of the last of the reigning Hohenzollerns, is not only alive, but vigorous. She lives in a small house in Brunswick, at Stresemanstrasse 5, among pictures of Frederick the Great, of her father Wilhelm II, and of her own wedding day. She is now 84. She went ski-ing until she was 80. She proposed a toast to peace and we drank it in pink champagne.

She was born in 1892, Princess of Prussia, Orange Hildesheim, and of fourteen other territories; and, besides, Duchess of Saxony, Holstein, Schleswig and of twenty other territories. Today she is a citizen of the Federal Republic of Germany, though on her passport she is described firmly as Princess of Prussia and Duchess of Brunswick.

The last title came to her on her marriage to Ernst August, Duke of Brunswick, and her wedding picture is among the first she shows a visitor. I asked why the men in the scene were carrying flaming torches. 'It was the dance of the torches in the evening,' she said. 'I danced with my husband, and then with my father; and then with the King of England, and then with the Emperor of Russia.' That was in 1913, the year before the deluge, and the last time those emperors and kings ever met.

The picture of which she is perhaps most proud shows her on horseback, in 1911, when as a girl of eighteen, she was installed as colonel in chief of the Death's Head Hussars. It is a martial picture. Had she wanted to be a boy? 'Yes, yes, yes, yes. I was so delighted when I got my regiment. I had six brothers, and of course, I was a half-boy.' She always liked to wear the Scottish kilt, because a man might wear that too.

When she was a girl, the Kaiser would tell them stories, and laugh, and slap his knees. In public he was not allowed to laugh. At the unveiling of one statue, the drape at first stuck, and then fell and enveloped the mayor, who crawled around on the ground like a tortoise. The Kaiser kept his face, but afterwards exploded with laughter. Once he broke a chair under him at a banquet and bore it for as long as he could, until, when he rose to make a speech, he remarked that they might bring him another because the chair he had been sitting on had now only three legs.

Then the war. In 1914 the Kaiser had felt betrayed. He believed, said the princess, that the King of England could prevent the war. This was the saddest and wildest misapprehension: how could he have believed that? 'He believed in the friendship of his cousin.'

Several times, here and there in the conversation, the princess said how much her father loved England. In 1912, when he had first taken her to England, to open the Victoria memorial (the great golden thing in front of Buckingham Palace), he brought her on deck as they approached the English coast and told her that for him the sense of England was always the smell of English hay. 'When we came for the first time,' she said, 'it was winter, so there was no hay.'

The war dragged on, dragging Europe down with it. In Germany there was privation, in Russia revolution. The Czar with whom she had danced, and all his family, were murdered at Ekaterinburg. How had she felt then? 'That it could happen to us all as well. After a lost war, we all had the feeling the Communists were coming up, and the whole country was nearly starved. They had nothing to eat.'

In 1918, the Kaiser abdicated in chaos and bitterness. The princess thinks the abdication was inevitable but blames it principally on Woodrow Wilson. 'The abdication was the only way to get an understanding with America, don't you see? Because they tried to impress upon the population that the Kaiser was at fault.'

The Kaiser went to exile in Holland, never to return. The princess lived in Austria and Germany and, in the 1930s, visited England. There she met the future Queen of England as a little girl coming in breathlessly from a dancing lesson and exclaiming 'Mummy, it's wonderful,' and at Chequers, Ramsay MacDonald, who wanted to know about Hitler. He thought Hitler was a simple man and told the princess, 'I'm a simple man, too.'

And what did the princess reply? 'I said if Hitler's for peace and not war, we're all for him.'

It was after this visit that Hitler, through Ribbentrop, made the modest proposal that the princess and her husband should arrange a marriage between their daughter Fredericke and the Prince of Wales, later Edward VIII, later the Duke of Windsor. And what was her reply to Hitler? – 'No. We don't push our children . . .' Thus spake the Hohenzollerns. Besides, said the princess, the Prince of Wales had other ideas at the time, or so she believed. It must be one of the more piquant ironies of a century disastrous for European dynasties that in 1912, on that first visit to England, Princess Viktoria Luise herself had been whispered in the press as a future bride of that same, much younger, Prince of Wales.

Was it true that throughout his exile the Kaiser hoped for the restoration of the monarchy? 'I believe yes. That in his heart, and he was a very religious man, he thought, "If God wills that I come back, I will come back." '

He believed in the Divine Right of Kings? 'In the Divine Right of the Emperor.' And did she so believe herself a Princess of Prussia through the will of God? – 'Yes.' Nowadays monarchies are different. There were constitutional monarchies. 'The young

Spain' – and she referred to Juan Carlos, King of Spain, simply as Spain, in the way that the King of France might be called, in a Jacobean play, France – 'had been educated for kingship by Franco.'

By the will of the Caudillo, as it were, rather than the will of God, Sophia, granddaughter of Viktoria Luise, is Juan Carlos's queen.

Throughout the interview the princess's German publisher remained, and often helped her to find a word or a phrase. She explained that although, having had an English nanny, she had learned English before even German, she had forgotten much of it.

At one point when the princess spoke of peace, I said Germany had twice this century plunged Europe into war: she denied this was so with the first. Well then, Hitler had been a madman? 'Yes,' she said. 'At last. By his successes he lost his senses.' But she had known of his slaughter of the Jews? Dachau, after all, was about eight miles north of Munich just off the main road, and had been there since before the war. She said she had not known until the last. In the war she had lived in a castle in the Harz mountains, but had not known until after the war that there was a concentration camp behind those mountains. She would swear it.

Her friend the publisher then told a story, which he had from a nephew of the princess's who was an eye witness, about the Kaiser and the Nazis. It happened that in November, 1938, the Kaiser's sons were with him in Holland in order to draw up a new settlement of the family property. While they were together, the news came of the Kristallnacht in which the synagogues of the German Jews had been burned. The Kaiser was distressed, and shouted at August Wilhelm, the only one of his sons who had joined the Nazis, that if he did not leave the party, he would throw him out of the family. The eldest son reasoned with his father, saying that if his brother did this, he would be murdered. The Kaiser relented, but still refused ever again to appear in public with August Wilhelm. That day the Kaiser cried.

In 1939, there was war. In 1941, still in Holland though by then in German-occupied Holland, the Kaiser died. Princess Viktoria Luise was with him and says that his last wish was that Germany and England should be friends. Four years later the second German war of the century ended with Germany not merely defeated, but by this time destroyed. Most of what used to be Prussia was parcelled out between Poland, Russia, and what became East Germany.

The princess wants to see a reunited Germany, and in her heart cannot accept Willy Brandt's Ostpolitik, which formally recognized the existence of two separate German states. In a country which was now in the east, her father had a hunting box. She remembers a church. The people were very loyal. 'And shall we,' she asks, 'now give them all up?'

But would it need a war to recover them? It must be done little by little, said the princess; at which her publisher,* mentioning that the princess was not a politician, took the opportunity to produce a locket, found only that morning, which was a gift of Queen Victoria to the princess as a child. The princess had forgotten it. It opens to reveal a portrait of Albert, the Prince Consort.

We had been drinking tea, but now pink champagne arrived and we drank to peace, of which the princess spoke much. I said the princess had lost everything. She took this to mean a lost Prussia, and began to talk once again of never giving up hope. But I had meant her own loss, not only of rank but of material possessions. The publisher grasped this and explained to her. 'Living in such a house. No servants.'

'That is correct,' she said, but her family had always been religious, and she prayed. I understood her to say that she prayed that, among other things, the young might have a faith of their own, and not have to go for ideas to Indian mysticism as so many did. Then she told me the story of the allegorical painting. It was at the time of the Boxer rebellions, she thought in 1901. It was to do with the holy rights of Europe.

The Kaiser had painted this? 'Yes, yes, yes. It was a beautiful allegory. Woman, in all sorts of armour.' There were the women of Europe arm in arm – German, Austrian, French, and Russian; her father had not kept the Russian out.

And the English? 'Yes . . . And in the clouds, there was the face of the East, China, a Buddha. Here stood all Europe . . . and looked up to that face. I never forget it, because I had to run through the room of my mother, and pass this picture, when I went to see my father. I always thought of the picture and thought, "My God, I only hope never, never, never . . . " ' Underneath was an inscription which said something like, 'Europe, take care of your holy rights.'

Did she have that fear of the East now? She did, and felt the English did not know how near it was. Russia was now on the other side, on the eastern side. Before, there had been Russia and Prussia between East and West. The Prussian peoples had been perhaps the sentinels for Europe. Now she feared Russia and China.

We walked out together from the princess's sitting room into an ante room. There is a doll's house, given to her by a long-dead Queen of Holland. There is a portrait of her late husband, who died in 1953: she keeps it surrounded with flowers.

There was again the picture of herself as colonel of the Death's Head Hussars. She said her mount that day was called Trilby, a wonderful horse.

Then again, the wedding picture. As she danced with the Czar, and as he talked to her, in English as he did with his own family, what did he say? 'He had wonderful eyes, very earnest, and very lovable. We danced, and he embraced me, and he said, "I hope you will be just as happy as I ." And I'll never forget that.' They were the last words he ever spoke to her.

26 May, 1977   **Terry Coleman**

The Kaiser's Daughter, the memoirs of Viktoria Luise, Princess of Prussia, is published by W. H. Allen.

Dock Green

Time flows back along the metropolitan Thames. On the Isle of Dogs – scarcely three miles from Tower Bridge as the gull flies and the heart of what used to be London's inner dockland – the cattle and sheep may be returning soon.

156

They were famous once. The marsh was so fertile that the flocks and herds were the fattest and most prosperous in the country, or so early observers claimed. The industrial tide swept them away and in turn fell with startling suddenness. In the up-river docks herons displaced cranes, naturalists and birdwatchers ousted the watermen, wild flowers and marine developers took what root they could. And now comes Hilary Peters, starting up her dockland farms.

She already has a flourishing one at Rotherhithe, and is now busy planning the Isle of Dogs offshoot, with official blessing, as part of next year's jubilee effort. Hilary Peters is no romantic. She is a professional landscape gardener who lives at Greenwich and has taken to strictly practical farming in an area she finds more salubrious than the spray-polluted, overdriven country-side. Her aims for the Isle of Dogs are modest but comprehensive – just one or two each of the whole livestock range to build a teaching farm. And why, if that old pasture was as lush as it was cracked up to be, shouldn't she produce a new prize-winning strain of mudchute sheep?

The mudchute is the great wasteheap left when they dug the Millwall Docks, unused at present except by bored local lads who ride round the crater on their motor-bikes. Maybe they will turn from this to farming, for Hilary Peters's idea – and she says the Greater London Council likes it – is for the locals to run the thing themselves.

She must be joking? Not at all, judging from the local support and help she gets for her already well-established smallholding in the old Surrey Commercial Docks just across the river. Not surprisingly there was all-round suspicion at first, from officialdom and surviving inhabitants alike, but Miss Peters says this is now quite gone. People bring along their waste to feed the stock, and the kids – after a preliminary burst of routine destructiveness – grew deeply interested when they found they were not only welcome but needed. Also it was something of a dare. Their docker grandparents may have kept hens, long before their time, but few of them can have seen or imagined anything as extra-ordinary as a goat or a goose.

This Rotherhithe farm near the old Greenland Dock now has a

herd of goats, several donkeys, hundreds of hens and ducks, rabbits and bees, working dogs and cats, a few people.

In atmosphere it seems to go back long before the days when the whalers sailed in from the Limehouse Reach, centuries before fat cattle squelched about in the rich mud of what was to become dockland. The scene is uncannily quiet. Perhaps it is now the only part of London where something near total silence prevails. It is away from frequented roads, beneath no regular flightpath; the river rarely gives a hoot. It is silent in a way the modern country-side is not. All you hear is the soft, complex serial music produced by the creatures of the non-mechanized farmyard. It could be an island of ancient (rather than modern) Greece.

Playing up to this classical conceit, the geese clamoured as I tried to find my way in through the high defensive wall – built not by Miss Peters but by the dock owners who protected their territory so effectively that a docker's family could spend their lives yards from a river they never saw. Several large dogs bounded up, not aggressively. One had a disused scrubbing brush drooping from its jaw, but games were discouraged in working hours. A billy-goat under temporary house arrest was muttering furiously at an outhouse window, feet on sill. Rotherhithe children were skilfully going about their rural tasks, as if in deepest Devon or Delos. Fleets of hens, ducks, geese, and goats sailed happily in an ocean of household scraps and waste vegetables from the markets.

Eventually, as she extends her agricultural activities, Miss Peters plans to use her Dutch barge to collect and distribute her fodder, thus bringing the river itself into the productive picture. She is given far more waste than the animals can eat. This prac-tical demonstration of how much waste our allegedly impoverished society automatically produces, and how it can be used by anyone with a mind to it, must be one of the lessons the young people of Rotherhithe are learning far more tellingly than from any lecture. They will also have the chance of learning to milk, maybe to ride, and certainly to respect such agreeable fellow-citizens of the world as ducks and goats.

Is it all just a happy quirk, made possible by a hiccup in time and industrial tide? In a sense, yes. The Port of London Authority would naturally be selling unwanted land to the highest bidders if these were around, rather than lending it to Hilary Peters. Yet now that her work has been accepted as socially productive it could take root. It goes along with one of the more auspicious currents of our time, the revolt against the brutalities of factory farming. (One or two of the Peters hens are ex-battery and would have some thrilling escape stories to tell if they could speak.) At the same time she has her feet squarely on the ground and can sell enough cheese, yoghourt, eggs and honey to make her farming self-supporting.

Mushrooms could be remunerative. Possibly fish could be bred in the idle dockwater where the slaughtered whales used to sail in, which would be restitution of a kind. She has five full-time colleagues. Two will be concentrating on the home farm at Rotherhithe, two more on (so to say) the Isle of Dogs puppy. The third pair will be attending to another teaching farm they are planning to start at Thamesmead, the huge and highly contro-versial riverside new town on the edge of Woolwich.

This is probably the most significant step of all. Public author-ities now belatedly recognize that sound roofs and central heating are not enough; that when old streets are upended into new tower blocks social trauma can result. Windows now get broken before the new blocks are even completed. This makes the author-ities – so well-meaning, so unimaginative – deeply hurt. Hilary Peters thinks people shouldn't be blamed if they resent having everything done for them. They like to do things for themselves. She has an idea that Thamesmeaders might take to farming in quite a big way.

27 November, 1976   **Norman Shrapnel**

A drop in pressure

The London Hydraulic Power Company – 'the magnitude of whose operations is rendered tolerably evident by the fact that there is scarcely an important thoroughfare in London in which men may not be seen from time to time laying cast iron pipes,' according to *The Engineer* in January, 1893 – is going out of business. Those pipes carried water at a pressure between 750 and 800 lbs per square inch, and in the years 1883 to 1932 the company's mileage went from a modest 7 to the present 180. The retreat is orderly, will be complete within six months or so, and is sad. After all, as Lord Armstrong noted in 1848, hydraulic power is 'characterized by great accuracy and softness of movement'. (He was an addict: before Victoria had been on the throne a decade, he had rigged hydraulic power to a crane at Newcastle's Public Wharf.)

Until recently, Tower Bridge took three-quarters of a million gallons a quarter of LHPC water to raise its bascules. Carroll Gibbons and his Orpheans could hardly have managed without its raising the cabaret floor at the Savoy (whose management are even now having to convert to humbler sources). Quaglino's lift swept flappers upstairs on the company's power brought in from the street. The Port of London used nearly eight million gallons a week. London's sewers were flushed by the spent water, which began life in the Thames and was swiftly returned to it. (One bright spot: over the years, the river has improved to the point where now it is necessary for the LHPC to chlorinate their storage tanks; they've got fresh water mussels in their pipes.) With hydraulic gadgets of one sort or another, you can lift a locomotive, crush the oil out of nuts, pump organ bellows, print books, or extinguish fires. None of this was lost on the nineteenth-century mind.

As far west as Kensington (for apartment blocks and small hotels), as far north as Islington (for small factories), and to the east and south (for railways and dockland use) you could have your machines connected. The small customers were never profitable unless densely concentrated: the docks and railways made up the difference. But containerization and Dr Beeching managed to shift the LHPC's best customers out of its reach. Now, all the users are having to move over to electric motors of their own.

Is anyone benefiting from the change over from the old, very civil engineering? Don Donnachie, the Geordie resident engineer at the last pumping station still working, at Wapping Wall (opposite the Prospect of Whitby, from whose bar he can detect any disaster at the plant by means of a Heath Robinson light he's fixed), is sceptical. 'The trouble is,' he says, from thirty-five years' experience with hydraulics, some of it in wartime submarines, 'electric motors are inefficient for frequent stop-and-start use.' Which is, of course, what a lift has to survive. 'In a few years there'll be a comeback. And in the meantime our network will have become useless. It'll cost hundreds of millions to replace.'

His chairman, Mr White, explains that electricity used to be the alternative to hydraulic transmission of power: both were generated by steam. But now electricity is not only competition, it is the cheapest way of generating hydraulic power, too. Over the years the price of electricity has shifted in favour of medium-scale users, and away from the LHPC's advantage. Between losing business and the battle against fuel costs, they have had to concede defeat. It's an awful parable on our times. We keep thinking we can do things better than our great grandparents did: from railways to windmills (which they were developing for electricity production), and not forgetting the bicycle, we ditch their ideas. At about the time we begin to watch windmill-driven television, ride bikes to the station, and have to start re-laying railway track, perhaps all those important thoroughfares will have to be dug up again.

15 January, 1977   **Richard North**

Gumboot democracy in sinking Venice

You can telephone a number in Venice and hear a recorded voice tell you how high your boots should be tomorrow, or how much water you can expect to find on the ground floor of your house. The calculations depend on where you are going and where you live in Venice, for some parts of the city are a fraction of an inch or even a couple of inches higher than other parts. This morning, unforeseen by me, the hotel where I was staying was on dry land. A coffeebar and a newsagent's close by were also dry, but all around was flooded with about two feet of water. Only Venetians with rubber boots could navigate the streets, go to church, or keep their morning appointments. Of course, Venetians have their rubber boots.

It is a clockwork flood. It depends on three things to make the clock start ticking: wind from the south, which we had last night and again today, a positioning of the sun and the moon (called in Italian *sizigia*) and a certain tilting of the floor of the Adriatic Sea. Last night we had the first two things. The water was expected to rise by 1.15 metres above the normal lagoon level, as it had on Friday night.

The forecast was a little off because the wind was not very strong. There was a metre of water in St Mark's Square this morning and that also is the prediction for tomorrow. Sirens will sound tomorrow morning as they did this morning, confirming the prediction and warning those about to go out. The water will subside before midday, if the wind from Africa, the *sizigia*, and the tilt permit.

For the past ten days, this has been a daily occurrence, appropriately coinciding with the tenth anniversary of the worst Venetian flood, that of 4 November, 1966, when St Mark's Square was six feet deep in water. That remains the record, included each day with the 'high water' report posted by the door of the bell tower standing in the same square.

Ten years ago, Venetians could expect high water or medium-high water an average of 100 times a year. Now the average is 150 times a year. Today's one-metre level, like tomorrow's, is still considered exceptional, but it may not be for much longer.

Venetians, along with other Italians, including those living along the banks of the River Po, which is expected to overflow at some points today, are mourning the death of at least thirteen Sicilians swept away by the flood in Trapani, west of Palermo. Three years ago there was a similar flood in Sicily and £652,000 was voted for a flood-control programme. As the television news announcer said today, that money has not been spent. The £315 millions appropriated in 1973 to preserve Venice from ultimate destruction, also has not been spent, or at least, not on Venice, save for a very small part.

So what else is new on the Rialto? Because of its high arch, the Rialto bridge is a good place to watch the flood come in and to watch it go away, carrying with it yet more of Venice's structure, which also suffered fresh cracks from the tremors felt here from the Friuli earthquake of 4 May.

Standing, bootless, on my little dry island this morning I saw a big burly man wearing a white apron emerge from the kitchen of a restaurant. Seeing the Venetians and others looking at the water which was then encroaching from all the side streets, he exclaimed to everyone, and to no one, as he marched by, 'Si, si, high water again! And all Italy will be moved to tears at the sight. Just as they were on 4 May.'

This is not a cynical but a fair appraisement of the electorate and the elected in this beautiful land which, when it does not have a bad government has a non-government which cannot even stop a flood from destroying Europe's most handsome city with clock-work regularity. And the clock is gaining time.

8 November, 1976   **George Armstrong**

The Road to Glory

When documentaries claim never-before-seen footage, I take their word for it, for one foot looks very like another. But the early Fascist film which David Rea coaxed from the Instituto Luce for Mussolini – *The Road to Glory* (ATV) was quite new to me. And yet I half thought I had seen it before. The fat marble, the fountains, the cast of thousands. The horses, outriders and runners and forums full for the balcony scene. It was Hollywood. It was *Ben Hur*. Well, Benito Hur. Probably Mussolini expanded to fill the architecture available. I dare say it's a variant of Parkinson's Law.

David Rea, the producer, who is Italian by descent, is evidently trying to redress the crude propaganda balance and present what TV Times calls 'perhaps one of the most fascinating, controversial and tragic figures of our time'. I like the touch of banker's caution in that 'perhaps'. When news came of Mussolini's death, hung by his feet from a meat hook with his little mistress swinging beside him, schoolboys grabbed young Rea and held him upside down. It could, I quite see, give one the other fellow's point of view.

It was a pitiful and grotesque death for someone who did as much for British morale as Tommy Handley. When Miss Violet

Gibson, described as 'a crazy Irishwoman', a phrase I would like to linger over, tried to shoot Mussolini she managed to put a tiny bullet right through his nose. A picture of the Duce with a large plaster on his nose and deeply reproachful eyes is hard to view with equanimity.

I have a friend (or perhaps had) who received a war wound in the bottom while serving with the Italian Navy. I don't know what we would have done at times without the Italian Navy. Or the extreme difficulty Mussolini encountered in subduing anyone from the Ethiopians to the Greeks. Or his partiality for spats and strange hats.

I greatly enjoyed early film of young Fascists who appear to have some difficulty deciding which arm to stick out in salute. There were also scenes of early Fascist thuggery which, one must add, were not such fun. Next week Rea completes the story of Mussolini's fall.

I think I would have preferred to the impartial, detached commentary some testimony from the Italians who loved him, gave their wedding rings to finance him, paved the piazzas with their upturned faces when he spoke, murdered and mangled and never mention him now. But, if asked nicely, they might.

2 December, 1976   **Nancy Banks-Smith**

Dire tribe

A new culture has been born in Italy, spawned in the violent climate of demonstration and clashes over the past few months.

Italian politics have become more and more like science fiction, with the official parties prevaricating while ultra-right and ultra-left make the running. With each scandal and kidnapping the borderline between reality and fiction becomes more blurred. The reality is strange enough but the culture emerging from this 'strategy of tension' is even more grotesque and deliberately so.

This new culture is as far from officialdom as the official Communist Party is from the radical 'spontaneous movements' it treats with such suspicion. The creators are often the same:

minority groups, feminists, homosexuals, the homeless and above all the students of the occupied universities. For them, this is *Anno Nova* – year nine from May '68. This is the year of the Metropolitan Indians and their companions of the group P38, students on the warpath against the barons of the universities. The professors had it coming to them in the overcrowded quagmire of the universities. But no one could have foreseen the violent irony of the attack.

Now it is not just stones that are thrown, but radio waves. Pirate radio stations all over Italy and some cable TV stations too, link up and co-ordinate events, call in support and reinforcements when needed and notify on police movements.

The Metropolitan Indians dress to disrupt. No university teacher can be sure of getting through a lecture without the intervention of plumed and daubed redskins placed strategically in the audience. He may be confronted with their jeers, their gauze masks and their favourite accusation: 'Enemy of the working class'. He may be forced to grant the minimum mark needed to ensure continuation of a state grant: 27 out of 30. While the Metropolitan Indians may force him to address the assembly on his knees or squirt him with a water pistol, the members of P38 claim to be armed with real pistols of that number.

Combine this with the belated flowering of drag on to the streets of the large cities and the punitive flying squads organized by the feminists to hunt down rapists and you have something that resembles a synthesis of early-twentieth-century Dada and post-revolutionary Russian agit-prop.

Arthur Cravan, intellectual and amateur boxer, who disrupted lectures at the Sorbonne seventy years ago by bursting in shooting real bullets from his real gun and shouting abuse at academia. Benjamin Peret, French Dada anti-politician, who would cross over the street to spit at priests and politicians.

Add to these the black humour of Jean Genet and Samuel Becket, the expanded language of James Joyce and you have something of the tones and codes of groups and movements who are fighting for what they call an '*area creativa*'.

In pursuit of this creative area alternative newspapers have proliferated. The Milanese feminists have one called *Sottosopra*:

a scurrilous pun on the traditional sexual position of below/beneath. The Metropolitan Indians have now started another in Rome, called *Oask*, it is a tabloid with an edition of 5000, deliberately based on the original Dada magazines: spiralling topsy-turvy layout, politics, Eskimo poems, satirical cartoons and vignettes mingled to the taste of the new barbarians. Spokesman Maurizio (no surnames used) explained: 'We want to break up and regroup in small provocation cells like those of the Dada movement: we want to provoke emotion.'

This ancestry in a previous generation of the cultural *avant garde* has not escaped Italian intellectual commentators like the philosopher and journalist Umberto Eco. Extraordinary interpretations crop up in traditional newspapers like *Corriere della Sera*. Eco has related all this to an extension of McLuhan's Gutenberg Galaxy into real life: the link up of sophisticated communications technology and radical unruly protest. He calls it 'a new eye on the index finger', and then goes off into a bit of cultural (rather than political) science fiction: 'A sort of genetic mutation in which the new technical instrument is seen as a natural extension of the body . . .'

By this he means the instant journalism of the radical groups, and in particular their use of radios. The most famous of the pirate stations was Radio Alice in Bologna, the voice of the students, which ran for over a year before being closed by armed and helmeted police last month. Now the prosecutor must decide whether the four radio operators can be charged for encouraging urban guerrilla activities because of the nature of the station's transmissions: monitoring of police movements during the tear gas riots and shootings in Bologna and the relaying of these to demonstrators.

While the police prepared to charge the station, the last panic-stricken broadcast words again reflected the dangerous confusion between reality and fiction that prevails in Italy: 'That film . . . what was it called? Katherina Blum (Heinrich Böll's *The Lost Honour of Katherina Blum*, or *How Violence is Born and Where it can end*) . . . well here they've got the same helmets, the anti-flak jackets, the Berettas at the ready . . . It's just absurd, just incredible, just like a film. I swear that if they weren't hammering at the door I'd think I was at the cinema.' A few seconds later the reality was clear enough. The last words of Radio Alice were: 'They've burst in. We've got our hands up.'

But the new culture of irony is not restricted to students and intellectuals. The weapon of satire was used at Easter in remotest Trapani in Sicily by twenty-five homeless families occupying the cathedral and expressed in the form of a play savagely satirizing the mayor, the trade unions, the political parties and all for their hypocrisy and inadequacy. The Radical Party, far to the left of the Italian Communist Party, staged an event that might almost be called a performance in a Milanese bank earlier that week. They collected 100,000 lire-worth of the spontaneous 'phoney' paper money in small denominations of 100 and 150 lire that has been run off by the big banks over the past year, and presented it to the Credito Italiano Bank. The manager fell into the trap and refused to change it into 'real' money, thus bearing out the Radicals' claim that 'the banks rob and the State is accomplice', and precipitating a near riot in which his regular clients sided against him and forced him to comply to the demands. The next target, the Radicals say, will be a Catholic bank since 'The banks rob and the Church is accomplice'.

And what does the official Italian Communist Party, allegedly the young force in European politics, think of all this? 'We are not amused' was the gist of it. What the spokesman said was: 'We repeat, satire and irony are the salt of life. Violence, insults and threatening letters do not amuse us at all.'

Hardly surprising then that the university professors who are members of the party are among the prime targets of the Metropolitan Indians. The example of Chile is cited. Before the coup, the radicals warned Allende of the danger of leaving 'culture', in the widest sense, to point forty and last of his programmes . . .

23 April, 1977   **Caroline Tisdall**

A jumbo-sized heartbreak

Sandra, a twenty-five-year-old Indian elephant, who has been with the Circo do Brazil for the past eighteen years, has died of starvation. Her companion and trainer for the past eighteen years, a German named Helmut Krone, abandoned Sandra on 22 December and since then she had refused to eat.

The circus, which is Italian, despite its name, was then performing in La Spezia, when the thirty-five-year-old Herr Krone reportedly fell in love with a local girl. She apparently told the circus man that he had to choose 'between me and the big tent' and the two of them left La Spezia in the German's caravan. The circus moved to Pisa, where it is now, and Sandra gave her last performance on Christmas Eve. She played a piano with her trunk, and danced a little waltz. After that, she was too weak to go on.

A specialist was brought from Milan and another from Paris, in efforts to save the young animal by intravenous feeding. The contents of a jar of honey were also poured down her throat, but rejected.

Italian frontier police were asked to stop the Krone caravan if it should be seen, with the hope that the return of Herr Krone would restore the elephant's will to live. He could not be traced. The two vets agreed that Sandra chose to die because she had been abandoned by her companion. She thus has given the world of circus lore its biggest broken heart.

6 January, 1977   **George Armstrong**

Flowers are not for girls to pick

Sharp beams of light catch a cluster of heads in the gloom of the Roundhouse restaurant, three actors, their hair dyed crimson and orange and brilliant green, chatter and giggle over their lunch. In the womby darkness of the auditorium, brightened by the big phalluses on the graphics around the walls, every exotic creature

168

waiting to rehearse is a man.

There are only male performers in Lindsay Kemp's show, *Flowers and Salome*, which opens at the Roundhouse on Monday. It will be Kemp himself who casts off the sequinned silk now shrouded in the wardrobe ready for the most famous strip-tease in history. Yet the artist who painted those phalluses and stuck on those 20,000 sequins is a woman. The dresser who dyed those dozen heads of hair is a woman. The electrician just now fixing the lights is a woman. Lindsay Kemp's entire backstage staff – not just the wardrobe and stage managers, but the company manager too – is female.

Odd? Sexist? Regrettable? Lindsay Kemp – vivid monkey face, neat, shaven head, capacious fur coat – ponders his company's sexual divide. He hadn't really noticed it until someone pointed out: 'I don't think about whether anybody's a man or woman – I just take the best people available.'

Kemp feels sorry to see the men apparently getting the fun and glamour, and the women the donkey work. 'I'm very fond of women and they're around me all the time. A lot of my students are women, and I might even prefer to sleep with women – it's just that I don't have enough time to experiment off the stage.' But for what he wants in his performers, precious few men are suitable: 'And even fewer women. That really is the rub.'

He wanted a woman to play Salome: he auditioned droves of them. But though they were often beautiful and talented, 'I couldn't find a woman who would turn herself inside out.' To him the essence of performance is 'total giving, absolute generosity, being all the things you are in private on the stage. I want to restore the excitement and danger of the circus in the theatre, and to do that one must first risk falling on one's arse, making a fool of oneself, dropping all fronts. It's difficult to find women who are prepared to subject themselves to the grotesqueries required. Women are more reluctant to fall on their arses. For some reason there are very few women clowns. Maybe they care too much about their dignity. The women that attract me are fabulous extremes of women – they're women plus, they're Medeas and Electras and Ophelias too – and I like men playing women's parts because they just seem to be more like women than women.'

Lindsay Kemp speaks more in sorrow than sexism when he admits he has found women wanting in this generosity on stage. Backstage, it's a different story. 'They give themselves to it utterly: they work extraordinarily hard.' And from what his hidden regiment of women say, they seem to have as good a time as their feathered colleagues in front.

Silvia Jansons, his graphic artist, left an independent existence as a teacher and painter in Australia to work with the company. 'I wouldn't normally have found myself in a mass production situation,' she says. But Lindsay Kemp has got her sticking on his Salome sequins and adding flurries of graded shaded feathers to his angels' twelve-foot wings. She can cope with that, she says, though she's never liked the idea of working for a person or an industry before.

'I don't feel I'm just sitting here gluing things on in isolation, or even in collaboration with Lindsay: because I see the whole of Salome as a work of art, created by a lot of people. I see everything I do – posters, panels, programmes, costumes, – as connected, and radiating towards a centre, which is the performance: and that is like a living picture. It's transient – it happens for two hours, the audience participate, and then it's over – but it's on again the next night, and it's something new and alive again.'

The girls in the company gather round a table and throw a bit of light on the dark backstage life. 'It's sad that people always assume that anyone who works backstage is just stagestruck, and doing it for second best, so you can meet the people – like being behind a sweet-shop counter, only a bit more on the spot,' says Gill Hebden who created the costumes. 'It's not true at all; though it's hard to realize how fascinating it is backstage, because all anybody sees is what happens in front. But the thing I like best is cutting the patterns for the costumes, making the shapes, and seeing them work and looking good. It's almost like performing – it's just seeing what you've done performing, rather than performing yourself.'

Linda Bates is the company manager; she confesses that she wanted to be on stage, until she 'started discovering all these things that go on backstage, and I got hooked. I have been on stage, but I get far more satisfaction about the finished production when I see a good show where all the lights work, nobody trips over anything, everything happens on time.'

These girls look so dedicated as they discuss their work. Okay, one can believe that it's fascinating, and that there's a sense of wholeness and lack of demarcation in this company. But are they sure that their hard work and love of it aren't being exploited by the male side of the operation?

'In the theatre you have to give yourself wholly,' says Linda Bates, 'because it's so demanding. I don't feel exploited, but I wouldn't care if someone was exploiting me because these are my responsibilities, and until I've done them, I won't go to my private life. I do think women often have a deeper feeling of warmth for their jobs, and that's very necessary in the theatre where you are handling people every minute and I can tell you, handling the stage carpenters is not fun. But I think that women have traditionally been the warm ones who keep families together, and I think that extends itself to their work. And that's part of what forms the basis of the Lindsay Kemp family.'

18 February, 1977   Janet Watts

For valour

Jean Rhys is a beloved writer, a rare category now, and these stories* will be a painful pleasure to readers who care for her. She has always laid her experience on the line with shocking candour, but in the lately recovered and cherished pre-war novels that still comprise the bulk of her work, the years have distanced pain and enhanced the romantic bloom her ardour gave to those encounters with the facts of love. In some of her new stories she is dealing with the heart conditions of age and loneliness, and their reality strikes home like the raw chills of an English winter.

The very arrangement of this collection – a retrospective exhibition of her life and talent – suggests that 'singular instinct for form' which her old patron Ford Madox Ford noted, something rare in an English writer, especially a woman writer. The

Sleep It Off, Lady; stories by Jean Rhys (Deutsch).

first five stories are breathing versions of myths and memories from her Caribbean childhood, making the violence and innocence of a receding world present and particular. *Overture and Beginners Please* and *Before the Deluge* bring an adolescent half-Creole girl to school in England and launch her precariously on the stage, springboard to deep waters in Paris in the twenties. One of four short pieces from that time of her life, *Kikimora* is in the author's most enamelled art deco manner:

' "What a very elegant dinner suit you are wearing," said Baron Mumtael mockingly. "Yes, isn't it? . . . Oh, I don't think it is really," said Elsa distractedly. "I hate myself in suits," she went on, plunging deep into the scorn of his pale blue eyes . . . '

With *The Insect World*, we enter lower and later circles of hell: the drained, deathly greyness of wartime London; then ageing, illness, a reclusive dream-haunted life in a shabby West Country cottage and a bitter ending in the title story. Not quite the end, however. After this apparently ineluctable journey into the dark, there follows just over a page of a revenant's vision of the house where she was born at the other end of the world. Read in isolation it seems too simple; in context, the effect is hair-raising, as if one were to find oneself switched in mid-sentence into the negative of that bright scene.

Its last sentence – 'That was the first time she knew' – gives a clue to the essence of Jean Rhys's quality. She is loved not just for a talent that seems as spontaneous and individual in its personality as physical beauty but for a special kind of courage. The eyes of all her heroines that see so much are the eyes of that child instructed in the reality of human loving by handsome old Captain Cardew in *Goodbye Marcus, Goodbye Rose* – a child with fewer illusions than other children but with a sense of life so strong that she will never quite accommodate to society's rationalizations nor even to being the prisoner of a sick old body, acquiescent in the cage of years.

It is a defiant form of that same existential valour which prevents the annihilation of personality by the most dreadful ravages of illness, something more vivid and vital than stoicism, tested here throughout a long life, and celebrated in brave fictions.

21 October, 1976   **W. L. Webb**

... are but shadows

It is a reassuring thought that most of the plays on the Elizabethan stage were as abysmally bad as the plays at the Royal Court and on the London stage today. No doubt it is a matter of what you expect. The drivel about sex, the self-pity, the 'finding out who one really is', the laborious satirizing of mothers and fathers, and the middle-class, the adulation of terrorism – all had its equally mechanical counterpart in the platitudes of hundreds of Elizabethan and Jacobean plays. The humour was as depressingly predictable, so was the rhetoric and the moralizing: even the verse was in most cases no better than the broken-backed diction yelled or mumbled by today's actors.

The quatercentenary of James Burbage's arena theatre, opened in Shoreditch in 1576, is not a bad moment to cheer oneself up with this reflection. *Plus ça change* . . . even the Arts Council and the university drama departments cannot do much worse than the companies which played at the Curtain, the Rose on Bankside, the Swan, the Globe, the Blackfriars, and all the others which figure on the excellent map of the then London theatre world supplied by Professor Bradbrook.*

The Red Bull survived the longest, continuing throughout the Commonwealth and mentioned in the *Historia Histrionica* of 1699 as 'one of the large houses open to the weather, and there they always acted by daylight'. Most recent was the Salisbury Court, opened in 1629, where fires were supplied in the private boxes and magnificent scenery was appointed for the more ornate productions, even though – as Ben Johnson protested – 'so many players were allowed to sit on the stage that the players were driven to act in compass of a cheese trencher'.

A scholar of Professor Bradbrook's calibre is, of course, equably aware of the shortcomings of the Elizabethan stage, just as she is of its glories: and she has an unrivalled sense of theatrical con-

The Living Monument: Shakespeare and the Theatre of his Time, by M. C. Bradbrook (Cambridge, £8.50).

tinuity. Although her study celebrates the quatercentenary she does not confine herself to matters of stage and theatre; every page reveals her encyclopaedic knowledge and has some striking comment or suggestion thrown out – she has produced a superb book both for the scholar and the general reader.

It begins with the sociology of the theatre, the relation of actors, audience and playwrights, and the image of Jacobean London as presented by Jonson and others: goes on to some admirable studies in detail of Shakespeare's tragedies and their use of setting and convention; thence to the romance plays and the particular problems of form which they pose and solve in enactment. The concluding section deals with Caroline masque and pastoral.

She is particularly illuminating on the use of elaborate death scenes in the theatre, as in Act 5 of *Antony and Cleopatra*, and the obvious pleasure that the audience took in this prolonged display of *Liebestod*. The appropriateness of death as an ending and proper concomitant of a play's span is one the moderns might do well to ponder – have we lost the art of expecting deaths and awaiting them with enjoyment, seeing the pistol on the table, as Chekhov observed, and looking forward to its going off and killing someone in the last act?

Professor Bradbrook points here to Dr Barton's valuable essay on *Antony and Cleopatra* – '*Nature's Piece 'gainst Fancy*' and her book on *Shakespeare's Idea of the Play* – two of the numerous and rewarding references to the work of other specialists and scholars in the field such as Frances Yates and Glynne Wickham, whose work on the acting of the time and its relation to social classes and events has been so much help to critical interpretation.

One of the most interesting asides in the book is on Lope de Vega, the great Spanish dramatist two years older than Shakespeare, who began to write his *comedias* for a theatre which had opened in Madrid two years before Burbage's. All is grist that comes to the mill of Professor Bradbrook's perceptions, for she points out, after analysing two of his best plays, how comparatively feudal and secure Vega's values are, as he shows them working in society, and by contrast how uncertain and unpredictable – to themselves and to us – are those of Shakespeare and his contemporaries.

174

For this is the real excitement in at least some Elizabethan drama. Even Macbeth, who has offended so obviously against the laws of kingship and degree, is imagined as judging himself, not being judged; and in Heywood's play of bourgeois realism, *A Woman Killed by Kindness*, the question of marital infidelity is seen in some sense as a kind of free-for-all, the imponderables lying about as intriguingly as they do in *Othello* – that drama of insiders and an outsider – or in the query about class and marriage left open in *The Duchess of Malfi*. Then as now a bourgeois audience 'did not know what to think', an excellent premise for live theatre if the dramatist can rise to the occasion, as he sometimes did then, and occasionally even now.

25 November, 1976   **John Bayley**

Actorgenarian

Richard Goolden had had an operation on what he called his bosom the day before we met. But thought nothing of it. Just a small portion snipped off for a complaint usually reserved for ladies, he explained cheerfully. 'I said, "What are you going to do with that – send it to the Director of Public Prosecutions?"'

He thinks equally little of his programme for the next few weeks. At 81 and in spite of arthritic twinges, he'll be giving his public two, three, even four performances a day. Afternoons and some mornings as Mole in *Toad of Toad Hall* at Her Majesty's (for the twenty-first or twenty-second time in his life, he forgets which), just opened; evenings as Bernard, the nice old bore with the story about Lloyd George in Tom Stoppard's *Dirty Linen* at the Arts.

He never opens a book for Mole, he says, and Bernard's a mere matter of tottering on stage and sitting at a table. 'Be careful that chair doesn't collapse,' he added concernedly. 'Somebody quite fat sat in it once and it went to pieces immediately.'

We sat each side of his fire in a room like the stage set of John Aubrey's *Brief Lives*. Peeling leatherbound tomes and yellowing folders stuffing the bookshelves; pictures, postcards, photographs brightening the walls, furniture, floor; collections of pens, pins, scissors, medicines, rulers, old coins, little boxes and cotton reels filling all available crannies. Even the tubes of Veginin looked antique. Good advice from Horace and Pascal and Baudelaire is carved on the marble fireplace whose centrepiece came off his mother's washstand, to which he is now adding Blake's opinion that 'Prudence is a rich ugly old maid courted by incapacity' (still indistinct after a whole year's scratching and chiselling).

Goolden didn't mind the mention of Aubrey – though 'I don't have a chamber pot here,' he pointed out in mild reproach – but thought he was far less cultured a man. Erudite, he would allow – 'I know a lot of curious facts, a bit of Greek and Latin.' He wore a shirt of pink, blue, green, and orange check, a crumpled red bow-tie, a green woolly cardigan that withstood the constant spinoffs from his cigarettes and coffee cup, and orangey check tweed trousers matching the orange handkerchief that bursts from his jacket's breast pocket (locale of the missing bit of bosom).

For a post-operative convalescent, he seemed alarmingly mobile – always up and down for something or other, to his own regret. 'Isn't busy-ness supposed to show some deficiency?' He lists household repairs among his recreations in *Who's Who*, and is attended by a maid who is 'nominally retired' (after forty or fifty years in his service) and only four years younger than him.

Goolden admits he's had rather a good life, though he quickly dismisses its pleasure as frivolity. He went on the stage because it was such fun there, though being 'half posh' he couldn't fulfil his real ambition – to be a music-hall comedian. But even at Charterhouse, his theatrical bent was clear, and his impersonation of the headmaster so good that whenever some dignitary like a bishop was visiting, he would be 'lugged over to do it in his drawing-room, to his face, at his wife's request'. The wife loved it, but the head wasn't quite so keen, and despatched Goolden to Oxford with the warning that 'he must aim at good taste in the use of his gifts'.

Did he? Well, he was certainly gifted with a taste for Oxford, where he stayed five years in spite of Warden Spooner's disapproval and observation, on Goolden's applying for yet another year, that he hardly thought the New College tutors would think he had 'added to the intellectual industry of the college'. Goolden couldn't help it: he just gets fond of places. 'I'm very peculiar. I take root. I settle down wherever I am. It was the same with Charterhouse – I broke down and wept when I had to leave – and with the army – I didn't want to leave France.'

Sure enough, Goolden even managed to enjoy the Great War. He must have gone in the wrong door somewhere, because he found himself a sort of sanitary inspector in the RAMC, and the two years he spent in a Picardy village created a bond he renews every year with a visit, though the little girls he once took black-berrying have turned into toothless grandmothers.

He brings out his photographs, sepia peasants in smocks and smiling girls in pinafores. 'The great love of my life,' he declares at one ravishing one. 'She was seventeen then. She's rather faded now she's seventy.' Why didn't he marry her? 'Oh, I never thought about it – marriage. I'm very fond of ladies.' So I see from all the photographs on the mantelpiece. 'One of Mr Cochrane's young ladies,' he says of one – 'not so young now, of course.' Yet he accepts that tranquilly, and rifles through the French ones saying He's dead – She's dead, without emotion. Doesn't he mind their loss? 'Oh, I don't know. You get used to it.'

His luck prevailed. Straight after Oxford he was hired by the just-formed Oxford Playhouse Company in 1923, with Tyrone Guthrie (another ex-undergraduate), Flora Robson, and John Gielgud, at £5 a week. So all he had to do was move his stuff out of licensed into unlicensed lodgings; and they still got jumped on by Proctors on the way from the theatre 'because we wore grey flannel trousers and went back singing arm-in-arm'. Then he went to Stratford, and an extraordinarily varied career unfurled, as his role-filled entry in *Who's Who* is proof. ('The secret of that is, I've been in so many failures.')

His memory is vivid and detailed, perhaps because he has enjoyed his life so much. He can remember the excitement when Ladysmith was relieved in the Boer War, and he remembers seeing Queen Victoria's funeral – or was it Edward VII's Coronation? – and making a noise meant as a cheer, but everyone thought it was a boo. He has lived in this Chelsea house for forty-five years – 'Oh, no, fifty-two' – and remembers when they had a bomb practically on the front doorstep, and his mother, a lady of great *sang-froid*, remarked that she hoped there wasn't another raid that night – 'I don't feel in the mood for it.'

Goolden seems to have survived pretty well intact, though he thinks 'your gusto goes a bit – you lose what I call *dynamic initiative*' (his italics make us both laugh). Yet he seems indefatigable in his fruitful fidgeting, reads so late that his neighbour comes to see what his light is doing on at three in the morning, and has a life-preserving knack of falling asleep if he's bored. He slept through barrages in the war, he's dozed while the dentist was filling his tooth, and he often nods off in *Toad and Dirty Linen* (where he's supposed to anyway).

Samuel Beckett has been a friend since Goolden played 'that man in the dustbin' in the first British production of *Endgame*. 'He comes here, but we don't talk about anything learned. And he hates going to the theatre, you know.'

Goolden never much wants to go to the theatre, either – to go anywhere, come to that: though 'when I get there I thoroughly enjoy it. But I get rather dug in, and I always seem to have too much to do, which is never worth doing when it's done.'

He goes to first nights, though, because he can claim them on his tax: and, of course, he goes to perform. Mole is a particularly good role for his arthritis, as that embryonic hunch is 'the only position I'm really comfortable in. So the more arthritic I am the better my performance.' And *Dirty Linen* came along just when he thought he'd 'more or less packed up'; and although it only earned the actors £6 a week at the Almost Free, now it's doing more handsomely at the Arts.

Though that isn't the point, for Goolden: and this is perhaps the greatest good luck of his life. He still enjoys being on stage as much as ever he did – so much that 'I'm always rather surprised when someone gives me a cheque at the end of the week. I think, Oh yes, I do this for money.'

21 December, 1976   **Janet Watts**

Pneumatic thrills

In yards of white lawn, with gold filigree at the hem of her robe to match her accessories – helmet and trident – Britannia looked the pick of the portlies in the somewhat despondent, camouflage-minded window of Evans the Outsize.

She'd no bra. By contrast with her Imperial bosom even quite sturdy busts outlined by teeshirts parading Oxford Street had the look of little doorbells. *Caveat emptor*, for her pectoral surge was plaster. Mortal magnificence wants props – and to be at peace with them, as a liner is with her tugs.

Not all would agree. I'm told, by a belle poitrine who goes without, that her bubs owe their exemplary high morale to her habit over twenty years of cupping them with her hands, whenever she ran up and down the stairs – or for cover.

In her case, she'd best make a friend of Martha Hill, a designer who soon had me believing that a 72-inch hip is more appetizing than a pair of Gouda cheeses – a simile which may come to mind because it's Rubens's quatercentenary. And who wouldn't rather spend an evening with the painter's Helena Fourment in Anvers, than a season in Brussels drafting the nations' laws?

The modern beauty with the cannon-breech thigh, soup-tureen shoulder and ashet belly, can compete very well with Fourment by investing in djellabas, caftans, ponchos, and pina-fores from Martha Hill in Marylebone High Street, and perhaps model as a wild ethnic plumpy.

I've just idled away an hour with Penny's Model Book and the Top Models Directory. How fragile they all look, what a thirst for an endomorph the procession creates. This is the civilization of the salad, in which shrimps with 38-26-40 figures dare to call themselves 'outsize'.

Could we beget a race of heroes on these meagre morsels? 'Thin ones to look at, fat ones to lie on,' said the Chinese – with 6000 years of sexism behind them. You'll counter that we don't need heroes, and there's something in that, not Chinese sexism, which is arguable.

However, I do think great Nature loves variety more than perfection, and that there's a high residual content of sexiness in sexism. As a pledge to variety when the healths go round, here's to model Fran Fullenweider, 44-36-60. May her bookings never decline.

From where I live, like a bat under the eaves of Marylebone, the trade for the full-and-wider figure seems to be getting a boost from pampered jades of Asia. The practised voyeur can sometimes spot deep in a smoke-glassed limo, a pair of fubsy gazelles lifting black masks to compare their dainty Harley Street nose jobs.

Then, their new retroussé snouts catch the whiff of Western corsetry. At the underpinners, Bradley's of Knightsbridge (actually two doors from Martha Hill) they place shipping orders for chiffon ponchos and red satin basques.

From hand-cups, through A- to Double-D cups, there are now, would you believe, E-cups? If you wouldn't, report to be ticked off for excess slimming. Right across the country women are moving up a cup or two – one of the more cheerful side-effects of the Pill.

Had E-cups existed when Baudelaire wrote his poem La Géante, in which he luxuriously compared a woman with a countryside, and curled up like a cat in the shadow of her breast, he must have worked them into his caprice – slung as a hammock perhaps. Baudelaire also loved exceptionally small women, which clears him of the charge of being obsessive.

Finally, the tale of Swanhilda Olafsen. But for her epic scale, the modern bra might never have been. It's credited to Pierre de Brassiere, but he was little more than a shrewd fellow with patents. It should take its name from the young engineer who helped Swanhilda in distress, Otto Titzling.

They both had apartments in a rooming-house in Minneapolis. She was a Rhine-maiden with ambitions to get on in opera, but her spectacular build could not be contained in the basques of the time. Otto's father built bridges, the son applied the same principles. The cantilever system adapted well.

That was the positive approach. In recent times opera singers have tended to fine down. There's a tale of a prima donna who went so far as to swallow tapeworms. Apocryphal, I trust. It's a great pity when a girl sheds the marvellous glow on her skin given by subcutaneous fat. And it's a great asset to be able to respond to the challenge, 'Astonish me!'

29 June, 1977   **Alex Hamilton**

The Case of the Unemployed Fiction Writer

The pages of the Ombudsman's reports, usually weighed down by bureaucratic jargon, yesterday crackled with the deft and passionate touch of light fiction. For there, lurking between the Case of Misleading Advice about National Insurance Contributions and the Claim for Compensation for the Effects of Motorway Construction, lay the torrid case of the Unemployed Teenage Girls' Magazine Fiction Writer.

All she wanted was an interesting temporary job until her freelance writing picked up. But she knew from the start that there was something funny about the Regional Unemployment Officer who interviewed her at the DHSS. He had 'the high colouring of a drinker, and it has been my opinion all along that he had a hangover on the relevant morning, he was certainly in a bad mood about something . . .'

What's more, he said her claim to type at sixty words a minute had got her listed as a copy typist, and though she thought the work beneath her, she must accept suitable work or eventually lose her benefit.

She went to the local Employment Service Agency. But if anything Mr Y was worse than Mr X. She spoke of her writing 'with enthusiasm', but he seemed 'to interpret such remarks as sexual. Like the other, he seemed to believe himself attractive to women and inferred that he wasn't faithful to his wife . . . which I must admit I took with a pinch of salt.'

She demanded to talk to someone who would understand her problems (a young woman, perhaps). She told him to 'pull yourself together' and 'stop behaving like a fool'. And then, while he was 'pulling faces and giving loud sighs', she suddenly realized who he looked like: that terrible man who interviewed her for the Training Opportunities Scheme two years earlier.

Breathlessly (no doubt), she continued: 'My teeth literally chattered and my hair seemed to stand on end. My mind seemed to whizz around like a one-armed bandit. I kept demanding explanations, and he sneered and fluttered his eyelashes and seemed to think this would mesmerize me into going . . . I stood my ground and told him I would kick him in the shins if he did not pay attention while I told him how repulsive he was.'

The Ombudsman, Sir Idwal Pugh, notes in his more prosaic style that 'clerks interviewing the public should be more carefully selected because "those with personality defects are too hard too cope with".' But, he concludes after a full investigation: 'I cannot find that the complaints against these officers are justified.'

26 November, 1976   Michael White

The woodlice which just drop in

Sir, – In the Chilterns, the roll-up woodlouse, locally called cheese-log, enjoyed a spectacular population explosion this spring. Our ground-floor bedroom became an assembly hall, and evicting the squatters became part of the nightly going-to-bed routine. Ultimately the brush and dustpan stage was reached (forty being a night's record); one had only to turn one's back to empty the pan and another three or four mini-mini-armoured cars would be careering out of nowhere across the orange expanse of carpet.

The climax was reached with the arrival of the acrobatic or ceiling cheese-log. Through a minute fissure in the ceiling paper oozed, very gingerly, first one, then another tiny black figure. The two friends did an excited little waltz on the fissure and then gingerly put a leg or two (they have so many to spare) on the flat ceiling surface. Alas, a fatal step: they dropped like logs on to what – or whoever – was underneath. ('Sleeping like a log'? Those logs never sleep). So, pasting cracks with Sellotape was the next chore.

Cheese-logs in the bath, the wash-basin, on the curtain, the window frame, on the walls in the airing cupboard (cosily among the clean sheets), finally sharing pillow and bed. Charming, friendly little creatures, no malice. But what's wrong with their own home that they need decide, in such multitudes, to share ours? – Yours,

Francis Cole

Coppshill,
Fingest,
Henley on Thames,
Oxon.
27 June, 1977

A pen mightier than the horde

Every day, in some corner of this country, you can be sure that a little boy or girl is sitting down and painstakingly writing, rubbing out, and rewriting a letter to President Carter.

It may be to tell him that Miss Lillian looks just like their own grannie, or that nine-year-old Amy Carter is great, or that so is her Siamese kitten. It may be to ask Mr President to please one day come down and visit our home town. But, when the envelope is delivered to the White House a different world of fantasy is waiting. Unless Mr Carter changes the system which he has inherited from his predecessors the letter will promptly be swallowed up by the hard world of presidential public relations. One of twenty 'mail analysts' will check through their index of correspondence codes. There on the list is P-814, the stock category for 'chatty letters from children'.

The letter will then be despatched to the robotype room in the Executive Office Building, opposite the White House, where a computerized message – the same one that all P-814s get – is ready to be punched out by one of the twelve MTSTs (magnetic tape selectric typewriters). The finished answer is clipped under the 'autopen' which neatly produces an almost perfect fascimile of Jimmy Carter's signature.

It is good enough to fool most children. Even adults are sometimes misled into thinking they have held the attention of the world's most powerful man for a minute. A favourite aunt is seriously ill in hospital. Relatives may write to the President asking him to boost her morale by sending a personal message. The robotype room and the autopen will then crank out PR-70, a signed letter letting the old dear know that 'you have our prayers and warm wishes always'. The widow of a policeman killed on duty is sent a PD. This is a letter which says: 'May God give you strength to bear the burden of your loss.' It is signed 'sincerely' and concludes with another mechanical flourish of the automated presidential pen.

The system of fake letters has grown enormously and some officials are complaining it has got out of hand. In President Kennedy's day there were four robotype machines. By Lyndon Johnson's time the annual peak of autopen signatures was 10,000. Last year, Mr Ford's signature was simulated on 191,578 letters. 'We are trapped by our own system. It cheapens the presidency,' one veteran staff member commented.

Mr Carter's eager new lieutenants were equally appalled to discover the correspondence production line. Mindful of Mr Carter's inaugural address – 'to be true to ourselves, we must be true to others' – they want him to scrap the robotype room.

One of the first decisions Mr Carter had to make when he took over in January was whether to have his signature put on the autopen. At first he refused. A few days later, when the mail began to pile up and his wrist ached, Mr Carter gave in. In a victory for continuity the autopen was reprieved.

Mr Carter has still to decide what to do about the whole system of coded replies to the American people. His staff are urging him to preserve an open Administration, and to maintain as much communication with the public as possible. Only yesterday the White House announced the despatch of 300,000 letters to citizens, selected at random from their census lists, asking for their comments on Mr Carter's energy policy. At the same time Mr Carter is being pressed to end the charade of the fake personal letter, part of the same mentality which produced the institutionalized deception of Watergate.

After all, he is being reminded by veteran White House officials, the system of coded replies is not just phoney – it is sometimes fallible. In 1973, a Vietnam war widow wrote to the White House

184

pleading for an end to the senseless war in south-east Asia. Back came the presidential answer. 'Thank you for your support of the Honourable Spiro T. Agnew.'

4 March, 1977   **Jonathan Steele**

A backhand to upset the brothers

In reporting the MCC's match against the Combined XI at Nagpur Henry Blofeld describes Lever as twice sweeping Jadeja backhanded through the slips for four. Although over the years I have seen a wide variety of weird and eccentric strokes, I cannot, in honesty, claim that this feat has been among them. I did once, however, have an eye witness account of a highly dramatic scene arising from this very cause.

The witness himself is worth a line of introduction. Cyril Foley was a man of many parts, having played cricket for Eton, Cambridge, and Middlesex. He had also taken part in various enterprises as diverse as the Jameson Raid, and an expedition in search of the Ark of the Covenant. Neither was successful but, in the latter case, biblical authorities might allow that he got some way towards his goal by hitting a couple of sixes into the Pool of Siloam. When I knew him, he was a staunch, but profoundly pessimistic, supporter of Middlesex, which county he was actively representing against Gloucestershire when there occured the incident in question.

Middlesex being in a strong position, 'W. G.' sought to delay their progress by bowling very wide to the off at that spirited Irish Baronet, Sir Timothy O'Brien. A couple of wides were enough to raise the Bart's pressure to bursting point and the next one he thrashed back-handed through the slips, doubtless to the accompaniment of a blood-curling Hibernian oath. Indeed blood was nearly spilt when the ball whistled past the ears of Brother E. M. Grace, who happened to be standing at slip. What fraternal alarm this caused W. G. is a matter for conjecture but, seeing his tactics foiled, he managed a fine show of shocked outrage. 'I'll tell you what it is, Tim,' he said. 'You'll kill my brother.' To this he

185

received the obvious reply. 'And a bloody good thing too,' retorted the Bart.

Baulked in the verbal as well, W. G. dropped the lofty hauteur and proceeded to straightforward threats. 'If you do that again,' he said, 'I'll take my men off the field.' Of course the Bart did it again and immediately found himself, except for a scared young partner, alone and monarch of all he surveyed, at which he relieved his feelings by thrashing stumps many a mile into the air. In the prevailing atmosphere this could have proved a costly gesture; for the Brothers, seeing the umpires unnerved, might well have lodged an appeal for hit-wicket.

Foley said that sanity might have prevailed at that point but for one 'Buns' Thornton, a famous hitter of the time, scenting the sporting possibilities of the Bart v. The Brothers, a contest of Homeric dimensions. Accordingly, having brought both parties to concert pitch by separate assurances to each of its complete propriety in the face of the other's unreasonable truculence, he was rewarded by a truly thunderous row. When W.G.'s beard had been all but tugged from its moorings (by its owner) his naturally high tenor was heard on rising key. 'I'll tell you what it is, Tim,' he cried above the din, 'I'll fetch a policeman to you.' This, said the narrator, was a suggestion so preposterous that the contestants momentarily fell silent, enabling lesser mortals to intervene and restore order.

Not all eccentric strokes have afforded entertainment on this scale, but many have added to the joy of cricketing nations. Some spring from genius. Victor Trumper had a habit of chopping yorkers to the square leg boundary. I remember seeing, from short-leg, much the same effect when George Gunn, suppressing a yawn, applied the old-fashioned draw to our fast bowler, Jack Durston. Nor was it a gentle deflection, but a lusty slap which sent the ball thumping into the Mount Stand fence.

As great a virtuoso as George and, in rather more aggressive mould, was Charlie McCartney, who loved to late cut full tosses and half volleys. When a young Jack Fingleton walked with him to open the innings of their Sydney club for the first time, the 'Governer General' tersely warned him to 'look out for the first ball'. This injunction 'Fingo' obeyed by making a good way down the track in anticipation of a quick single, and was nigh decapitated when the ball came straight back like a cannon shot. The striker apologized for what was an obvious misunderstanding, saying that what he had meant was that he always liked to hit the ball first straight back at the bowler's head. 'It upsets 'em,' he said.

Some unorthodoxy is born in prudence. Ewart Astill, a humorous and agreeable man, frankly stated in his latter days that he did not intend to be maimed at his time of life. Having astonished the cricket world by taking 120 off Larwood, almost exclusively from the square cut played from a discreet range, he set out for the West Indies to meet Learie Constantine at his fastest. But, when he made a strategic withdrawal, in this case the impish Learie kept shooting at him instead of the castle so that soon, according to a reliable if unofficial spokesman, the action was taking place in the no-man's land between the wicket-keeper and the square leg umpire. When Learie did take a shot at the stumps it was said that the defender, with legs at full stride and bat at the extreme extension of his arms, was still a foot inside the line of the ball which missed the leg stump by the same margin.

My old friend and captain, Nigel Haig, unabashedly pursued something of the same philosophy, occasionally with surprising results. Playing against Surrey at Lord's, he made a superb square cut off Alf Gover which must have been at the fence in a trice – had it not, after travelling a yard or so, knocked the leg stump out of the ground. That was in 1932 and the next year in the same fixture Alf contributed to another spectacular stroke. He bowled a bouncer at Bernard Atkinson, a large powerful man, who met it with a Wimbledonian overhead smash. The ball sailed back over Alf's head to land just short of the Nursery for six.

But whenever the subject of unlikely strokes arises, my mind inevitably turns to Jim Smith, who demonstrated what a vast range of glorious and unexpected effects could be achieved by one great agricultural swish with eighteen stone behind it. As I write I see the ball a pin-prick in the sky, and pity the babbling gaggle of fielders gyrating on the possible area of arrival, to say nothing of the harassed captain trying to remember all their names at once. Not that it mattered, for he was almost certain to nominate the wrong one.

Fresh in the memory is the day against Hants when Jim and I ran a leisurely two, abandoning an easy third to see just what would happen when the ball returned to earth. It was worth it. The ball brought down mid-off (Lionel Tennyson, trundling backwards with arched back, and head at maximum elevation) with a thud that shook St John's Wood and, deflected from the vertical to the horizontal by the heel of his hand, shot up to Father Time for four. To add a further touch of drama the concussion had riven Jim's mighty blade from splice to toe.

Last season we saw the West Indian batsmen play every beautiful shot in the book. For this let us be grateful; but I cannot think of any reigning batsman who brings to his craft the *fun* which Denis Compton did, either in his own crease or, as occasionally happened, when he turned up unexpectedly in his partner's or, more frequently, when he got stranded between the two. Perhaps this is too stern an age for buffoonery.

19 January, 1977   **Ian Peebles**

Tome rule

When it comes up mud, and the jumps in the country vanish in fog, books make a better bet than horses. At seventy-six, Eric Hiscock should know: most of his life he's tipped both with zest. 'Never touch 'em after October,' his dad would say, 'they're after the Form Stakes and a long price, to pay their winter keep.' His dad, butler to Frank Bibby who owned the Bibby Line, plus most of the GWR and a one-eyed nag called Glenside that won the National, was not referring to books. In winter the book odds shorten.

The heap of advance proofs from publishers that Hiscock has gutted in a lifetime would certainly frighten the horses. As the author of a column addressed to a phantom of his own imagination called the wideawake retailer, featured in the old *Smith's Trade News* and since its demise, in *The Bookseller*, he has been for twenty-five years a buzz in the ears of the bird-witted scout, the star-gazing publisher and the brain-fagged agent. For some, if

Hiscock hadn't plugged a book it became somehow insubstantial, ethereal; almost as if it hadn't been written.

He's very kind, easily moved – a great Boo-hooer. Publishers urge that he's generous to a fault. This is just. He's generous to several faults, usually theirs. And a testimonial from him is undoubtedly a moist, enveloping experience, like a cloudburst of sponges. He is a unique figure. Portmanteau words he loves – he's the book loreate, the gossipedlar who is met with champers from Paternoster Row to Bedford Square. He admits freely, even gladly, to an anti-intellectual bias. Fine writing he can get at home, his flat's full of it. But his poor old friend the wide-awake retailer has his shelves filled with money he'll never get back, result of reviewer's recommendations. He's trying to make a few pennies for him. So never mind if egghead sheets knock his best-sold choices.

Unluckily for him, he has no competition, because now that he's sired a runner himself, and Arlington is big with his book*, who is to prime the tills of all those alert traders? Naturally, he's been able to arrange half a dozen reviews without actually writing them himself, and Lsd-wise their winter keep is paid for, since Corgi have bought softcover rights for £2000 and the Book Society has taken 2500 copies. Still, there's a gap to be filled and it behoved me to do the decent thing and borrow his plumage and style, take a dinner off him in his local Mayfair fish restaurant, swig his mix of brandy and champers, and stand by in his flat for revelations. They came, I am privileged to tell you, thick and fast, and I don't know when I last had a more spoiling evening.

He's not a total stranger to the bookwriter's chore, since some years back, he authored a surveyola of the publishing scene called *Last Boat to Folly Bridge*, for which the hectic style of the Whitefriar column was not quite suitable, and which he means to come back to and improve. On form, I'd lay plenty of six-to-four that Hiscock's new starter, replete with blood and mud and the smear of buggery in the trenches of the Kaiser's War, will find the going more to everybody's liking.

Book is *The Bells of Hell Go Ting-a-Ling-a-Ling*. Tome treats

The Bells of Hell Go Ting-a-Ling-a-Ling

of his experience as an under-age soldier – he joined the Colours at fifteen years and one month, and put the infant into infantry – and his deep uncarnal attachment to two youths barely older than himself amid losses too deep for tears. It's a down-to-the-frightened-earth account of the trio's travails, mortal in one case, and of the leching predator who officered them and trumped up a Field Court Martial (when he accidentally shot himself through his Lance-jack's stripe and arm), in order to separate the true lovers. Reading it in proof sixty years on, says Hiscock, he wept anew. It was like a dream, that haunts him yet, from which, unless the book provides relief, the awakening comes never.

Remarque, Blunden, Sassoon, Williamson, Jones; these and others uttered their valedictory complaints about The Great War mainly around 1928–29. How come that a man so immersed in the book swim has left it till now? It must be remembered, he says, that he was in every aspect a late developer. For a couple of years after the War he was in a daze. A shop girl called Doris in Oxford taught him his heterosexual manners; he was a buyer for the W. H. Smith's in the Cornmarket; later in London the first great man he met was Sir Godfrey Collins, who gave him the idea that he could better himself and hired him in a taxi between Pall Mall and King's Cross to work alongside nephew Billy and grow old with him building up a general list; the second great man was Beaverbrook who wanted a runner for the *Evening Standard* book page; the man who encouraged him to write was that sheet's lead reviewer, his dear friend, Howard Spring, who succeeded Arnold Bennett, and whom in turn he persuaded to write a novel, for Collins, which Spring delivered with a dedication to Hiscock, saying that it was long and dull enough to go well in America and if it didn't he would never write another. It was called *My Son, My Son*, and sold a million copies.

There has been another reason for the long delay, ever present, ever censorious, in the shape of his wife Romilly Cavan, who died very recently. As you may know, he says, giving me a shrewd, tight look, authors are jealous people. Romilly liked his life as a journalist, she admired and hated his style, which she thought was common, being herself in the Virginia Woolf mould, but she did not want it to add up to a book. She was the book-writer.

'Do you have a copy of a book – I can't remember the author's name but a lot of people say he looks like me – and it's all about a starving author who, on hearing about the defeat of the Public Lending Right Bill, goes berserk in a library, strangles the librarian, runs off with the overdue books fines tin, buys a gun and shoots the six MPs who threw the Bill out?'

He met her at a publishing party, the first Dent's ever gave, in the spring of 1934. The occasion was the publication of her first novel, *Heron.* She was twenty-one and lovely, and the publicity man John Hadfield had pushed her along in his direction to do herself a bit of good with the man from the *Standard.* She was dark Irish, very introverted, her real name Isabel Wilson. The chemistry worked and he took her home that night.

Bringing her out was no sinecure. All their days together he had to drag her to parties. She could listen, if she liked people. She liked best to sit and think, and write. Dark Irish, very secretive. It is strange, for him, gossip-fired, to have had forty years with such a secret woman. They were lovers to the end, but when he came in she tidied her writing away. Showed him only the finished work. But devoted. The money that came to him on the side a dozen ways, because he's made with extra fingers to accommodate all the pies he finds, she salted away without telling him, so the book-makers would never see it. She left him a packet in building societies. He loves to spend money. 'You are sitting opposite,' he said, 'a man with £25,000.'

She wanted success of the order that would make him a lead story. And of course, it was beyond his power to contrive that. She was an egghead writer, he wouldn't say unreadable, but very difficult. No success was ever big enough for her. She couldn't stand to have Edna O'Brien mentioned in the house. Her books must not cross the threshold. Sorting out her effects after her death, he opened a cupboard and came across the complete canon of Edna O'Brien.

In 1940 she had a success with *Beneath the Visiting Moon*, with Heinemann. Spring picked it as a Choice. But there was a paper shortage. She said: 'I won't do it any more, I'll write plays.' He encouraged her. Like a fool: in his opinion the theatre ruined her.

Noel Coward titled her first play, *I'll See You Again*, which he read while fire-watching at the Globe, and with varying success she wrote in all a dozen, while Eric baked his pies in the book trade.

The pies go on. One of the first was *Pie* itself, done over the Moo-Cow bar in Whitefriar Street. In its pages he gave a new lease to the author of Billy Bunter, whom he found on his uppers in Hampstead, smoking tea-leaves in his pipe. Down the booksy years, he's made many others; got Peter Cheyney going; brought Agatha Christie to Collins; took over Daniel George's job picking the Book Society Choices, reading thirty proofs a month; sold space; fed paras to diarists . . . Today he's in daily touch with New York and Warner Brothers paperbacks as a scout, has an itch for the agency game, plans to go into a new publishing venture as managing director, a topic on which my gabby lips are sealed.

Overall, he says, he is ahead on books, on horses and on women. But one must progress, that is what life is about. He hates to be lonely, but whenever he is, he bends his mind to a couple of novels, a thriller called *Tether's End*, and a story set in the Thirties (to avoid libel) about an old married fellow with a young girl, called *To Mary With Love*. He finds that young women who chat to him in his flat are very much besotted by his Thirties records and know the words.

But how has he stood the relentless march of geese and swans in book form over the years? Not to be stupid about it, he says, he is Virgo, and that is the sign of the energetic, the neat and the disciplined. And sometimes friends lend him houses in exotic parts, as they did when Romilly died and he wanted to finish *Ting-a-Ling*. In Haut de Cagnes, where Connolly once wrote *The Rock Pool*, and it hasn't changed much from being the Lesbian HQ of those days, he had a villa overlooking the sea, where for five weeks he could work from six to six. And play in the evening. It came out, with all the deliberation in the world, on Armistice Day. He asked me, very douce, if I had liked it. Yes, I said, I did.
12 November, 1976   **Alex Hamilton**

Thinking about Erich

Reading Isherwood in wartime Penguins and in New Writing was an experience of pure romance – pure in the sense that style and content seemed as plain as water, with nothing in the manner to account for the fascination. Why was one so gripped? In this account of himself in those days he says he tried in his Berlin novels 'not only to make the bizarre seem humdrum but the humdrum seem bizarre.'

The intensity of his romance with Germany – as a place of pure otherness – comes across in every word. There was a simple reason for this. For Christopher, as he refers throughout the book*

*Christopher and His Kind, by Christopher Isherwood (*Eyre Methuen*, £4.50).

193

to his earlier self when the entire German language – all the way from the keep off signs in the park to Goethe's stanza on the wall – was irradiated with Sex. For him, the difference between a table and *ein Tisch* was that a table was the dining-table in his mother's house and *ein Tisch* was *ein Tisch* in The Cosy Corner.

The Cosy Corner was a cafe for homosexuals to which he was introduced by Auden, and where he found his first friend, a charming Czech boy called Bubi. But what makes everything he writes compulsively readable seems not connected with homosexuality as such but with states of mind and awareness common to all kinds of threshold excitement 'irradiated with sex'.

He and all he writes about become like the properties in *The Eve of St Agnes*, staring like 'carved angels, ever eager-eyed.' (Virginia Woolf called him 'nipped' and 'jockey-like,' with 'quicksilver eyes'; a less charitable friend referred to him ten years later as 'a dehydrated schoolboy'.)

Perhaps his style is a secret of youth and of the innocent eye; in *Lions and Shadows* he described his feeling for the cinema and for the otherness inherent in its gestures – lighting a cigarette, walking down the street. In my teens I remember being absorbed by these aspects of his prose, and its spell still works; the undercover sexual aspect of the stories, taken for granted then, is replaced now by total openness and a great deal of sexual gossip, much of which is amusing as well as informative. But the real interest is still elsewhere in the kind of meticulousness which made the study of the Isherwood parents so absorbing, and created a new world of perception in post-war novels like *The World in the Evening* and *Down There On A Visit*.

The meticulousness covers an immense toughness, both qualities reminding one unexpectedly of an author whose 'watchful dark bridge-player's eyes' and 'shy warmth' fascinated the young Isherwood – is his real status that of the sensitive man's Somerset Maugham? There is a sentimentality in both which expresses itself in the syntax as a form of almost excessive lucidity.

Isherwood's hero and spiritual father as he felt – the leader of his 'tribe' – was E. M. Forster, but it is possible to wonder whether Maugham wasn't a more natural father, and whether Forster's own reservations about his brilliant young devotee don't reveal this. (The real legatees of Forsterian baroque were Denton Welch and Angus Wilson.) Isherwood says of Christopher: 'He knew all the tricks of modesty and never boasted except in private'; he has cultivated a lack of illusion about himself comparable to Maugham's carefully acquired lack of illusion about human beings.

This comes out in the record of his long love affair with Heinz – the Otto of the Berlin stories – with whom he travelled over Europe and made immense efforts to get naturalization papers or at least work permits. Money flowed, but Heinz was eventually deported back to the German police, a labour camp, and service in the army during the war, which he miraculously survived.

Had some part of his will consented to Heinz's arrest? Had his helpless behaviour concealed a cold decision to let the police set him free from Heinz and his problems? Those moments of mysterious joy that came to him sometimes – why did they make him feel guilty? Wasn't it because this joy was joy in his new freedom? But as the frankness itself begins to arouse suspicion, humour breaks in.

Christopher's widowhood lent glamour to his image. If he had been parted from a wife a few sympathetic girls would have been touched by his plight and asked themselves: 'couldn't I make him happy again?' In Christopher's case, the sympathizers were young men who asked the same question. He encouraged them all to try.

The real cure, though, was that of the professional. 'I must write. If I can't, I'm lost.' Interesting to speculate whether either Auden or Isherwood could exist in any form today; their display of talent depended on an intolerant but civilized society, with rules on which they depended as much as they had done at prep-school, whereas contemporary society is as tolerant as it is un-civilized. Their private games, attitudes and conspiracies would attract little attention now, though Isherwood's formidable will and vitality would presumably find itself some niche in modern culture, and not necessarily as a homosexual, for the book stresses on every page how much his 'tribal' identity was formed by rejection of the orthodox tribal gods.

'Girls are what the State and the Church and the Law and the

Press and the Medical profession endorse and command me to desire. If boys didn't exist, I should have to invent them.'

Auden distrusted this ideological rather than hedonistic attitude, accusing the author of 'repressed heterosexuality', and expressing fears that he would sooner or later defect. (Nearly forty years have passed since then and Wystan's fears have been proved groundless.)

Auden had remarked on the 'bright eyes' of the immigration officer who politely questioned Christopher on his reasons for wanting Heinz to come to London, and said afterwards that he must have taken in the situation at a glance 'because he's *one of us*'. Isherwood was seeking his 'homeland', where homosexuality was natural and accepted, and hoped he had found it in Germany, where in 1930 the criminal code seemed about to legalize it. The Nazis changed all that, and in 1934 the Stalin government withdrew the revolution's 1917 recognition of individual sexual rights (Nazis referred to sexual bolshevism and Communists to 'fascist perversion').

Isherwood suggests that the only real motive he and Auden had for supporting and preaching communism was its promise of a free sexual society. At the time of their departure for America he found himself saying to Auden that he 'couldn't swallow another mouthful' of the popular front, the party line and the anti-fascist struggle, to which Auden answered: 'Neither can I.'

It is a bracing thought that talent can feed on and be fed by irresponsibility in this way, and that the mutual cry of 'Goody!' the pair exchanged when they found this out signified a further development for both of them, in terms of their personalities and their art. Goethe's old platitude about seeking and struggling is not mocked, for each was in his way in search of love – this is the moving fact to emerge from the book – and each in time found it. Isherwood defines it as that part of oneself that only exists in the loved one's company: his ideal was a permanent relation.

One of the sharpest stories in the book is about the Jewish film director Viertel, with whom Isherwood collaborated in 1935 on a modest hit called *Little Friend*. He used to tell a contemptuous tale about a male prostitute who couldn't perform unless he 'thought about Erich'. To the womanizer Viertel this was immensely comic, since everyone knows that sex among queers is just mechanically promiscuous. Christopher, who had concealed his 'tribal' allegiance, wondered what Viertel would say if he told him a comparable anti-Jewish story.

31 March, 1977   **John Bayley**

Return of the Iron Man

You may remember Lawrence's red trousers. What a different place England would be, he thought, if the men could wear red trousers. Well, they can and do, and England is indeed transformed, but not in the way Lawrence hoped. In *Gaudete**, a dream of animal energies released, Ted Hughes offers us his red trousers to wear. They seem to have come from the old Hammer Films wardrobe, and effect no transformation whatever.

The book is a narrative poem, the story of the last day in the life of the Reverend Nicholas Lumb, which he spends in his normal parish-visiting – on top of Betty in the quarry, in bed with Mrs Evans, hard at it with Mrs Davies in the potting shed. An iron man indeed. No wonder some of the locals are beginning to ask what goes on at those W.I. meetings. Actually, there's toadstool in the sandwiches, and they celebrate the ancient religion orgiastically in the basement of the church, a lot of naked women in animal masks, and the vicar in his antlers.

Once the men have put one and one together, Lumb's finished, but not before the dumb housekeeper Maud, smeared in pigeon's blood, has found her tongue and denounced him for wanting to run off with delicious eighteen-year-old Felicity, soon to be knifed with the sacrificial dagger . . .

This ridiculous hodge-podge could have made a campy horror-film, and indeed started life as a scenario. The trouble is that Hughes wants it to be taken much more seriously than that. Since Beauty, asleep, is still beautiful, there are careless strokes of genius on most pages, all at the level of rendering sensation. He has

* Published by Faber & Faber

always been good at telling us how things feel, and in language that is recognizably our own – of a man worn out running, 'His knees tangle with their chemical limits.'

But Hughes can't and won't think. The sex and violence give way to nothing else, and so don't liberate. The poetic naturalism of Shakespeare, immersed in human motive, doesn't interest him; his characters have the depth of a comic-strip. Although there are gestures to a metaphysic that might give a meaning to all the flailing in the hay, they are incoherent and unconvincing. *Gaudete*, simply, is a fantasy that has enslaved its creator. There is no room here for intelligence, and that is why the dignity of myth, which Hughes was doubtless hoping for, escapes him. Adam, Prometheus, Odysseus – they are all capable of thought. No one in *Gaudete* is. The whole enterprise fails if rationality is invoked.

The book ends with a series of tantalizing, fragmentary poems which reflect upon the narrative. They don't redeem it, because they can neither endorse his fantasy nor shake it. 'His one-eyed waking/Is the shorn sleep of aftermath' – however inflated, that is an admission of defeat.

Hughes is a genius, a Samson in his strength, but lacking wisdom. Strong but blind, Samson got nowhere, till the last time, when he pulled the house down on his own head.

19 May, 1977   **Martin Dodsworth**

In the Valley of the Moon

We met Anaizan, one of the last of the smuggler-poets of Sinai, in the Valley of the Moon, high above Eilat. He led us from the wide plateau of compacted sand, big and even enough to land a medium-sized air liner, through its coronet of jagged peaks to his encampment at Ras Rida'abi.

It was late afternoon. At the far end of the plain a mirage was draining with the sunlight. In the encampment the women and boys were driving home the sheep and goats from the pasture. Anaizan's youngest, a tiny, handsome child with mature black eyebrows and a serious mouth, padded over the hill with the last stray camel.

Later, around the campfire, where the boy but not the women joined us, we asked how old he was. Anaizan reflected. Well, he was born after the conquest (the war of 1967). When the next war came, he was just finishing nursing. Since the Bedouin women nurse their babies for two years, that made him about six.

We had come as travelling companions of Clinton Bailey, a lecturer at Tel-Aviv University who has been studying the Bedouin at close quarters for the past eight years. We were honoured guests. A windbreak had been erected and blankets spread on the ground. We were bidden to make ourselves comfortable while Anaizan and his family busied themselves with the demands of hospitality.

Twigs of the white, desert broom were gathered for tinder. Slim trunks of trees, ready felled and trimmed, were dragged to the fire and pushed gradually to the centre as they were consumed. A big brass kettle was filled and put on the flames. Then to a mixture of bleating and incantation, Anaizan slaughtered a sheep. The blood was drained, as required of good Moslems, and Anaizan smeared some of it on our Land-Rover, a sign to other Bedouin we would meet later in the desert that our host had done his duty.

The nomads save their sheep, worth £30 or £40 each, for special occasions. The meat is eaten fresh, which means it has to be cooked slowly. Anaizan's womenfolk, with their black veils and embroidered dresses, boiled the mutton in a distant tent.

For the three hours it took to become tender, we huddled around the fire, sipping innumerable small cups of sweet tea and bitter coffee. Anaizan or one of the older boys fastidiously rinsed the cups after each round.

The Bedouin talked endlessly in the loud, declamatory Arabic that is their everyday speech. Bailey joined in, interpreted, and added his share of stories, lore, and history. He had been to a Bedouin trial near El Arish, and had a tale to tell of double dealing by a young ambitious drug-smuggler, of assaults, revenge, and reconciliations made and broken. Anaizan, his face burned almost negro by the sun and wind, his beard a stubby steel grey, listened rapt to Bailey's English, guffawing with recognition every time one of the litigants was named.

He tossed in an anecdote of his own about saving two English-women on runaway horses near El Arish long ago. They were the wife and daughter of 'Mister Jarvis,' Claude Jarvis, who governed Sinai for the British in the Twenties and Thirties. Jarvis gave Anaizan £5 as a reward.

The Bedouin relish a good story, however familiar it may be. Our driver Alfonso, a Swiss with an Israeli wife, recalled a night he once spent in another encampment. The sky was black and clear, the stars brilliant and the moon full. Alfonso told his hosts about men landing on the moon. They attended in fascination, marvelling among themselves, interjecting with scepticism when he said the astronauts had brought back moon rocks. 'Go on,' they mocked, 'they must have taken them from here.'

When Alfonso came to explaining how they had made the journey, his Arabic ran out. He did not know the word for rocket. He tried aeroplanes, which the Bedouin see every day, and mumbled about aeroplanes without wings. As his embarrassment deepened, Alfonso's host took him gently by the arm and whispered: 'Tell them Apollo 15.'

Around Anaizan's fire, the conversation turned naturally to smuggling and to poetry. Until the Israelis and the Egyptians sealed the borders, running hashish from the Arabian Peninsula to the Mediterranean was a major trade among the Sinai nomads. The smugglers, who travelled farther and mixed in more diverse company than most, were welcome raconteurs, news bearers, and above all, poets.

The poetry has declined with the smuggling and with the trickle of younger Bedouin into urban jobs to which they commute from their goat-hair tents. Clinton Bailey estimated that among the 70,000 Sinai Bedouin there were now only twenty poets, most of them, like Anaizan, men in their sixties or older.

The acknowledged laureate of these desert troubadours is Anaizan's elder brother, Anaiz, a poet-over-the-water whose exile and dishonour dominated the night's conversation at Ras Rida'abi with the weight of legend. Fifteen years ago he was caught and imprisoned in Egypt for smuggling. Although he is now a free man, he has never been allowed back. His brother and his sons, 'brought up to be men' by Anaizan, listen to his voice and his poetry on Cairo Radio's *Voice of Sinai*.

'My brother is in prison,' Anaizan said in one of his poems, 'but that is no blight. Looking after your interests is no reason for shame.' The real dishonour was that two of Anaiz's three wives let themselves be enticed by their husband's cousins instead of waiting for his return.

The twin themes of faith betrayed and fortune overturned pervade Anaiz's poetry, subtly rhymed and rich in desert imagery. His cousins, he says in one poem, have become 'like a pack of hateful hyenas, crouching low beside fetid pools to drink when no wind blows, conveying our stench to others'.

In a more lyrical passage of the same composition, the exile dreams of a feast in the oasis of Wadi Wateer: 'How sweet to sip the cup down among the palms and hear the peal of the Mauser where the wadi bends, smelling the embers of broom with lamb upon them. To see friends reclining in the shade of the shelter beside girls with even teeth, darkened eyes, and tattoos as green as the pasture of spring.'

As men who can neither read nor write, the Bedouin poets compose in their head, moulding their sinuous Arabic to the rhythmic pattern of the one-stringed fiddle. They draw on a data bank of lines and metaphors, remembered and reworked.

To demonstrate his facility, Anaizan improvised a Ballad of Dr Bailey the day after we left his camp. The song, rhymed and formed, described the mountains and valleys we were driving through, the questions asked, the answers given, the sights and the stories.

The temperature was down towards freezing at Ras Rida'abi when the first meat was brought to Anaizan's guests. We began with tender cubes of liver, grilled on skewers, followed by mugs of mutton broth. The meat itself was served with big dishes of greasy rice, which we took as instructed in the right hand and squeezed into dumplings.

Mercifully, no one offered us sheep's eyes. We ate and were satisfied. Only then did Anaizan and his family tuck into the rest. The hospitality, like the poetry, conformed to its convention.

2 March, 1977   **Eric Silver**

A star is born beside the dustbin

Mr Graham Hosty, of Huddersfield, has discovered a nova with nothing more to help him than an O-Level in astronomy, keen eyesight, one half of a broken pair of binoculars that cost him £10, and an observatory housed in a wooden shed in the yard of his back-to-back house.

It is an astonishing achievement and one that eludes most astronomers in a lifetime of scanning the night skies. Mr Hosty, a twenty-seven-year-old postman, says he believes that he is only the second man in Britain in fifteen years to have discovered a nova, a star that surges into sudden brilliance and then fades over the succeeding months.

In his little wooden hut yesterday Mr Hosty described himself, perhaps with a hint of self-mockery, as 'the director of the Crosland Moor Observatory'. He is a member of the Nova Patrol, a group of about fifteen amateurs set up six months ago. Each member is given regions to patrol for novas; his beat is six regions of the Milky Way.

On the night of January 7 he took his monocular, which had a prism loose, and set it up on a rickety tripod near the dustbin, a good vantage point when he turned his attention to the constellation Sagitta. It was misty, there was glare from the street lights, and he was aiming straight between the chimney pots of Nos. 89 and 93 Blackmoorfoot Road – not the best conditions for a backyard astronomer or indeed any astronomer.

'I had got five minutes into the sweep, around the area Alpha Sagitta, when I saw a star I had never seen before,' he said. 'I was absolutely amazed. Immediately I realized that what I was watching was probably a nova. For a moment I was frozen by the sight. Then I recovered and became a serious astronomer.'

First he had to make sure that it was not what is called a variable star. He drew the area, noted the position of his discovery and checked it against the catalogues of the region. It was not shown as a variable star. He wrote his report and telephoned the news to Mr Guy Hurst, of Northampton, founder of the Nova Patrol.

Asked how he had managed to discover a nova with makeshift equipment ahead of the professional astronomers, Mr Hosty said: 'Amateurs have a much better chance of discovering objects because they are always searching the sky on clear nights. Professionals don't use their telescopes so much. They are more concerned with the study of Quasars and objects that are deep in space.'

Mr Dennis Holroyd, a part-time tutor in astronomy, described his colleague, Mr Hosty, as 'an exceptional observational astronomer'. The British Astronomical Association has circulated details of the discovery to its members, and has already received confirmation of the sighting from Mr Hurst.

The discovery will be given a number, and the name of the man who discovered it will be recorded, but there will be no official record of how the nova was found by a man standing by a dustbin in a backyard, looking through the remaining half of a broken pair of binoculars. Truly, *Per Ardua Ad Astra*.

14 January, 1977   **Michael Parkin**

The Bugatti Royale road to ruin

It was something of a sacred moment when the factory foreman broke the padlock on the store at the red-brick textile mill at Mulhouse and rolled back the sliding door to reveal the fabulous treasure of the Brothers Schlumpf.

In industrial mythology it could become the equivalent of the breaking open of Tutankhamen's tomb. On the 25,000 sq yds of floor space covered with immaculate red carpet were 584 veteran cars, all in perfect running order.

Apart from Fritz and Hans Schlumpf, now on the run in Switzerland to escape French arrest warrants, only three people – until today – had ever been taken on a tour of the lines of Rolls, Bugattis, Mercedes and Hispanos that the brothers had built up at the cost of ruining their mill industry. Signor Amedee Gordini, the Italian-born car builder who is one of the privileged three, describes it as the 'Louvre of the car industry'. Today, the 500 millworkers were admitted to view their display.

'Its value is beyond price,' Signor Gordini said, which is hardly an understatement as Bugatti Royales sell for as much as £70,000 each. The Schlumpf brothers had thirty of them as well as an array of models dating back to an 1878 steam car.

The opening of the garage followed a court order to seize the cars for auction to pay off an unrevealed amount which the Schlumpf brothers, who are Swiss, are accused of embezzling.

Until the factory nearly went bankrupt, the brothers had been considered pretty good bosses. Even in the middle of the War they opened up a 1000-place canteen, community hall, and library which made their factory the envy of a string of mills around the eastern French town near the Swiss border. But since the brothers arrived in 1939, factory gossip has centred mainly on their obsession with veteran cars. It is still remembered that a young factory worker was fined more than £50 by the brothers for peeking into a garage to have a look at a newly delivered Buick.

Railwagons were regularly shunted into the factory enclosure, carrying old cars hidden under canvas which were then rushed into the secret storehouse for restoration. One train brought in eighty veteran cars imported from the US, and a special squad of one hundred bodybuilders, painters, upholsterers and mechanics recruited from Rolls-Royce or Mercedes was kept working in isolation from the rest of the factory to put the cars in perfect working order.

Hans Schlumpf kept guard on his bicycle, with unending patrols to check the work and keep away the curious.

But such eccentricity was impossible to hide. One day a special train arrived with a complete sixty-five-seat passenger plane which the brothers wanted to use as a private restaurant. Another truck brought in a cinema organ and lorries brought in loads of turn-of-the-century gas lamps. It was only when the factory was threatened with bankruptcy that the brothers considered opening their museum to the public. They installed three restaurants and lighting worth £100,000 which they paid for out of the factory takings. They intended to charge about £6 admission.

The only visitors will be the millworkers, who say they will occupy the museum until the cars are sold by auction, although there is a chance that Mulhouse or the French Government will step in to stop the collection being broken up.

Someone will also have to worry about the brothers' latest obsession – mountain goats. More than one hundred are running wild around the factory.

8 March, 1977   **Paul Webster**

A Country Diary: The Lake District

Five summits in the Blencathra area, collected on a short May Day of sunshine and storm, were the start of a modest but blatant peak-bagging challenge. The aim is to traverse all the 203 listed tops of more than 2000 feet in the district within three months – a suitably pointless but conceivably enjoyable task for an old-age pensioner. All the ground has long been familiar but seeking new ways up and linking summits together into horseshoe rounds might require a little ingenuity. An unconventional ascent of Blencathra by ravine and crag with a final scramble up the patchy snow, still hanging like a tattered lace collar below the summit, was an encouraging start with close-up views of sheep clinging to the rocky upper slopes like the seabirds on St Bees Head. Not a breath of wind on top, dazzling sunshine on the snow patches, and unrestricted views for thirty miles but, five minutes later, a great black pall crept over the mountains and I was in a thunderstorm of driving rain and hail. Ahead, visibility shortened to yards but, curiously, through a bright gap below the black cloud to the south I could see the sun still shining on the High Street snow gullies. But the rigours of my new game meant a trudge across featureless moors to collect undistinguished tops around the desolate valley of Bannerdale before winding back along the skirts of the mountain wall to Threlkeld. Few people nowadays go into these lonely dales in the corner of the national park, but one hundred years ago, Bowscale Tarn, with its legend of two undying fish, was a big tourist attraction for Victorians 'doing the Lakes'.

9 May, 1977   **A. Harry Griffin**

Organ nut bolts with bits

Detectives in Hertfordshire are looking for a thief they describe as an 'organ nut', who for the past few weeks has been visiting churches and chapels in the county and selectively stealing small parts from the organs.

The detectives and rural clergy are convinced that someone somewhere is attempting to build his own organ. It is thought unlikely that some mighty Wurlitzer is being surreptitiously constructed. The missing parts – pipes, knobs, console items – are more suitable for a less ostentatious, garden shed creation. Put together, however, they are worth thousands of pounds.

The thief is threatening to cause widespread discord in the county and villagers are being urged to keep a watchful eye on particularly remote places of worship and to report the presence of strange cars or possible intruders. The 'organ nut' has to be caught before Hertfordshire's organs become silent.

He seems to have started pulling out the stops and other such things three or four weeks ago – no one is sure exactly when because at first his activities went undetected. In one case it was only when a specialist organ tuner had been called to rectify an apparent technical fault that the theft came to light. 'You've lost some pipes,' said the bemused tuner as he reappeared from within the organ.

Most of the troubled parishes come within the rural deanery of Berkhamsted, over which the Rev. Keith Arnold has oversight. 'We're convinced it is not a scrap thief at work,' he says.

Obviously the pipes could be valuable for scrap; but experience has taught him that greater quantities are taken in such circumstances and they are usually flattened by stamping before being taken away. 'This can only mean the parts are being taken by someone wanting to build their own,' he says. 'After all, owning your own organ is both fashionable and prestigious. There are many people, even organ societies, who set about building or restoring old organs. It is an estimable hobby. They build organs while others build buses or save Rolls-Royces. Most people use

the honest markets, however, but a number will do it this way, and
it is difficult to stop.'

So it is that tomorrow the people of Buckingham, Winslow,
Chesham, Potten End, Great Gaddesden, Berkhamsted, and
surrounding areas will be peering behind the console louvres, and
counting the organ pipes to ensure that for the moment, at least,
everything is intact.

2 April, 1977   **Baden Hickman**

Small minority

A dwarf talking: 'The weasel has nothing on me in getting to the
bar. There is nothing but legs. You don't see people. All you see is
legs. To find a path, you have to predict which way these enormous
legs are going to move. You are not dealing with *people* at all at this
level, you are dealing with legs. You have none of the conventions
of saying: "Excuse me", because you cannot say: "Excuse me" to
a knee. A knee is an object. So you get to the bar first.'

The dwarf is twenty-five years old and three feet nine inches
tall and his head is as high as one's navel. He is a man who protests
he is not a midget and insists the distinction must be made clear.

He is a member of a minority seldom written about, more
rarely still interviewed; but for which there could be more hope as
the knife-edge nature of British politics gives more weight to
minority groups of unheard-of kinds. Would it be a total surprise
if the next election were to be decided on the basis of which party
was willing to promise National Health stilts at football matches?
In the meantime, David Rappaport assured me he would settle
for an educational system which did not teach children to accept
the normal and reject everything else and for electric light
switches which do not force dwarfs to make spectacular leaps in
public places.

There was, said Rappaport, a difference to be noted between
his sort of person and midgets (of which there are about 3000 in
this country). Midgets developed to the stage of nine-year-olds,
were not fertile, had high voices and were sometimes 'rather silly'.
Dwarfs only stopped growing, but continued to develop. 'I was

the son of a taxi driver who became a school teacher and a mother who was also of normal size,' said Rappaport. 'I suppose I first realized I wasn't like other children in my first year of school. The other children were fascinated. It was quite a positive thing, really. A whole gang wanted to be my friends. As for the others, I developed a technique of toe-stepping which is very effective. Most people stamp down on the instep with the ball of the foot. If you use the heel you get a real crunch. I used to do it at five, but I don't do it now. I have calmed down and mellowed.'

Rappaport spent his 'different' childhood in Hackney and Ilford. He did not suffer greatly from bullying. 'I was below the rules, you see. The bully would pick on a weed but not a dwarf.' He learned the dwarf's first rule of survival: be sunny in the face of chiding.

He first fell seriously for a girl when he was in the sixth form. 'She was a Scot, very open and honest and forthright. She had short hair, a round face, turned up nose, grey blue eyes, very nice figure, good at hockey. The relationship was pretty sexual. Petting. We didn't sleep together. The sexuality was mutual, though. It fizzled out about the time we left school and that was mutual, too.' At university (Bristol was easier than the 'sexual show-off' world of the disco) he read psychology, took part in revues and learned to live with his dwarfishness. He could look at men five feet tall and say to himself, 'He is short': he himself was outside the rules. He found that women like to be protectors as well as be protected.

Getting a job as a teacher caused trouble. At Bradford, Rappaport was up against a selection panel which reacted to absolutely nothing he said. Eventually a woman said: 'Are you trying to prove something to yourself?' Rappaport bit his tongue on the reply: 'Oh hell, I am not trying to prove anything, I know I can get on with children, that's all.' Later he got a job at Wakefield. He could get on with children better because, in height, he was on their level, he said.

Rappaport had a bad year last year: married to a woman of normal size, a house owner, claustrophobia set in. He is now living in a commune in London, has taken to acting, has appeared in *Illuminatus* at the National Theatre, and is in the production of *Volpone* which opens at the National tomorrow. With such satisfactions, his life has more in it than those of many dwarfs. He is still worried about high light switches and lift buttons. But chiefly about the public reluctance to look dwarfs in the face as human beings.

Meanwhile Rappaport and his kind try to see the advantages. It is possible to get past almost any officious doorman simply by walking straight past and mumbling something incoherent. No officious doorman wants to tangle with a dwarf.

25 April, 1977 **Dennis Barker**

A drop of the hard stuff

The question *'Est-ce que l'eau est potable?'* which, after *'Comment se trouve madame votre femme?'* is the first to be asked of an English host by a visiting Frenchman with any pretence to urbanity (and which, the roles being reversed, is never asked by an urbane Englishman because he knows the answer to be that it is not) has been given a new dimension by the makers of *Canada Dry*. They have taken their rights over the distribution of Buxton water as a complement to their whisky, and they expect it to find a market in the South-east because 'drinkers there find that the local water tends not to mix as well with spirits as, say, the granite-based waters of the North'. This is all very polite, but what it means, shorn of its geological overburden, is that although in the sense of not being immediately fatal, and of not containing more than 1000 p.p.m. of the faecal bacterium *E. coli* which used to be the curse of Rangoon, the South-eastern tap water allows the technical answer 'yes' to the Frenchman's question, it is, on the other hand, not fit to drink.

The water authorities will advance many reasons why London water should be so unpleasant, even seeking refuge in the chalks and clays which, as with 'the granite-based waters of the North', influence the taste or want of it. And it is probably true that water which simply sinks through clay has a less interesting history than a mountain stream which, meandering through the igneous fissures and fluorspar caverns of the Peak, takes in those stimulating trace elements which gush forth in the springs of Buxton and Matlock. But even London's clay water would be drinkable if so many people were not drinking it in succession. The truth is that in order to keep down *E. coli* (the scourge of Basra) larger and larger quantities of disinfectant are poured into the water as it is lifted from the sewers until the question becomes not 'Is the water drinkable?' but 'Is the chlorine dilute?' Malvern water has not been a great success. Evian is tolerable. Vichy ranks supreme. But if *Canada Dry* keep the price down (the raw material, after all, is free) they will find that Buxton is the table-talk of London, aye, and of Woking and Beyond.

12 November, 1976   **Leader**

Grape expectations

You stand on top of a ladder with a flattened dustbin-thing strapped to your back, and inside it there are enough grapes to provide the juice for twenty-eight litres of wine, plus the waste which will make *marc*, and you're ready to die. The ladder leans against a pretty trailer which is already half-full of grapes, glistening: ladybirds and spiders are idly nudging through the bounty; wasps zip busily around. You pick the most intensely populated insect area, the area with the most tiny breathing, feeding bodies, and with a mighty thrust of the small of the back, and a slump of the right shoulder, you sling the grotesquely heavy load down on top of them all. So far, this miniature carnage is the nearest to pleasure you've felt since *l'hotte* was hoisted on to you.

A brief survey of the mountainous clouds heaped up behind the Château des Ducs at nearby Duras, Lot-et-Garonne, or of the Turnerish mists, or, on an occasional dazzling day, of a hornet, its bomber-load of venom at the ready, heading for the next vineyard, and then back to work. There are seven cutters with their scissors all clipping away in an attempt to overload their panniers by the time the porter can return down the row to them: their backs are aching, and their watches working to rule, too. Two huge alsatians play and fight endlessly, mockingly playful, a sideshow for the weary.

The *vendage* is an intense period in late September, about two weeks' worth, when the French countryside shakes off the leisurely pace which alone ensures rural endurance and undertakes a harvest which has the labour force working like it's a hundred yards' dash in hobnailed boots (or, more accurately, in mud-encrusted espadrilles). Old men in dungarees ease aching bones back into harness. Married ladies whizz about on *vélo-moteurs*, dividing their days between family and field. Young men take holidays from urbanized jobs in the towns and go back to their parents' farm. The farmer's wife alternates between the vines and the kitchen, where twice a day she must provide *La Soupe*, a six-course gastronomic ecstasy, the lunchtime version of which is intended to send workers out into the afternoon session too full and drunk to notice that the human frame was never designed to go through such struggles just so that an entire civilization can forget that it's gone mad, and can burble *In Vino Veritas* into its cups.

One terrible day, early on in this divinely tortured period, before habit had set in like embalming fluid, I picked up a book by an English vineyard proprietor from Bordeaux, Allan Sichel. In it he remarks that the wines of the Côtes de Duras are rather mediocre. This portly expert is now dead. Lying flat on my back, my lumbar region draining exhaustion into the mattress, I could easily have done the deed myself. The wines of the region are, in fact, exquisite, perfect, and if they are not classically great or celebrated, then that is because they have the good sense not to get involved with the frightful snobbery of the vinicultured.

The grapes, if they're white, are pumped from the trailer into a circular press like a big tube, whose ends can be squeezed together. The juice floods down into a concrete draining area, is filtered, and runs out into a vat. From there it is pumped into fermenting cisterns. Half the red is also pressed, the other half sits in the fermenting juice as it comes. The team filled two trailers a day, each one yielding enough to make two vast barrels of wine.

The quality of each session's pickings was measured with a specific gravity float for sugar content – *le degré*. Long faces met the announcement that some of the white was *neuf* (it improved a lot); tremendous miming of drunkenness greeted the red when it registered *quinze*. Some smart men in Cardin-inspired blouson jackets and handbags turned up in a big white Peugeot with a car radio-telephone, and pronounced themselves pleased. They were buyers, and clearly very important, picking their way through the muddy puddles in their dapper shoes. One wrong word from them about the vintage and I'd have let their well-heeled tyres down.

In the stone-built barn, with rat-traps and beams, and cobwebs, and three low wattage naked bulbs, the misty inert grape juice is allowed to mutter and fizz its way into intoxication. Around the vat with the red wine there hovered in exclusive attendance a drone of gnats, all of them the colour of their liquid diet. They must be all alcohol by now, and take no interest in nibbling humans, as they keep station with slurred flight.

The wine making was miraculous: nothing added, nothing taken away. I never saw anything go into the juice except kamikaze insects, a bit of mud and a sprinkling of sulphur. They were magical surroundings, with pipes and piratical tubs and barrels, and the curiously animate liquids doing their vital thing all around.

Each night we assembled at eight for the second meal of the day. It was a lighter affair: a mere five courses or so, and no liqueurs. We were all sleepy: seven of us, and the household's half of the frolicsome twosome, dead to the world like a sharp-eared rag on her doggy blanket. Across a language barrier which would have made Hadrian's Wall look diaphanous, dictionary to hand, a lesson, delivered with immeasurable patience and some hysterical giggling, took place. Ribaldries, agriculture, politics, all these were coaxed into one's mind: whatever pathetic French I speak, I suppose it now has the equivalent of a West Country burr.

Once again, the chickens, ducks, guinea-fowl, turkeys, goats, cows, pigs; the fig trees and plum trees, the vines, the vegetable plots; and above all the skills of a *cuisinière* of ineffable deftness, gave up their best. A last hobble across to bed, and a whole new intimate encounter with the meaning of the word 'repose'. As one fellow-worker observed in the vines one day, 'You can't really call this a holiday, can you? But I suppose it's a change for you.'

6 November, 1976   **Richard North**

212

It's lipsmackin', easyeatin', bellyfillin'. . .

Along Wisconsin Avenue, which runs through the heart of middle-class Washington, Roy Rogers, the faded cowboy hero of the 1940s and 1950s, is earning a pleasant retirement income.

He runs a highly profitable and rapidly expanding fast food establishment. Every evening the car park is full of station wagons; inside, families grab cheap hamburgers and fried chicken.

According to the Bureau of Labour Statistics, the daily scene at this branch of Roy Rogers's chain and at similar junk food outlets is so pervasive that it has become a stereotype. The average American family spends more money on transport than it does on food. But although the proportion of family expenditures spent on food declined from 24.4 per cent in 1960-1 to 20.1 per cent in 1972-3, the amount spent on cheap meals in restaurants went up.

As Americans became more affluent they also spent less of their money on reading matter. The latest BLS survey of 20,000 families showed that the proportion spent on books, magazines and newspapers went down over the decade from 0.9 per cent to 0.6 per cent.

The big shift in spending was on the car. It was not just that people bought more cars. (The average family had 1.3 cars in 1972 compared with one in 1960). They were buying larger, more lavish cars and using more petrol to run them. The survey was made before the big jump in petrol prices in 1973 and the trend towards higher spending on transport is presumed to have accelerated.

Officials explained that the declining proportion of income spent on food did not mean less consumption per person, because family size itself was decreasing. They did not explain why American families did not insist on better quality food, nor why in the most productive agricultural country in the world, bread should be almost inedible and people should tolerate the substitution of milk and cream by 'non-dairy products' in many restaurants.

The convenience of places such as Roy Rogers's is undeniable. The fried chicken comes in foil, the hamburgers and chips in paper, and the drinks in throwaway cups, all of which patrons dump by themselves in bright red dustbins as they go out. Costs are kept to a minimum and a family of four can save mother two hours in the kitchen, eat and drink for about $5 and get back into their station wagon in fifteen minutes flat.

Convenience foods have created so much of a cult of their own taste that the trend may be irreversible. Last week 200 children at a junior high school in Rosyln, Long Island, walked out in protest when the board of education tried to provide a salad for the annual picnic instead of Ring Dings, Devil Dogs, Yankee Doodles, Yodels, and Funny Bones.

One child called the new menus extreme. 'We don't want to be pawns of a nutrition chess game,' he wrote in the school paper about the board's experimental programme, which culminated in the salad for the annual picnic.

20 May, 1977   Jonathan Steele

The turn of the corkscrew

They've just opened a new Yates's Wine Lodge in Leeds. It's smaller and smarter than most – there's a carpet on the floor – and it's set rather self-consciously, as if it hasn't got comfortable yet, in a basement under a new shopping precinct in Boar Lane.

Yet in most other respects the new lodge in Leeds retains the traditional characteristics shared by all those gauntly grand Victorian Yateses dotted around the country. The decor is more modern but it's still unfrilled functional, and the clientele looks interchangeable with that of any other Yates's Wine Lodge.

The new lodge in Leeds replaces one which was closed for clearance nearly three years ago. Any other business might expect some difficulty in picking up after a three-year gap. But Yates's isn't like any other business.

'It was just as if we'd closed as usual the night before,' said the manager, Mr Wilf Norris. 'The first ten customers to come in were exactly the same people who were the first ten in three years ago, and in the same order.'

You find that with Yates's. I asked Mr Norris how working there differed from working in any other bar. 'I don't know,' he said; 'I've never worked anywhere else. I've worked for Yates's since I was thirteen, bottling up. I did fourteen years in the Strand before I came here.'

The first time I went into a Yates's Wine Lodge was on the day I got engaged. It wasn't so much a celebration as a tactful smoothing over of the row about the ring, but we ordered half a bottle of champagne between four of us. The pensioners checking their pools looked as if they thought we'd won.

I've learned since that it was an even more sensible move than I realized. Yates's non-vintage champagne is, I'm told, highly regarded. The family drink it themselves, and the only person I know who drinks champagne all the time buys it by the crate.

That's the other thing about Yates's. Despite the down-market image, people who know what they're drinking know that Yates's products are chosen by people who know what they're choosing.

It's not too long ago that the executives of – let's say – a nationally-known sherry firm were regularly seen drinking Yates's Delissimo Cream in the Albion restaurant in Manchester. They knew it was the same sherry as their own label – before that was degraded eight times – and only two-thirds their price.

Yet the wine lodges have somehow acquired a distinctly dismal reputation, as if drinking Yates's was only a hiccup away from drinking meths. There are exceptions, of course – the Blackpool lodge, which provides splendid value in its basement restaurant, has its seasonal complement of show-biz stars in the summer and politicians in the autumn. The imposing Nottingham lodge still has a trio playing every evening except Sunday.

But the characteristic Yates's customer is working class, elderly, and often female with overdone make-up. Richard Boston pointed out that every pub seems to have a little old lady sitting in a corner with a bottle of Guinness. Yates's is full of them.

Perhaps it's because of the relatively low price policy. Or maybe because of the starkly spartan atmosphere of most lodges which, with their high ceilings and bare floorboards, their pillars and rails for propping yourself upright, seem clearly designed for the determined and joyless business of taking the quickest route to oblivion.

In Oldham, they say, the regulars used to write their requirements – Guinness on Friday, pale ale on Wednesday – on the soles of their shoes, so that they could order the next round just by raising the foot, without going through the hazardous business of rising from their seats.

And just round the corner from a Liverpool lodge, there's a police station known as the billiard hall because you're in off the white – Yates's Australian white wine, which is said to be regarded as a panacea by some and by others as 'lunatic soup'.

But the widespread impression that Yates's is just a drop away from Skid Row or the drying-out clinic is somewhat at odds with the firm's idiosyncratic reason for being. Its origins go way back to the Victorian temperance movement – Yates's motto, people tend to forget, is 'moderation is true temperance'.

In the 1880s, when the lowest orders seem to have spent most of their time drowning their sorrows in beer and gin, perhaps it wasn't too cranky to suggest that the answer was to provide draught wine as a civilizing alternative. Especially if your family business in the wine trade was missing out on the mass market. What Victorian entrepreneur could pass up the chance to combine profit with reforming zeal?

Peter Yates, the founder of the firm, was brought up in Preston, Lancashire, by an aunt in the wine and spirit business who sent him to Spain to learn about wine while his younger brother Simon went to America to study business methods.

The first lodge opened in 1884 in Preston, which was also the home of a less-well-known chain of temperance wine lodges, Addison's. (They have, for instance, a bottle shop in Wigan.) Addison's was the older firm – their wine lodge is listed in a Preston trade directory as early as 1869 – but Yates's took it over by marriage in the 1940s.

The brothers' combination of specialist knowledge, business acumen, and philanthropic purpose led to the growth of a catering empire with headquarters in Manchester and wine lodges in most northern industrial towns from Nottingham to Newcastle-upon-Tyne, and as far south as Worcester. There are two in London – that at Avery Row was apparently frequented by morning-suited waiters from Claridge's.

At one time the firm owned its own laundry, behind the Ashton-under-Lyne lodge; its own bakery, behind the Oldham lodge; and its own farm at Bosley, near Congleton in Cheshire, where they still have a country pub, the Harrington Arms. There is still a Yates's butchers, in Tib Street, Manchester, and a flour mill behind the Oldham Street lodge. They own restaurants like the Merchants in Manchester and an hotel, the Grand, in Douglas, Isle of Man.

It would be unjust to dismiss the temperance lodges simply as a self-protective, pre-emptive strike at tee-totalism. Peter Yates himself practised moderation in both eating and drinking, and used the lodges to promote his ideas.

'The staff have strict instructions not to serve anyone who shows the slightest sign of intoxication,' notices used to warn. The lodges still close half an hour before the pubs – a bell is rung ten minutes before time – and most will only serve beer in half pints.

The idea was to cut down on drunkenness by importing good quality wines and selling them from the wood in ample measures at prices that ordinary people could afford. Yates's still serve wine in the old Imperial measures – a 'sample' and a 'dock' – and spirits in the generous 'club' measure of one-fifth of a gill (compared with one-sixth in pubs).

Fortunately for those who are initiated into the Yates's free-masonry, the firm remains a private limited company wholly owned by the family. Its managing director is Peter Yates's grandson, Sir Richard Martin-Birr, a former sheriff of Manchester who was knighted for his services to the (then) Territorial Army. The family are still sent to Spain to learn about wine. They retain their legendary contacts in the trade.

One of the surviving eccentricities is that the firm, like the family, shuns publicity to a degree which must be unknown in the licensed trade. Telephone calls, even to named executives, are intercepted and not returned; letters go unanswered if they're from the press. Consequently very little ever appears in print about Yates's. It is typically eccentric that one of the most informative pieces on the firm appeared in the *Manchester Free Press*.

And the family still seems to be committed to retaining the style and traditions of an institution which has become an integral part of the Northern working-class sub-culture. The old paternalist, do-gooding tone is still there in the notices in the lodges today, apologizing for the prices and grumbling mildly about taxation – not special pleading, just a suggestion that the level is 'unreasonable'.

Yates's may have lost their competitive edge on price cutting, faced with an operation like Augustus Barnett. But their prices are still reasonable – and not only for wine. Bottled Guinness is 19p in the Oldham lodge, compared with 26p in a none-too-pretentious pub (and a wholesale price just under 13p). Their own label spirits are about 50p a bottle less than branded lines, even at discount prices. They still run a mail order service from Blackpool.

Peter Yates was one of the first to insist that, in the interest of sobriety, food should be available throughout licensing hours, and every lodge still boasts 'something good to eat at any time of the day'.

The idea was taken further in the 'Tee-total Taverns' (the sign is still up at the back of the Oldham lodge). Between closing the bar after lunch and opening again for the evening, the lodges served tea, and hot soup which, at 2d a bowl, was said to be so nourishing you could live on it.

'His views on food reform were original,' one obituary said of Peter Yates, 'and for many years he advocated the use of wholemeal bread exclusively and would serve no other in his premises.' He started his own flour mill to make stoneground, unbleached flour which Yates's still sell in their bottle shops, packed in cloth bags with the motto: 'The whiter your bread the sooner you're dead.' Another enthusiasm was for cigar smoking as against the cigarette habit. Yates's still sell their own brand, El Cuervo, although you can no longer watch them being hand-rolled. The bottle shops also sell their own brand of tea and, presumably through the association with Portugal, three sorts of sardine – in olive oil, tomato, and spiced.

Between the wars, Peter Yates used to tour his wine lodges making little speeches to the customers advocating his ideas on healthy living – such as the correct anatomical attitude for sleeping (on your stomach) – and a reduction in the speed limit for motor-cars.

Peter outlived Simon – he died shortly before his ninetieth birthday in 1944, at Fordingbridge in Hampshire. He is still commemorated in the wine lodges with the issue of Founder's Day port, which is specially selected for the customers to drink a toast to the founder on his birthday, April 22. At the bargain price of around £1.65 a bottle, it tends to be snapped up within a few days and sales are limited to two or three bottles to each customer. Even the labels, it's said, have become collectors' items.

If some of Peter Yates's ideas now seem a trifle quirky, others are clearly coming back into fashion, like his advocacy of wholemeal flour. The trendy wine bars which have sprung up in most cities in the past few years seem to charge a premium for very ordinary plonks, while for years Yates's have been selling extremely good wines on draught, in generous measures and relatively cheaply.

The business still makes a considerable profit – something in excess of £173,000. It must look like a very tempting morsel to a city speculator with its assets (most lodges are hugely built on corner sites in town centres), its devoted staff and loyal customers, and its scope for development. One shudders to think what would happen if it fell into the hands of a big brewery or a steak-and-fairy-lights conglomerate.

13 June, 1977   **Robin Thornber**

Bruhaha

On the Afternoon After the Morning After the Night Before, hundreds of thousands of Scotsmen waken with a heavy head and their 'breath like a badger's bum' and reach for the Barr's Irn Bru, a remedy to a night on the bevvy, which has reached mythical proportions and million pound profits for its makers.

They have been flogging the stuff to the Sassenachs for some years, but it is in Scotland that the true majesty of this amber concoction can be seen. The street hoardings entreat you to sample Scotland's Second National Drink, and provide a Guide to Your Local Barrs. 90,000 gallons are consumed each week. Five million gallons each year. It outsells lemonade, even though

I would not have thought you could put it in whisky.

'Funnily enough you can,' says Robin Barr, son of the company chairman.

Pull the other one, Robin, it's got haggis on it.

'No, reports are reaching us that they are mixing it with whisky in Fife.'

Funny people the Fifers.

'No. It has been in the papers and one diarist asked me what I thought of the idea. I said it sounded disgusting and, alas, he quoted my comment.'

Have you ever tried it in Scotch yourself?

'Good lord, no.'

Barr's soft drink factory lies along Glasgow's Gallowgate near Parkhead Cross. On one side stands the Eastern Necropolis, on the other a Catholic Church, and at the back there is Celtic Park. We are ushered into the boardroom, an unprepossessing place where A. G. Barr glowers down at us darkly and the walls are ranged with bottles of the company's products and a few of their competitors. Over in Ireland, Robin found a bottle of Rangers lemonade with a crusading knight, or was it King Billy, emblazoned on the bottle.

'Now is that not a splendid sight,' he says, holding up a particularly gaudy label and then musing quietly on the wondrous inventiveness of soft drink makers.

Could Robin tell me what is in his best selling potion?

He could not, except to quote the declaration on the bottle. 'As required by law,' he tells me, 'it contains sugar, salt, caffeine, carbon dioxide, citric acid, colouring, iron, in the form of ferric ammonium citrate, and a blend of fruit essences.' Only Robin and his father know the proportions.

The first bottle of Iron Brew, as it was then called, rattled off the production line in 1901 along with other company products like Wee MacGreegor, Hop Bitter Beer, Dinner Stout, and Dandelion Stout. In 1946 the government got uppity about misleading brand names, the family went into a huddle, and so was born the phonetic Irn Bru. Ironically the legislation never came to pass. Those were the days of organizations like the Glasgow and West of Scotland Aereated Waters Manufacturers and Beer Bottlers

Defence Association, a nasty little cartel who had ways of dealing with pop squeaks who tried to undercut the fixed selling prices.

'Would you care for a cup of coffee?' inquires Robin.

'But I thought you would be offering us a sample of the Bru.'

Robin looks as though we are spies from Coca-Cola and orders coffee.

Robert Barr started work as a cork cutter, preparing stoppers for soft drink manufacturers in Falkirk in 1830. The family is from Ayrshire where there is a village called Barr. By 1880 Robert's son, also called Robert, opened the family's first soft drink factory. Today there are manufacturing and selling outlets throughout the UK. They bought Tizer the Appetizer in 1973 for £2.5 million. And yes, they do make Irn Bru south of the border. In Edmonton, London. Profits last year, just announced, were £2.2 million.

'We are,' says Robin proudly, 'the largest specialist soft drink manufacturer in Europe.' Others sell more? 'Even in the UK there is Beecham and Cadbury-Schweppes. But we don't make pills, do we?'

Now there is a thought. Irn Bru pills.

That other Glasgow institution, Billy Connolly, has a warm place in the heart of the Barr family since he took his love for Irn Bru on to the stage and into the television studios. He has dedicated a wee ditty, quite unsuitable for reproduction in a family newspaper, to Mr and Mrs Barr 'who saved my life on so many Sunday mornings'. Down for a London concert, invited members of the press were sent bottles of the liquid to encourage their attendance. The packages looked and felt like the hard stuff and many was the long face when the wrapper was ripped open to reveal the teetotal truth.

Robin Barr is not saying how much Mr Connolly has helped sales. The guy might come banging on his banjo at Parkhead Cross looking for his ten per cent. But for two characters there is nothing but praise. Ba Bru and Sandy advertised the wonders of all Barr's drinks from 1932 until 1973 in the form of a strip cartoon which ran in almost all the Scottish newspapers. The bubble captions were excruciating but the effect was stupendous to behold.

During the war there were Ba Bru ack-ack gunners firing giant size bottles of Barr's drinks at unsuspecting Jerry. Sadly, for the duration of the hostilities, Irn Bru was not available in civvy street. The characters were a straight pinch from Kipling's *Sabu, the Elephant Boy*, although as the Race Relations pressure got tighter, Ba Bru got lighter until, says Robin, 'he ended up as a white boy in a turban'.

Sociologically, Barr have a contribution to make to the mores of the British. Take this for example. The farther south you go, the shorter is the life of a returnable pop bottle. In Scotland you get twelve trips, in North-east England eight trips, in the Midlands five trips. By the time you get to London, you only get one and a half trips, which is why the company only uses non-returnable bottles there.

Does this mean that the farther north you go, the meaner the people are?

'That is primarily . . .' There is a pause as Robin recognizes the dropping of a tartan clanger. 'I would not be accused of saying that the Scots are mean, but the social habit of returning your bottle to recover your money is certainly stronger the farther north you go.'

It is time to leave the boardroom and go below for a touch of the soft stuff. We are put into the hands of Mr John Sneddon, production manager, who accompanies us round a variety of amazing machines in a great hall heavy with the pungent aroma of Barr's Irn Bru. No one can hear to speak. The crashing of the bottles, running at 400 per minute, being unloaded, unscrewed, washed, filled, screwed, loaded, is more than a man can stand, which no doubt accounts for the women operators.

The din is broken from time to time by the sound of an exploding Bru bottle. Years ago, in my tender Glaswegian youth, I had a splendid bomb recipe which included mixing certain proportions of Irn Bru and vinegar plus one or two other ingredients which I am not telling you or Robin Barr.

'It's more popular than milk, ye ken,' announces John when we get to a quiet bit.

Does he drink it himself?

'Och aye, it's awfu guid for the kidneys.'

How much is the staff allowed to drink?

'As much as they want.'

Average consumption?

'About four bottles a day. It gets hot in there in the summer.'

Upstairs in a smaller hall, gleaming aluminium urns contain the concentrated mixes of Strike Cola, lemonade, Irn Bru, and more. Cissie Scott is in white-coated control. Perhaps you get used to the smell; it is a place of heavy vapours. John leads us back down to the loading bay.

He brandishes a bottle of Irn Bru at photographer Don McPhee who has been courageous/foolish enough to admit that he has never tasted the stuff.

A sign on the wall reads: 'No Smoking – this is a food factory.'

Don raises the bottle to his lips.

Loaders and lorry drivers fall silent in awe.

John smiles menacingly.

'Quite tasty,' says Don.

Wise chap Don.

14 February, 1977   Raymond Gardner

Blind Man's Bluff

The Scottish National Party can be forgiven some of its Tarzan-like utterances immediately after the Government's defeat on the guillotine motion on the Devolution Bill. But second thoughts were taking place yesterday, and they were perfectly illustrated by a story told by the party's leader at Westminster, Mr Donald Stewart, at a full SNP group meeting last night.

Mr Stewart (who would pronounce his own Christian name as Tonald) told how he had seen a well-known blind character standing at a crossroads in his own home town of Stornoway. A dog walked up to the blind man and relieved itself down his trouser leg. To Mr Stewart's astonishment, the blind man took a chocolate biscuit from his pocket and offered it to the dog.

'That was a very Christian thing you did to the tog (sic),' Mr Stewart remarked to the blind man. 'Not at all,' the blind man replied. 'I was only trying to find which end his mouth was so that I could kick him in the palls (sic).'

Her Majesty's Government may take warning – if the SNP looks less belligerent today than it did on Tuesday night, it may be trying to identify the right place in which to deliver its kick. Jesters do oft prove prophets.

Peter Hillmore

Anne stays above Ulster reality

Princess Anne yesterday encountered what must be for her a rare phenomenon: three young girls who did not want to be photographed with the royal person.

The reason was depressingly simple. The girls live in the Catholic ghetto of Short Strand, in East Belfast, which is to monarchism rather as Cheltenham is to Stalinism.

It was indeed brave enough for the girls to be in the royal presence – at a reception for the Princess in Hillsborough – and it would have been even braver for the Princess to be in Short Strand. In fact the only sight she had of Belfast was a fleeting glimpse from her Queen's Flight helicopter, as it whisked her to Hillsborough Castle, in County Down.

Hillsborough, though indisputably in Northern Ireland, looks and feels like an outpost of Sussex. The castle, former home of the governors of Northern Ireland is a gracious sandstone pile presiding splendidly over a village of antique shops, smart bars, and Georgian houses. Yesterday, the only indications of Ulster reality were the army road blocks in the village and the armed policemen posted around the magnificent castle grounds.

The scarlet Wessex helicopter looked entirely appropriate to the setting as it approached its landing ground in a meadow near the castle. The instant the machine landed, a hand emerged from the pilot's cabin to affix a small royal standard to a miniature flagstaff by the window. Simultaneously, the Daily Express reporter doffed his Russian-style fur cap (because, he claimed, of the strong draught from the whirling rotor blades) and the Princess disembarked.

She came as President of the Save the Children Fund, which

performs good works in more squalid parts. The Ulster members are the most successful fund raisers per capita in any part of the UK. They are also responsible for thirty-three projects in their own region, including play groups and clubs like the one in Short Strand, from which the three young girls came. One playgroup they run is in the visitors' compound at Maze Prison, Long Kesh, where small children visiting their fathers are amused during the rigorous security checks.

The work of the fund in Northern Ireland, as the Princess remarked to 200 workers, is carried out in circumstances of unparalleled difficulty and indeed great personal danger. But yesterday was not a time for grim reality. There was pheasant for lunch – a piece of information obtained by a colleague at the cost of a stern ticking off for talking to kitchen staff – photographs on the terrace, and chats with SCF stalwarts and with members of the regional Royal Jubilee committee.

For the press there was a small ante-room off the elegant drawing-room where the Princess addressed SCF members, complete with a relay loudspeaker, and a cramped view of the guest of honour. One of the double doors had to be closed, a Special Branch man explained, because otherwise there would be a direct line of fire between the press and the Princess.

24 March, 1977   **Derek Brown**

Day of the dog-collars

I've borrowed my dad's brown trilby and been to Cheltenham races. I knew it was cracked up to be something, but never anything quite like this. St Patrick's Day gone mad. The festival starts at Paddington, where first-class, non-stop morning specials leave on the half-hour full of the buffeting champagne and cigar gentry, every man Jonathan of them smirkingly knowing a thing or three . .

I caught the orthodox second-class. More Irish. They know a thing or two of that as well. So they tell you. Our buffets were more scruffy. Brown ales and scarce a Wills Whiff to be seen. Everyone deep into the Sporting Life. All wide-eyed expectation

225

as a cover for furtive, blotchy-faced despair. And, quietly, in corners, sheepishly studying Timeform as if a breviary, a host of Irish clergy.

And once at Cheltenham Station, in the long queue for buses and taxis, you can't finish your count of the dog-collars. Sunday clerics with the glint of midweek sport in their eye. And, I'd bet on it, twice as many again in civvy collar and tie and having told their abbots and bishops that they're off for their annual treat on the mainland of some unsuspecting convent school or whatever. Certainly Cheltenham's racecard could be printed in Latin and half the fancy could read it.

Mark you, Cheltenham Races and the Catholic Church have long been hand in glove. A lively settlement of Romans was established there by refugees from the French Revolution. And when the merry Captain Berkley founded the race meeting below Cleeve Hill in the early part of last century, the Irish brought over their relatives, who in turn brought their nags, to join in the fun. Many stayed there and then. Indeed, 100 years ago Cheltenham had to build itself a new cemetery, for, as the old refrain went:

The churchyard's so small and the Irish so many
They ought to be pickled and sent to Kilkenny.

To the Bible-thumper, Dean Close, the horse racing Irish of Cheltenham were the pet hate ahead even of drink. 'Papist gambling and profligacy,' he ranted in 1835, 'are essential concomitants of horse racing.' But he failed to wipe even a smile from their face and he stomped off to Carlisle.

Cobbett failed too. 'Cheltenham on race day is the resort of the lame and lazy, the gourmandizing and guzzling, the bilious and nervous . . . ' Now that's the sort of thing I would have been thinking of if I'd caught the first-class.

Hey ho, but what a lovely jig the Irish give to the prim place. Not that the residents stir to wake out of their doze, unless they're hoteliers or traffic wardens or shopkeepers. One daft local grocer, for years now, has made a tradition of presenting a posy of jasmine and a packet of Polos to the Queen Mother as she's chauffeured past his shop on her way up to the course.

The Queen Mother has a horse called Isle of Man. 'Good luck to the Isle of Wight,' said the grocer in his blushing confusion.

But the Queen Mother seemed beamingly oblivious as she accepted the gift.

Yesterday, bewildered but rubbing shoulders with the clergy, with shady Cockneys and nobs from the shires, I chanced across our film critic, Mr Malcolm, looking knowing like everyone else, even more so he in his porridgy oatmeal coat. With flamboyant confidence he gave me Chekhov 'for classical reasons' to win the first race. It lost. He was certain about Flitgrove for the second. Not a flicker. Well, Birds Nest for the third. Nowhere. I console him with the posy I'd bought specially in case I met the Queen Mother. But he won on the fourth when I didn't bet. So I gave him the packet of Polos in celebration. To the uninitiated, Cheltenham is no place to find the winner. Bet now, if you are looking to be converted to the one true faith . . .

17 March, 1977 **Frank Keating**

Brief encounter with the SAS

Chance encounters with members of the Special Air Service Regiment are supposed, more by legend than by record, to be as unpleasant as they are infrequent. The torch in the eyes at 3 a.m., the cold press of the blue steel in the back of the neck, the muffled bark of a silenced machine pistol from a passing van – such is the popular vision of the SAS, highly professional men pursuing enemies of the state by highly uncivilized means.

But my chance encounter could hardly have been more civilized. He was dressed in a three-piece, charcoal grey pinstripe suit, with a blue-striped shirt and a red woollen tie. His shoes shone mercilessly black. He was sitting, back to engine, in a first-class compartment of a southbound train which meandered through ten hours of a bitterly cold night from Scotland to the English Midlands, and until we changed trains near Birmingham, the only obvious assumption one could make about him was that he was an army man, and an officer. But then he mentioned he was going on to Hereford, which prompted the question – SAS, then? And he turned out to be, not just SAS, but one of the regiment's most senior officers.

The ensuing two-hour conversation over coffee and milk (he drank the milk, although it was seven in the morning) could scarcely have been more illuminating about the regiment's operational activities in Northern Ireland. The SAS, until Mr Wilson put them in on 7 January, had only operated twice before in Ulster, once in 1972 and once again in 1974. 'Both operations were quick in-and-out jobs, both in Belfast, and from our point of view, both were accomplished satisfactorily.' Satisfactorily, F – as we shall call him – explains in another part of the conversation usually meant that members of enemy units had been, to use the CIA's favourite phrase, 'terminated with extreme prejudice.' The regiment had never once operated with the army's notorious Mobile Reaction Force, as had been suspected. 'They did that all on their own,' F snorted.

When the single squadron from the barracks at Hereford was flown to South Armagh 'the men were delighted. We had felt for a long time that we had the only answer to the border problem and we were all very enthusiastic about going out and wasting a few of the Pira (his current army jargon for the Provos). How wrong we were.'

The regiment on the ground in South Armagh at the time, a Scottish infantry unit, made it clear they knew nothing of SAS methods. 'Understand you chappies work in groups of four,' said one officer to F. The SAS man protested this was nonsense and that the benefit of his regiment was that there were so few hard and fast rules. 'Yes you do,' said the Scotsman, 'I read it in *The Soldier*, and that's how we've prepared things for you.' And so, instead of squirming through culverts in County Louth, picking off Pira officers with pump-action shotguns in the still of the night as they had hoped, the SAS men had to spend their first week patrolling, in the uniform of the Scotsmen, in fours.

One tactical scheme was to send Scots platoons marching up to the border to act as decoys while hidden quartets of SAS men would hide and open up on the expected IRA ambushers. But the Scots grew weary of being used as bait in such sport, and after a while the ploy was abandoned. This was two months or so after the SAS came in, and morale among them all was deadly low. Then a plan was conceived, by F and others, and approved by the GOC. The SAS could operate as they wished, though preferably in the uniform of the resident regular unit (the Scots were being replaced by Paras, the unit from which many SAS men had been seconded, anyway) and they could use traditional, though preferably non-fatal methods. Their target was to be the top ten Pira men in the region. 'Well, we got four of them,' said F, 'and the other six have been chased away down south. The area is pretty clear of them now – you can tell how much quieter it has become.'

The precise circumstances of 'getting' the men cannot as yet be told. One, Mr Sean McKenna, was arrested by the British after having supposedly been dragged over the border from his hidey-hole in the south; two were arrested by the Gardai on SAS advice; and one, Peter Cleary, was shot dead at point blank range on 16 April.

'There has been a lot written about that killing, mostly wrong,' said F. 'The fact is there were five of us involved in the arrest. We radioed for a chopper to take him out, but because the RAF boys are so bad these days, all of our men had to be used to hold up landing lights to let the machine get down. Cleary was being held by just one chap, and, of course, made a run. He grabbed the soldier's rifle by the barrel and tried to pull it away, the soldier squeezed the trigger three times and got him in the chest. And he was quite right to do it.'

The helicopter eventually got down and took away the body. 'A few years ago the RAF could have landed with three lights, which would have meant we could have guarded him. But not any more. They always want five.'

There was the famous border-crossing incident last May, still the subject of litigation and diplomatic anger. 'Their map readings were a bit off. They thought this vehicle checkpoint was one of ours but it turned out to be one of theirs. And you know, but for one bloody Garda, we could have been allowed home. But he rang Dundalk and, of course, was told to hold our chaps. It was all pretty demoralizing.'

Yes, one of them had been a Fijian soldier. 'Frankly we only normally use Fijians at night – and do you know, of all the blacks we use for nightwork Fijians are much the best. Much stealthier than the rest. But they suffer terribly from the cold – if you've ever seen a blue Fijian you'll know what I mean.'

All the SAS men involved served out their time in Ireland, F said, 'and then went off elsewhere'. Two of them are said to be in Oman now back serving the Sultan, which is the other principal activity in the regiment. F doubts very much that the others will appear in court.

Increasing the size of the SAS commitment to the Irish border (and the cities now, it seems probable) will be difficult in F's view. 'All our squadrons are now committed in various places around the world,' he said mysteriously. 'We've no one left. And the standard of training in the army is such that we have a very high failure rate among potential recruits. But we'll just have to get bigger. Do you know the Russians have three brigades like SAS? South Armagh has shown we're effective in this kind of war, I think, but we need many more men if we are going to be effective in Europe. Maybe Ireland will help MOD to let us boost the strength, in which case all this will have been well worth while.'

11 December, 1976   **Simon Winchester**

Massacre at Thammasat

The photographs of the killings at Thammasat University, which the world's press printed last week, like all atrocity pictures dehumanized not only the murderers but also the victims. Who could see people – real people – in those twisted bodies, those charred limbs sticking out from an obscene bonfire?

This is a story about a girl to whom these pictures were more than just a jolting sight at breakfast to be put out of mind as soon as possible, or simply a dramatic indication that a time of political crisis had arrived in Thailand, a nasty end to an unstable little democracy. It is a second-hand story, and the one without names, because the girl, rightly or wrongly, feels herself in danger under the new military regime which was installed here directly following the Thammasat battle.

But she lives in Bangkok, is in her early twenties, is a former student herself, and is an aspiring writer. She is a member of the student generation that went on to the streets in October, 1973, and brought down the military government of Thanom and Prapas, with help, it is true, from the army and the palace. In those days the euphoria of such young people was almost tangible. A parliamentary democracy was set up.

The right wing was still dominant but it was a saner and more sensible right wing. Men like Kukrit Pramo, the best of the three prime ministers of the period, were opposed politically by the Left but applauded privately as democrats who were 'good for Thailand'. Our girl talked revolution sometimes but preferred reform, and, like most of the so-called 'left-wing' students, she is, by English standards, not much more than a middle-class radical.

Or at least that is what she was until she opened a Bangkok evening paper on Wednesday and saw the mutilated body of a young man hanging from a tree. He was not the love of her life, but he was a boy she knew well, with whom she had perhaps had an affair, with whom she had travelled in the countryside on one of those middle-class student forays, mainly unsuccessful, to 'get close to the peasants'. He was a Leftist, a mature student, and a big talker. She had admired him, but sometimes she had wondered if he was quite as clever or as brave as he thought he was.

The next day she arranged the photographs of his abused body on her desk and wrote a poem, crying as she did so. Here is part of it:

'Yesterday was the darkest day of our time,
Tense enough as I was while walking on the street . . .
The evening paper was on sale.
I picked one up and turned to the middle page.
Where are you Kom? Come and tell me.

You're not the dead body hanging on the tree in that picture.
My legs walk no more. I was trembling . . .
Kom, my dear brother, I believe you.
You have fought in every way:
I'll hurry to catch up with you again – fighting in all ways.'

Her friend Kom had died at the end of one of the most unequal battles imaginable and one about which many questions are still unanswered. Students from Bangkok's universities were inside Thammasat on Tuesday as a protest against the continued presence in Thailand of the former military ruler Thanom. The situation was bad but not disastrous until the word went out that the students were heavily armed. Military radio stations whose ultimate controllers are unknown constantly broadcast these rumours as facts, adding the assertion that Vietnamese agents were in the university with students.

This was a sophisticated black radio operation that is one of the legacies of American counter-insurgency training. To cap it all, the broadcasts discovered an insult to the royal family in a bit of street theatre the students had put on to pass the time. Nobody knows who planned this skilful 'blacking' of the students.

Nor is it clear who ultimately issued the orders that brought to the university area scores of thousands of Village Scouts, an anti-Communist village self-defence force who have no business in cities and no legitimate police role, and other anti-Communist right-wing groups. But the myth of great student firepower eventually overwhelmed the police who, when a small negotiating party was fired on from the university, requested reinforcements.

What they got were units of the border police, specially trucked in, a paramilitary force with heavy weapons for counter-insurgency. They blasted their way into Thammasat against hardly any opposition. The best police intelligence – after the operation – is that there may have been two light machine guns as well as a score of M-16s in the university. The police treated the students like prisoners of war.

Some students died from police automatic and recoilless rifle fire during the battle – probably about thirty. But the worst fate was reserved for those few, like Kom, who tried to escape from the front of the university. There they were captured by a howling mob of Village Scouts and Red Gaurs (bulls), a right-wing student group, and killed.

It seems that the four died in this fashion. The worst irony is that Kom, who believed that the peasantry was the backbone of Thailand and that the really valid political work was with the peasants, in a sense died at their hands. 'Sister,' he told the girl, 'turn your back and you'll reach the main road soon.' He meant that the road to social change was in the villages and not in the cities.

What in the end is clear is that everybody at Thammasat on Wednesday, in the battle that destroyed Thai democracy, was being manipulated – the students themselves by the unbearable provocation of Thanom's continued presence, the Village Scouts urged on by the hate-filled imaginings of the radio stations, and even the police, half convinced they were in a major fight.

12 October, 1976   **Martin Woollacott**

Blood on the waves

By midday on 8 September the waters of Hvalfjordur – Whale Fjord – had turned a dark viscous red. The last catch of the Icelandic whaling season had been brought in, nine male sperm whales in all. Thousands of shrieking Arctic gulls were already feasting on the blood of the first three to be processed. The great carcass of the next in line lay grounded by the ramp, ready to be winched up to the blubber strippers and bone cutters. His black hulk was covered with gulls picking at the molluscs and algae. As a pathetic reminder of his mammal status and thirty million years of procreation, now threatened by seventy-five years of intensive hunting by man, his limp penis, whiter than the gulls, hung exposed to human gaze for the first time.

Then the chains tautened and tiny figures, dwarfed by the black mountain, guided it up the ramp into the station. When the blood-letting cut was made, the thick red fluid gushed out for ten minutes, running waste down the ramp and gulleys, food only for the gulls. It wells out like that because the explosive harpoons used to hunt the whale cause massive internal haemorrhage. Each harpoon weighs 160 pounds and strikes at sixty miles an hour. On striking, four barbed warheads open inside the animal and release a grenade which explodes. The whalers at Hvalfjordur, waiting by with the next five carcasses floating round their boats, estimated that it can take up to an hour for the whale to die.

After the blood had drained the processing was quick. The blubber was stripped off in regular bands and cut into neat squares. Some would become the traditional Icelandic dish – *hvalrinka* – slices of rancid fat stored in silos and eaten raw in January and February. The bulk is processed into sperm oil in the oil plant behind the whaling station. The rest was sawed through and divided up into mounds of intestine, stomach, and entrails for meal and fertilizer, the piles of meat for animal food. These were sperm whales and their meat is not palatable for humans. They are the Icelandic whaler's second choice, the first being the fin whale. If these are brought in within twenty-four hours of killing they can be eaten as whale steaks, Japan and Scandinavia being the main markets though whale meat accounts for only 0.8 per cent of Japan's protein intake. The gut is set aside for tennis rackets, and the teeth of the delicate lower jaw are used for traditional 'scrimshaw' carving.

Hvalfjordur is Iceland's only inland whaling station, sole holder of a strictly controlled licence from the Icelandic Government. It was established in 1948 by Loftur Bjarnason and is now run by his son, the thirty-three-year-old Kristjan Loftsson. Both father and son adhere to the quotas and regulations imposed by the International Whaling Commission and the Icelandic Ministry of Fisheries, and believe that these are necessary and right. In the past, Iceland was the victim of massive over-exploitation of whale stocks by Norway and Britain in particular, Norway's catch topping 1300 in 1902. In 1915 the Icelandic Parliament, the Althing, banned whaling and it was not reintro-duced until 1948.

Now the station at Hvalfjordur handles about four per cent of the world's total catch and this in turn represents one per cent of Iceland's exports. The Icelanders feel that their policy on whaling is conservative. They adhere to their quotas – 1121 for the coming season – control the minimum length of whales caught, do not pay bonuses for illegal catches as some other countries do, catch only male whales since the species is polygamous, and work under the watchful eye of an inspector from the International Whaling Commission. Every year the inspector comes from a different country of the seventeen members of the Commission. In

September, he was Japanese, and the previous season he was Norwegian. The whaling season lasts only four months as opposed to the six months allowed by the IWC. Iceland feels her observance of the rules is borne out by the fact that she does actually succeed in catching her quota while other countries fail to meet their quota through overfishing and every year the quotas have to be dropped.

Four whaling boats operate out of Hvalfjordur, employing some fourteen men and keeping to a two-hundred-mile radius of the station. In all the industry, including processing and freezing plants, provides work for a maximum two hundred people, and some of these are students from the university doing summer work.

The world spectrum of whaling is neither as conservative nor as regulated as in Iceland. Evidence presented at the eleven-day conference of the United Nations Food and Agriculture Organisation organized by the Advisory Committee on Marine Resources Research in Bergen in September bore out what the conservationist pressure groups have been saying for years. The evidence indicated that not only were stocks dropping because the quotas for the catches were set too high, but that the mean size of catch was also diminishing. The average sperm whale caught in the nineteen-thirties weighed forty-seven tons, now it is down to twenty-seven tons, and is reflected too by the mean oil yield, down from 29.9 barrels per whale in 1970 to 21.6 barrels in 1974, and that in spite of more efficient extracting processes. The implication is that the stock of mature whales has dropped off and is not being made up. Thirty-eight feet is the estimated size of a sexually mature whale. The permitted catching length is only thirty feet.

Blame can be placed squarely in three directions: massive overexploitation by the factory fleets of Japan and Russia in particular, since they take ninety per cent of the catch; relative scientific ignorance about the social, breeding, and survival habits of the whale; and the failure of the International Whaling Commission to care for anything but the commercial interests of its seventeen member countries.

The International Whaling Commission was set up in 1946 'to provide for the conservation, development, and optimum utilization of the whale resources'. In 1974 one of its own delegates from Mexico condemned its record in light of her experience: 'This Commission will be known in history as a small body of men who failed to act responsibly in terms of a very large commitment to the world, and who protected the interests of a few whalers and not the future of thousands of whales.' In 1972, a United Nations ten-year moratorium on whaling was voted in by the Conference on Human Environment in Stockholm by fifty-three votes to nil. Since then growing awareness, not just of the danger to whale stock but of possible repercussions on the whole ecosystem if the largest mammal was driven to extinction, has led to persistent lobbying that responsibility should be taken out of the hands of the self-interest of the IWC and placed under a United Nations body with adequate scientific monitoring.

Yet four years later, in spite of management reforms in the IWC virtually nothing has changed, except that quotas have had to be drastically reduced. The 'exploiters' club', as conservationists call the IWC, still goes uncontrolled. It has its own Scientific Advisory Committee which advises only on what it is asked to advise on. The member countries of the IWC appoint this committee, and it is not obliged to disclose its findings. Scientific information gathered by the committee is presented on the Friday before the annual conference of the IWC meets on the following Monday, allowing no time for comment or consideration by the scientific community, or independent observers.

Then there are failings in the structure of the IWC which mean that militantly pro-whaling countries can block the passing of reduced quotas. Three-quarters of the votes are needed to pass a motion, and a powerful grouping of countries can be enough to tip the balance. At the last IWC conference in London in June for example, reduced quotas of sperm whales were recommended by the Scientific Advisory Committee. This was opposed by the combined votes of Japan, Russia, Denmark, South Africa, and Australia, while Norway abstained. The direction of such voting indicates which are the most pro-whaling countries. The other problem is that not all whaling countries belong to the IWC. Members are Australia, Argentina, Canada, Brazil, Denmark, France, Holland, Japan, Iceland, Mexico, Norway, New Zealand,

Panama, South Africa, United Kingdom, USA, and USSR. Non-members, who take at least ten per cent of the world catch and do not observe quotas, include China, South Korea, Portugal, Spain, Chile, and Peru. These countries refuse to join the IWC, which in turn refuses to affiliate to the United Nations.

Where the protection of specific kinds of whale is concerned, the IWC has a gloomy record. In 1955 its own Scientific Committee warned that the blue whale, the largest of the lot and the size of thirty elephants when full-grown, was depleted in stocks almost to the point of no return. Yet the blue whale was hunted for a full ten years more, and it was not until 1965 that it joined the bowhead, grey, and Northern Right whales on the protected lists. To these the Right whale and the humpback were added, although the IWC at one point actually took the commercially extinct humpback off the protected lists.

Now that these species are all protected, full commercial pressure falls on the fin, sperm, sei, and minke whales. The biggest proportional drop in population is estimated to be among the fin whale stock, since these were too swift for the whalers before high-speed ships, powered harpoons, and the Asdic depth-sounding methods of hunting were introduced. Scientific observers are also concerned about inadequate calculations for quotas of both sperm whales and sei whales, while the hunting of the smaller minke (maximum size thirty feet) still seems to be unregulated, even off the northern shores of Iceland. Pressure is now being exerted for a total ban on all species by Friends of the Earth, the World Wildlife Fund, Project Jonah, and the Greenpeace Foundation. Meanwhile, quotas permitted by the IWC have dropped in such a way as to suggest that they too are aware of the urgency of the situation. The 1975-6 quota for both hemispheres was 32,576. For 1976-7 this was dropped by 18.4 per cent to 26,581. For sperm whales alone the 1974-5 quota was 23,000, dropped to 19,040 in 1975-6, and then again in 1976-7 to 11,991 in spite of the lobby from the pro-whaling countries.

Protectionists and conservationists are now concentrating on two main areas to consolidate the arguments for a ban on whaling. The first is the development of alternatives for the products which make the whale desirable and commercially attractive. The

237

second is the furtherance of scientific study of an animal about which we still know lamentably little.

In the past five years, since the United States imposed a ban on the import of all whale products, the development of alternatives for sperm whale oil – the biggest commercial attraction – has progressed rapidly. The main users of sperm whale oil have traditionally been the motor industry and the leather trade, and they accounted for the bulk of the 461,600 barrels of oil produced in 1975.

The motor industry, worried by the possibility of shortages, has largely phased out whale oil in favour of products produced by a range of oil companies who have been able to find chemical equivalents for the stability and high pressure and temperature resistance of the whale product which made it a favourite for the gearboxes of high-performance cars and tractors. Companies who now have commercially available alternatives include Chevron, Century Oil, Sun Oil, Standard Oil, Shell, Duckham's, and Lankro Chemicals. BP, who now own Duckham's, have strangely enough been slower off the mark.

In this country, a ban on all import of whale products 'except sperm oil, spermaceti wax or ambergris, and those products incorporated abroad into manufactured goods' was imposed in 1973. Since oil is the main attraction it was obviously a half-hearted ban, and difficult to control. In no way did it make up for this country's guilt in overexploiting the blue whale and in introducing the concept of factory ships. Britain is no longer a whaling country since this contribution to depletion of stocks helped to make the runs out of Hull unprofitable, but she still imports some 8000 tonnes of whale oil per annum – roughly the equivalent of 3000 whales.

Although the motor industry has phased down its use, the leather industry here still accounts for forty per cent of the oil, and has proved less willing to develop alternatives than the motor industry. The attractive qualities of whale oil in tanning and fashion leather processing are the suppleness it gives, its stability, and lack of smell. Some leather manufacturers now use alternatives like Synthol LCT and a whole range from Lankro Chemicals or Hodgson Tanning Products. Others have stuck to sperm oil and

238

the powerful British Leather Federation has proved uncooperative in spreading the message.

Products which are treated with the oil include soft gloves (many of which are in fact exported to the United States), pastel-shaded fashion leather clothes, and the shoe uppers of the British Shoe Corporation shops (including Saxone and Dolcis) and Marks and Spencer's, who feel that there is 'no case to be answered'. Cosmetics account for less use in this country than in the past, but imported European lipsticks and face creams still contain spermaceti wax in spite of the fact that France is likely to impose a ban.

Of the sperm oil imported into this country, about a quarter is re-exported in refined form. In 1975, 1778.6 tonnes worth £493,358 went out to nine major markets, headed by West Germany. The major handler of sperm oil in this country is Highgate and Job, an Australian combine, whose largest shareholder is in turn Dalgety Ltd., who are the major suppliers of both hides and oil to Britain: a full circle.

Recently Customs and Excise, who have in the past released figures on the country of origin of oil and its port of entry, have been requested no longer to do so. This will make the conservationists' task in monitoring supplies more difficult. A lobby for a Private Member's Bill to ban oil imports has begun, and should complement the effect of the Endangered Species (Import and Export) Act which was given Royal Assent on 22 November.

This will hopefully galvanize Edward Bishop, Minister of State for Agriculture, Fisheries, and Food, into action, since as recently as last year he told the House of Parliament that 'the sperm whale is not considered to be in danger' and that he had confidence in the quotas set by the IWC.

Mr Bishop's complacency is in marked contrast to the urgent tone of the Bergen conference in September. Here it was felt by scientists and conservationists alike that the calculations of the IWC in establishing the catch quotas were totally inadequate. More scientific research was needed, and the findings of any scientific advisory body should be available to the community at large before being implemented by the IWC. Proposals for marine wildernesses in which whale stocks could recuperate and be studied were made.

The problem of ownership of resource was raised: who do the whales belong to? Here again it was felt that the United Nations should be responsible and not the IWC which only cares for the commercial aspect. This was placed in the context of our general ignorance of almost every essential aspect of the life of a threatened species, its relationship to the entire ecological cycle, and threat to the stability of this cycle if whales were hunted out of existence.

10 December, 1976   **Caroline Tisdall**

The nucleus of doubt that lingers

Sir, – Have I missed it or has no one yet mentioned why, nuclear reprocessing being so safe, the business-like Japanese are content to send theirs to be done here, on the other side of the earth, at great expense, instead of doing it themselves?

Ernest Roth

Threeways,
Vicarage Lane,
Kent.
22 June, 1977

Bomb happy

You can hardly open a newspaper nowadays without reading about some totally uninformed person who's got up on his hind legs and started bleating on about the dangers of nuclear power, fast-breeder reactors, plutonium and all that stuff. It's all cobblers, of course, and at last a few people who know what they're talking about are beginning to answer back.

Last week, for example, Mr Simon Rippon said that nuclear energy is actually the safest form of power available, and he's in a position to be completely objective. No axe to grind at all. He's European editor of *Nuclear News*, which is the publication of the

American Nuclear Society, and you can hardly ask for better than that.

He's not the only one either. There was an article in *New Scientist* last week in which the chap said he'd read an article in an American magazine called *Atom News* which reviewed a book called *The Health Hazards of Not Going Nuclear* which puts the whole thing in perspective. What he says is that . . . that's very kind of you, same again please, large pink gin.

Cheers. Where was I? Oh yes, nuclear power. All these do-gooders, so-called conservationists, self-styled ecologists and other assorted wets of all complexions keep spouting all this rubbish about building windmills or something because if we have these nuclear fast-breeder reactors then a tiny bit of nasty stuff might leak out some time in the next million years, or someone might pinch a bit of plutonium and make an atom bomb. It's most unlikely, you know.

Apart from which, the dangers have been wildly exaggerated. Let me ask you one thing. Who are the people who've had most experience of being on the receiving end of nuclear energy? That's right, the Japs.

Completely transformed the place. I'll tell you what I think. I think if we dropped a couple of atom bombs on Leyland's tomorrow I bet that in six months we'd be producing transistors and cameras and Hondas and Datsuns so bloody fast you wouldn't be able to move for them. That's what I think. But that's beside the point. The point is, um, I've forgotten what I was going to say. Oh yes, I was starting to tell you about this article in *New Scientist* about the article in *Atom News* about the book called *The Hazards of Not Going Nuclear* which is by Professor P. Beckman, published by Golem Press in Boulder, Colorado, for $10.95 and worth every penny by the sound of it, because this Professor Beckman makes pretty good mincemeat of your anti-nuclear chappies.

For one thing he says they're all mediocrities in their own fields, and I bet he's right – pink gin, large one, no water. What's more he takes a hard look at the alternatives, wind power and the tides and solar power, that kind of thing. Take solar power. Terribly dangerous. Professor Beckman, obviously a bright chap, points

out in this very important book that it could be a killer. I'll tell you
how if you let me get a word in edgeways. Well, supposing everyone has solar cells on top of their houses. Sooner or later they'll
want to climb up on to the roof and inspect the things, and
Professor Beckman points out that if you have all these people
climbing ladders then some of them are going to fall off and kill
themselves.

Good grief, is that the time? Large pink gin, please, and this'll
have to be the ABL. Absolutely bloody last. Awful lot of work to
do this afternoon. When you think about it you have to agree
Professor Beckman is right, don't you?

I'll tell you something else. More people die in hospitals than in
pubs, and that's a fact. What's more . . . you're not going already,
are you? Stay for just one more. ABBL. Large pink gin, please, no
water and go easy on the pink bit. Cheers.

15 January, 1977   **Richard Boston**

Rich man's law

Whenever I go into the Law Courts in the Strand – and despite
appearances to the contrary, I do my best to keep out of the place –
I am always struck by the crude blasphemy of the building. It is
an ugly Victorian pile built in the style of a Gothic cathedral.
Inside, the atmosphere is religious – high vaulting arches, echoing
footsteps, scurrying figures. You half expect to see an altar at
the far end or hear a choir chanting legal psalms in a side-
chapel.

The lawyers who bustle in and out of the building presumably
see no incongruity in the setting. To them it makes abundant sense
to regard the law as a sort of God in honour of whom it is very
right and fitting to build a magnificent shrine resembling Westminster Abbey. They see themselves in their better moments as
priests, dedicated to the service of this deity. Indeed counsel at
times can be heard using religious metaphors – 'the majesty . . .
the pure undefiled stream of the law' – to win over the better class
of judge.

242

Personally, I have come to regard the Law Courts not as a cathedral but rather as a casino. 'Las Vegas' could be put up over the main entrance in neon lighting without offending my susceptibilities. Who loses and who wins are matters of pure chance. When a judge starts to sum up at the end of a case it is for me as if someone has twirled a roulette, and we wait anxiously to see if the ball will land up on red or black. In the long run the only winners in this game are the lawyers, bewigged croupiers hauling in their fees, while their clients stagger out into the night, vowing never to go near the place again.

As with gambling, the rich are at an advantage. They can afford to double the stakes and go to the Court of Appeal, or treble them and go to the Lords. The poor player is more likely to throw in his hand and cry quits if he loses in the first round.

It was as a life-time gambler and a millionaire, that my recent adversary, Sir James Goldsmith, approached his litigation against *Private Eye*. To begin with, there was the choice of criminal libel. This was a rank outsider, which a non-gambler might not have thought of. At the time Goldsmith made his original application to bring criminal libel proceedings no one that I spoke to among the legal fraternity thought he had a hope of bringing it off. There had not been a case against a newspaper, so it seemed, since Lord Alfred Douglas accused Winston Churchill of deliberately losing the Battle of Jutland in order to cash in on some shares on the New York stock market.

In fact the survival of the criminal libel law illustrates a notable feature of our legal system. It is one of those ancient and unexploded bombs which have been kept on in the legal armoury just in case they might come in useful when all else fails.

Most people's conception of what distinguishes a criminal from a civil libel is that the former is so serious that it is likely to cause a breach of the peace (I always found such a breach of the peace hard to imagine, until recently when Lady Falkender wrote in a magazine article: 'I once heard someone angrily deciding to go along to *Private Eye* and punch Richard Ingrams for something he'd printed about them.')

It is not only the layman who has this mistaken idea about breach of the peace. Lord Denning himself, at a later stage in the proceedings, admitted that he thought that that is what it was all about. Not so. For in a case in 1936 (Rex v. Wicks) one Mr Justice du Parcq decided as follows: 'There is however in our judgement no ground for the suggestion made at the Bar that it is incumbent upon the prosecution to prove that the libel in question would have been unusually likely to provoke the wrath of the person defamed.'

You could compare and contrast du Parcq's view with that of a famous Lord Chief Justice, Lord Coleridge: 'There ought to be some public interest concerned, something affecting the Crown or the guardians of the public peace (likely to be broken by the alleged libel) to justify the recourse by a private person to a criminal remedy by way of indictment. If either by reason of the continued repetition or infamous character of the libel, breach of the peace is likely to ensue, then the libeller should be indicted; but in the absence of any such conditions, the personal squabble between two private individuals ought to be permitted by grand juries, as indeed it is not permitted by sound law, to be the subject of a criminal indictment.'

In any other sphere Lord Coleridge's greater rank and reputation would count for more than that of the unknown and obscure Justice du Parcq. But that is not the way the law works. Because du Parcq spoke out in 1936 his view is apparently considered binding until such time as it is overruled by the House of Lords. When Mr Justice Faulks conducted his rather desultory investigation into the libel laws a few years ago, he regarded the judgement in R. v. Wicks as the last word on the subject.

But once you remove the 'Breach of the Peace' criterion, how do you define a criminal libel? This was the awkward question confronting Mr Justice Wien (now famous for his ruling in the recent Guardsman rape case) when he came to sum up in Goldsmith v. Pressdram.

He concluded that because (a) the libel was a serious one and (b) that Goldsmith occupied important public positions, therefore the application should be granted. Wien's criteria, if applied generally, could logically result in a flood of criminal libel actions – Harold Wilson, Jeremy Thorpe, Reginald Maudling – where would it all end?

Wien's unexpected verdict was a perfect example of the element of pure chance which operates in the law. A 50-1 outsider had romped home. One beneficial effect was to confirm my view that if your lawyers assure you that you have a strong case – as mine had done here – then it is safe to assume that you will lose. The opposite is also the case.

Curiously enough the only other battle in the Goldsmith campaign where the lawyers were confident of victory, we also lost. This concerned the *Private Eye* distributors, 33 of whom had been sued by Goldsmith at the beginning of the case. Sixteen had done a deal with him: he would drop his action and in return they would agree never to sell *Private Eye* again. It was not only to the layman's eye that this looked wrong. Lawyers agreed that we should apply to the court to have the actions dismissed on the grounds that they constituted an abuse of the legal process. Initially the application was successful but in a higher court, Mr Justice Stocker overruled the Master's decision, and his ruling was upheld in the Court of Appeal.

But here arose another typically legal anomaly. Lord Denning supported the Private Eye claim. Denning is the only judge in recent years to command general respect. He is a Pope John figure appealing to the public in spite of all their suspicions about the institution which he represents. The simplicity and directness of his language is in marked contrast to that of his brother judges.

Yet if you talk to lawyers about Denning you will find they regard him as a rather lovable old crank. The reason is that his judgements err in favour of what is obviously right rather than what is merely legal. To a lawyer, Denning is 'unsound'. So it was in our Distributors case, Denning, in spite of his eminence, was overruled by the two judges sitting with him. In no other game would a man of Denning's standing be trumped by two comparative nobodies.

Denning went further than just damning the Goldsmith writs. He affirmed that there was no case in which a subordinate distributor had been found liable to a plaintiff, except when prior knowledge of the libel had been brought home to him. Where would it end, he asked? Not only would distributors and bookstalls be at risk, but clubs and common rooms as well.

All this would seem to be no more than common sense. But common law and common sense are not the same thing. As it happened, this matter of distributors' liability was something about which I felt deeply as for over fifteen years Britain's two biggest distributors, W. H. Smith and John Menzies, have refused to handle *Private Eye* on the grounds that they would be held liable for any defamation. Here was Lord Denning telling them: 'There might be papers so bad that a distributor should handle them only at his peril; but there would have to be very strong evidence before it reached that point . . . Even though a paper may be scurrilous, it is not to be banned on that account. No such ban has hitherto been imposed on newspapers. Nor should a start be made now.'

It was some such point that I myself had tried to make when I went in 1974 with Paul Foot to give evidence to the Faulks Committee on defamation. The Committee grouped round a large table in the Law Courts, included a number of eminent laymen like Lord Ballantrae and Mr Harman Grisewood. But their puzzled expressions were proof that they had long since given up trying to understand the issues which they were being asked to adjudicate.

The lawyers had taken the thing over. This was not because of any superiority of intellect or even any greater knowledge on their part, but rather to the fact that when lawyers talk about the law, the normal human being begins to think about something else. Why is this? It is, I suppose, because the lawyers are not interested primarily in truth and falsehood, or in right and wrong. Most of the time they seem to be engaged simply in playing an elaborate game, a game which consists of making up the rules for the game by referring to other games that have taken place in the past.

To the sane man the whole process seems rather repellent, and in fact, the only laymen who actually enjoy the law are lunatics, one or two of whom can always be found hanging about the Law Courts in the same state of furtive excitement which other more rational men might evince when frequenting a strip club. To them a judge is the equivalent of a sex symbol, his summing up as thrilling as the Dance of the Seven Veils.

Personally I have found no experience so depressing or exhausting as a day spent in court. Part of the reason is that whatever is said seems to bear little relation to what is going on outside. Even the language is different. In the Goldsmith case his lawyer Mr Lewis Hawser, QC, kept using words like 'vilification' and 'opprobrious' which no other class of person would ever dream of using. (Imagine saying to your wife 'Don't be so opprobrious, my dear'.)

In the unreal atmosphere of a courtroom, jokes cease to be funny. A paragraph in *Private Eye* which would set the table on a roar across the road in El Vino's assumes in court an awesome gravity – 'It would be hard, My Lord, to imagine a more disgraceful calumny.' People sometimes talk of a case being 'laughed out of court.' I have never heard of it being done and would like to meet the lawyer who is capable of such a feat. Anyone who could reduce a jury to helpless laughter would deserve a life peerage for services to humour.

All such things, the lawyers might argue, act as a healthy deterrent. A man will wait until he is really ill before he goes near a hospital, such is the chaos and incompetence which are rife within those buildings. So too potential plaintiffs, the lawyers could say, will think at least twice before embarking on litigation. Unfortunately it does not work like that. Thanks mainly to television, lawyers, like doctors, enjoy a high reputation. Politicians and civil servants are subjected to regular attacks. Judges are probably the least criticized of all powerful public servants, and barristers who are, after all, only embryo judges, are dignified figures in three-piece suits, with quiet reassuring public school accents. (This picture could easily be dispelled if each lawyer was compelled to have fitted to his desk a taxi-meter which would click up the man's fee at regular intervals.)

It is impossible not to wonder nowadays which of our institutions – even which newspapers or which television programmes – would survive in the totalitarian system which will probably come into being sooner or later. It is depressing to think that all those lawyers are probably safe. One or two like Lord Denning would be put out to grass on account of their old-fashioned notions of liberty, but the majority would quite happily soldier on under whatever dictatorship, right or left, had taken control. And the fees would continue to roll in.

If you have a son of eighteen or nineteen, anxious how to safeguard his future in the uncertain times that lie ahead, I would advise him to read for the bar.

30 July, 1977   **Richard Ingrams**

'On the one hundred and eighty-fifth day of Christmas,
my true love said to me . . .'

Index of Authors